Decriminalizing Domestic Violence

GENDER AND JUSTICE

Edited by Claire M. Renzetti

This University of California Press series explores how the experiences of offending, victimization, and justice are profoundly influenced by the intersections of gender with other markers of social location. Cross-cultural and comparative, series volumes publish the best new scholarship that seeks to challenge assumptions, highlight inequalities, and transform practice and policy.

1. *The Trouble with Marriage: Feminists Confront Law and Violence in India,* by Srimati Basu
2. *Caught Up: Girls, Surveillance, and Wraparound Incarceration,* by Jerry Flores
3. *In Search of Safety: Confronting Inequality in Women's Imprisonment,* by Barbara Owen, James Wells, Joycelyn Pollock
4. *Abusive Endings: Separation and Divorce Violence against Women,* by Walter S. DeKeseredy, Molly Dragiewicz, and Martin D. Schwartz
5. *Journeys: Resiliency and Growth for Survivors of Intimate Partner Abuse,* by Susan L. Miller
6. *The Chosen Ones: Black Men and the Politics of Redemption,* by Nikki Jones
7. *Decriminalizing Domestic Violence: A Balanced Policy Approach to Intimate Partner Violence,* by Leigh Goodmark

Decriminalizing Domestic Violence

A Balanced Policy Approach to Intimate Partner Violence

LEIGH GOODMARK

University of California Press

University of California Press, one of the most distinguished university presses in the United States, enriches lives around the world by advancing scholarship in the humanities, social sciences, and natural sciences. Its activities are supported by the UC Press Foundation and by philanthropic contributions from individuals and institutions. For more information, visit www.ucpress.edu.

University of California Press
Oakland, California

Library of Congress Cataloging-in-Publication Data

Names: Goodmark, Leigh, 1969- author.
Title: Decriminalizing domestic violence : a balanced policy approach to intimate partner violence / Leigh Goodmark.
Description: Oakland, California : University of California Press, [2018] | Includes bibliographical references and index. |
Identifiers: LCCN 2018011165 (print) | LCCN 2018015037 (ebook) | ISBN 9780520968295 (ebook) | ISBN 9780520295568 (cloth : alk. paper) | ISBN 9780520295575 (pbk. : alk. paper)
Subjects: LCSH: Intimate partner violence—United States. | Family violence—United States—Prevention.
Classification: LCC HV6626.2 (ebook) | LCC HV6626.2 .G667 2018 (print) | DDC 362.82/925610973—dc23
LC record available at https://lccn.loc.gov/2018011165

26 25 24 23 22 21 20 19 18 17
10 9 8 7 6 5 4 3 2 1

For Doug, Juliet, and Carter, as always

There is no such thing as a single-issue struggle because we do not lead single-issue lives.

—AUDRE LORDE

Contents

Acknowledgments

On some days, writing a book is a labor of love. On others, it's unimaginable torture. And those are the days when you're grateful for the colleagues, friends, and family who provide the support and encouragement you need to keep going—and you're glad that you get the acknowledgments section of your book to thank all of them.

This book would not exist but for Claire Renzetti. Claire is a mentor, a supporter, a dear friend, and my idol. No other individual (in my opinion) has made as significant a contribution to the field of intimate partner violence research and no one else does so with the wisdom, humor, and warmth that Claire brings to every project. Which is why I keep doing projects for Claire, and why I will be fully employed (by her) for the next several years. Thank you so much, Claire.

Maura Roessner was enthusiastic about this idea from the first time we talked over coffee, and didn't blink (okay, maybe she blinked a little) when I told her the title. Her support of this project and her encouragement have been invaluable to me.

Thanks to the cohort of colleagues and friends who continue to push the envelope on the relationship of law to gender-based violence: Donna Coker, Deborah Weissman, Julie Goldscheid, Aya Gruber, Aziza Ahmed, Carrie Bettinger-Lopez, Brenda Smith, Margaret Johnson, Joanne Belknap, and Angela Harris. Thanks also to my restorative justice friends, particularly Gale Burford. I couldn't write a book entitled "Decriminalizing Domestic Violence" without expecting some serious pushback, and your work, as well as your comments and critiques both on this book and on the articles that preceded it, have helped me to develop an argument that (hopefully) will withstand that criticism and offer something valuable to the conversation. I'm grateful for the benefit of your insights.

I am unbelievably lucky to be teaching at the University of Maryland Francis King Carey School of Law. Thanks to all of my colleagues, but particularly Dean Donald Tobin and clinic codirectors Michael Pinard and Renée Hutchins, for their encouragement and support. My research assistants, Neda Saghafi and Chelsea Van Orden, fielded every bizarre request with alacrity and good humor and provided invaluable feedback. They are both going to be amazing attorneys, and I'm proud to have worked with them.

Parts of this book were adapted from law review articles that appeared in the *Harvard Journal of Law and Gender* and the *Florida State University Law Review*. Thanks so much to the student editors of those journals for their input and ideas.

Like many people who are passionate about what they do, I tend to bring my work home. Which means that my family has heard enough about gender-based violence to last them a lifetime. Thanks to Doug for twenty-five years of love, support, and editing, for being willing to single parent both at home and abroad so that I can learn and work with advocates around the world, for your sense of humor, and for the thousands of things that you do to make our lives better. And to my children, Juliet and Carter, who have sat through trainings and court and lectures and been in many places that caused people to question my parenting, thank you for being the amazing people that you are. I am in awe of you every day. I can only do this work and stay happy and relatively sane because of the three of you, and I love you dearly.

Introduction

For the last thirty years, the United States has relied primarily on one tool to combat intimate partner violence—the criminal legal system.[1] But that system has been ineffective in deterring intimate partner violence and has had problematic, sometimes destructive, consequences for people subjected to abuse, people who use violence, and their communities.[2] This book argues for taking a different path, one that incorporates economic, public health, community, and human rights policies. Decriminalizing domestic violence—deemphasizing the criminal legal system's role in responding to intimate partner violence—will enable the United States to develop a multifaceted and, ultimately, more effective policy approach.

This story begins with women like this one:

> I said "no more" when I got punched and had hair pulled out; there were big clumps in my hands. He threw chairs at me. I remember being on the floor screaming. It was a nightmare. . . .
>
> I ran to my neighbor. She let me in which is amazing. He banged and screamed on her door until the police came twenty minutes later. . . .
>
> The police arrived and said, "Did anything happen?" The house was in pieces; chairs were broken everywhere, and my hair was out of my head, hanging on my shoulder, and the cop said, "It looks like nothing happened."[3]

Criminal laws that could have been used to address intimate partner violence had always existed, but by the 1970s those laws were inconsistently enforced in the context of intimate relationships. As one woman recounted, "[E]verytime I went to the authorities, they laughed at me stating that they, the law, would have to see my husband kill one of us before they could help."[4] Rather than make futile appeals for help to police and prosecutors, antiviolence advocates created shelters and community-based services for people subjected to abuse. In the 1980s, however, the antiviolence movement began to publicly question why intimate partner violence was not treated like other crimes and to enlist police and prosecutors in their efforts to change law enforcement policy. The turn to the criminal legal system began in earnest in 1984, when the United States Attorney General's Task Force on Domestic Violence called for strengthening the criminal legal response to intimate partner violence. Former prosecutor Jeanine Pirro, a member of the task force, explained, "We believe [intimate partner violence] is a criminal problem and the way to handle it is with criminal justice intervention."[5]

Since that time, enhancing the criminal legal system's response has been the primary aim of intimate partner violence law and policy. Focusing on the criminal legal response resulted from a number of factors, including the historical failure of the criminal legal system to respond to intimate partner violence, the belief that intimate partner violence is a public problem requiring a state response (rather than a private family matter), and a tendency to address all social problems by "governing through crime."[6] Some police officers and prosecutors were slow to accept their new roles in responding to intimate partner violence, despite the enthusiasm of the antiviolence movement for increased intervention. Recalcitrant law enforcement officers were forced to act, however, by mandatory policies adopted by states and localities. Those policies were driven by research (later questioned) on the impact of arrest on intimate partner violence, lawsuits brought by antiviolence advocates, funding incentives through the Violence against Women Act (VAWA), and the active lobbying of the antiviolence movement. Over time, police officers and prosecutors in many jurisdictions have come to embrace their role in combating intimate partner violence and often lead interdisciplinary efforts to address the issue.

Originally housed in the Violent Crime Control and Law Enforcement Act, funding through VAWA, first enacted in 1994 and reauthorized several times since, created powerful incentives for police, prosecutors, and courts to invest their time and energy in developing and implementing criminal legal interventions. Since VAWA's passage, the Office on Violence against Women has awarded $5.7 billion in grants. The majority of that funding has been dedicated to the criminal legal system, and over time the disparity in funding between grants to the criminal legal system and those to social services has grown substantially. In 1994 62 percent of VAWA funds were dedicated to the criminal legal system and 38 percent went to social services. By 2013 social services authorizations made up only about 15 percent of VAWA grants. Fewer total dollars were devoted to social services in the

2013 iteration of VAWA than in the original 1994 legislation.[7] In fiscal year 2017, VAWA's two largest grant programs combined to provide $266 million to the criminal legal system. By contrast, VAWA allocated $30 million to housing, despite repeated studies showing that housing is the single greatest need identified by people subjected to abuse. VAWA also encouraged antiviolence nonprofit organizations to collaborate with the criminal legal system as a condition of funding, diverting staff, resources, and attention away from other facets of the response to intimate partner violence. As a result of these law and policy initiatives, the criminal legal system is the primary response to intimate partner violence in the United States today.

Since 1984 the United States has steadfastly committed to the criminalization of intimate partner violence. That dogged persistence might be justified if the criminal legal response had proved successful. But there is reason to question whether criminal legal interventions are having an appreciable impact on intimate partner violence. Since 1994 rates of intimate partner violence in the United States have fallen—but so has the overall crime rate. From 1994 to 2000 rates of intimate partner violence and the overall crime rate decreased by the same amount. From 2000 to 2010 rates of intimate partner violence dropped less than the overall crime rate. No reliable social science data ties the drop in the rates of intimate partner violence to criminalization or to increases in funding and criminal legal system activity spurred by VAWA. Crime has declined and the funding to address intimate partner violence has increased, but the problem persists.

The turn to the criminal legal system to address intimate partner violence coincided with the rise of mass incarceration in the United States. As criminologist Beth Richie explains, "Right alongside of our evolution as an antiviolence movement came the conservative apparatus that was deeply committed to building a prison nation. That buildup fell right into the open arms, as if we were waiting for it, of the anti-violence movement that had aligned itself with the criminal legal system."[8] Incarceration rates have multiplied by five times during the life of the antiviolence movement. The United States incarcerates approximately 2.3 million people, with another 5 million under the scrutiny of parole and probation officers. While the criminalization of intimate partner violence may not have been the primary cause of the increase in incarceration in the United States, scholars have argued that the turn to criminal law to address intimate partner violence contributed to mass incarceration. Richie notes, "They took our words, they took our work, they took our people, they took our money and said, 'You girls doing your anti-violence work are right, it is a crime, and we have got something for that.'"[9] The numbers of people incarcerated for intimate partner violence are substantial. In Vermont, for example, an estimated 20 percent of the state's prison population as of 2014 was incarcerated as a result of intimate partner violence.

In 2014 and 2015 criminal justice reform was at the top of the policy agenda for both progressives and conservatives. Efforts to reduce the prison population focused on releasing nonviolent criminals, primarily drug users. To make a significant dent in the prison population, however, the United States must confront the prosecution and punishment of violent criminals. About half of all prisoners are serving sentences for committing violent offenses, including murder, rape, kidnapping, sexual assault, and other forms of assault. As Marc Mauer and David Cole have explained, "Even if we released everyone imprisoned for drugs tomorrow, the United States would still have 1.7 million people behind bars, and an incarceration rate four times that of many Western European nations."[10]

Policymakers have been willing to discuss cutting sentences for violent offenses or paroling those convicted of violent offenses in order to shrink the prison population. But intimate partner violence is rarely part of those conversations. For example, the Sentencing Reform and Corrections Act, a bill intended to address the problem of mass incarceration in the United States, would have decreased mandatory minimum sentences for a number of crimes—but created new mandatory minimums for some crimes of interstate intimate partner violence. While mandatory minimum sentences were decreased for a number of crimes in Iowa in 2016, mandatory minimums for crimes of intimate partner violence increased. In the context of intimate partner violence, advocates and policymakers continue to be more concerned about underenforcement—how law enforcement's failure to adequately police or prosecute crimes of intimate partner violence undermines the use of criminal law to prevent or deter instances of violence. These are arguments for more criminal legal intervention, not less. And underenforcement of the criminal law, particularly in low-income communities and communities of color, is a significant concern. As law professor Alexandra Natapoff has argued, both underenforcement and overenforcement are "twin symptoms of a deeper democratic failure of the criminal justice system: its non-responsiveness to the needs of the poor, racial minorities, and the otherwise politically vulnerable."[11]

But activists and scholars concerned about the disproportionate impact of law enforcement interventions on marginalized communities, and skeptical about the achievements of thirty years of prioritizing the criminal legal response in the United States, have begun to consider what role the criminal legal system should play in responding to intimate partner violence. That reassessment is driven by concerns that the criminal legal system is ineffective, focuses disproportionately on people of color and low-income people, ignores the larger structural issues that drive intimate partner violence, robs people subjected to abuse of autonomy, and fails to meet the pressing economic and social needs of people subjected to abuse. While the criminal legal system may serve some of the needs of some people subjected to abuse, it does not provide a comprehensive or effective response to the multifaceted problem of intimate partner violence.

Is the criminal legal response "working"? Working can be measured in a number of ways. Working might mean that rates of violence are decreasing, that people are being deterred from committing violence, or that deploying the criminal system has changed community norms on violence. A system can be said to work only when its response is helpful in some way and when people are willing to use that system. If people subjected to abuse are harmed rather than helped by turning to the legal system for assistance, it is not working well. When the justice needs of those the system was meant to benefit go unmet, a justice system is not fulfilling its purpose.

Intimate partner violence is a complex problem requiring a multidimensional solution. Crime is only one facet of intimate partner violence. Intimate partner violence has economic, public health, community, and human rights dimensions as well, all of which affect the experiences of people subjected to abuse. Criminalization has negative economic consequences for individuals and communities. Criminalization implicates questions of human rights and squanders funding that could be spent on public health prevention measures. Myopically pursuing criminalization as the answer to intimate partner violence undermines and diverts time, attention, and resources from untested but potentially successful strategies for deterring and responding to intimate partner violence. The failure to address any one facet of the problem complicates and magnifies the damage that intimate partner violence can do. The criminal legal response cannot address all of the facets of intimate partner violence—indeed, no one solution could do so. But relying primarily on the criminal legal system to respond to intimate partner violence has displaced serious policy attention to and funding for these other dimensions of the problem.

What kind of problem, then, is intimate partner violence? Both demographically and conceptually, intimate partner violence is a gender problem. According to the United States Centers for Disease Control and Prevention, 36 percent of women and 29 percent of men experience rape, stalking, or physical assault at the hands of a partner during their lifetimes. These statistics (and studies on men's and women's use of violence) have bolstered the claim that intimate partner violence is gender symmetrical: that women and men are violent and experience violence in roughly equal measures. But intimate partner violence is quite different for men and women. Women are much more likely than men to experience overlapping forms of abuse (stalking, sexual violence, and physical violence); most men experience only physical violence. Women are almost twice as likely as men to be subjected to severe physical violence. While men are most often hit with a fist or kicked, women experience a range of violent victimizations, including having their hair pulled, being strangled or suffocated, beaten, or attacked with a knife or a gun, in addition to being hit with a fist or kicked. Moreover, intimate partner violence has a more significant impact on women's daily lives. Twenty-nine percent of women report that intimate partner violence has caused them to be fearful or concerned for their safety, experience posttraumatic stress disorder (PTSD), miss more than a day of work, or has created a need for services including health care, housing, or legal assistance. Nine percent of men are similarly affected.[12] Treating intimate partner violence as a crime has also had gendered consequences (for example, the increase in arrests of women following the adoption of mandatory arrest policies described in chapter 2).

Conceptually, intimate partner violence has long been seen as a gender problem. The earliest theories on intimate partner violence held that the unions of masochistic women and abusive men produced intimate partner violence. The antiviolence movement of the 1970s and 1980s (originally called the battered women's movement) began as a response to violence against women, and early law and policy initiatives were specifically intended to benefit women. The movement characterized intimate partner violence as a means of "reinforc[ing] male dominance and female subordination within the home and outside it. In other words, violence against women . . . is a part of male control. It is not gender neutral any more than the economic division of labor or the institution of marriage is gender neutral."[13] The state's failure to intervene to prevent intimate partner violence bolstered those patriarchal norms. More recent scholarship argues that intimate partner violence by men reflects the impact of toxic masculinity on the socialization of men. The use of violence in intimate relationships (and other contexts) is a predictable occurrence in a society in which stereotypical masculinity is highly valued and in which violence is strongly associated with masculinity.

Gender is also at play when intimate partner violence occurs in the relationships of lesbian, gay, bisexual, and transgender (LGBT) people. Intimate partner violence is a significant problem in the relationships of LGBT individuals. Law professor Adele Morrison has argued that victimization is gendered female and violence is gendered male, regardless of the biological sex of the person who is victimized or uses violence.[14] But law enforcement officers often dismiss violence between same-sex partners as mutual, regardless of the elements of coercive control that may be at play in the relationship. In those cases, violence against gay men is seen as a fight among equals; lesbian battering is dismissed as a "cat fight."

For transgender individuals, violence is gendered along a number of dimensions. Violence against transwomen or by transmen can serve to reinforce traditional notions of patriarchal power within trans relationships. Violence can also be used to police binary gender roles and to punish "transgressions" of gender norms. For example, offenders rape transmen to send the message that despite identifying and presenting as men, because they can be raped, they are still vulnerable to violence, and therefore, considered female. Finally, violence can reinforce stereotyped renditions of gender identity, with transmen using violence to assert their masculinity and transwomen perceiving themselves as more feminine because they are being abused.

But the fact that intimate partner violence is gendered, and in many ways gendered female, does not mean that it affects all women the same way. Women's experiences of violence vary tremendously by race, ethnicity, socioeconomic status, and disability. The interplay of women's identities creates and reinforces the oppression that they experience as a function of intimate partner violence, a concept known as intersectionality. Intersectionality transformed the discourse of the antiviolence movement. The early battered women's movement was largely driven by and built around the norms and needs of white middle-class women. Their faith in the deterrent power of criminal law spurred the drive to treat intimate partner violence as a criminal matter. From the beginning of the antiviolence movement women of color foresaw the problems that criminalization would create for their communities, but those concerns went largely unheeded in the rush to institutionalize criminalization in law and policy.

While the antiviolence movement has embraced the language of intersectionality, it has failed to work to change laws and policies on criminalization that disproportionately negatively impact low-income people, people of color, lesbians, transwomen, and other marginalized communities. Women of color and other representatives of marginalized communities have repeatedly questioned whether the policy choices made by the antiviolence movement contemplated or comprehended their unique needs, identities, and positions. Reconsidering criminalization could help us to better understand the ways in which policy choices around intimate partner violence affect various communities and, ultimately, could transform law and policy so that it better meets the needs of the most marginalized people subjected to violence.

As questions are raised about how best to address the problem of mass incarceration and as criticism of the criminal legal response to intimate partner violence increases, the time is ripe to seek alternatives to the criminalization of intimate partner violence. Some antiviolence advocates are asking whether decriminalizing intimate partner violence might be not only possible but necessary if other responses to intimate partner violence are to be explored. As law professor Angela Harris has asked, "If reliance on the criminal justice system to address violence against women and sexual minorities has reached the end of its usefulness, to where should advocates turn next?"[15] The conversation about alternatives to criminalization in the context of intimate partner violence could also be part of the solution to mass incarceration. Decriminalizing domestic violence might provide a starting point for rethinking incarceration as the default response to violent crime in the United States.

This book will argue that existing research does not justify the United States' continued investment in criminalization as the primary response to intimate partner violence. Criminalization does little to prevent intimate partner violence. What it accomplishes comes at a substantial cost. Criminalization has failed to deter intimate partner violence. The criminal legal system harms some of those it was meant to protect and exacerbates the conditions that contribute to intimate partner violence.

Chapter 1 offers a brief history of the criminalization of intimate partner violence. After considering the benefits and critiques of criminalization, the chapter asks whether criminal law theory justifies the criminalization of intimate partner violence. Chapter 1 concludes that the theoretical basis for criminalizing intimate partner violence is weak at best, and that a persuasive case could be made for decriminalizing intimate partner violence.

If not primarily a problem for the criminal system, what kind of problem is intimate partner violence? Chapter 2 argues that intimate partner violence is an economic problem, imposing substantial costs on the economy, on people subjected to abuse, and on people who perpetrate violence. The chapter examines the relationship between economics and intimate partner violence, explains how impeding access to economic resources limits the autonomy of people subjected to abuse, and explores the link between economics and perpetration of violence. Finally, the chapter considers the structural economic factors that exacerbate intimate partner violence.

Chapter 3 looks at intimate partner violence from a public health perspective. Because intimate partner violence is associated with a host of adverse health consequences, eradicating that violence has clear health benefits. The public health approach views intimate partner violence as a preventable problem and sites prevention efforts at multiple levels across the social ecology—individual, relationship, community, and societal. Chapter 3 documents primary, secondary, and tertiary prevention efforts involving engagement with men and adolescents and explains how preventing adverse childhood experiences could significantly decrease intimate partner violence. Chapter 3 concludes with a look at how population level interventions could also prevent intimate partner violence.

Chapter 4 views intimate partner violence through the lens of community, surveying the research on the relationship between community characteristics and intimate partner violence. The chapter examines the links between social supports and collective efficacy and intimate partner violence. The chapter discusses a range of community-based responses to intimate partner violence, including community organizing, community accountability, and community-based justice, and argues that community-based responses could shift societal norms around intimate partner violence and provide meaningful justice for people subjected to abuse.

In chapter 5 intimate partner violence is cast as a human rights problem. The chapter explains the legal framework of international and regional agreements governing state responses to intimate partner violence and the specific rights safeguarded by those documents. The chapter introduces the concept of due diligence, which requires governments to intervene positively to prevent, protect, prosecute, punish, and provide redress in cases of intimate partner violence and explores how that concept has been actualized in case law and policy. The chapter also considers the relationship between human rights and the criminalization of intimate partner violence and looks at how international human rights norms have been applied to intimate partner violence in the United States. Finally, the chapter argues that using a human rights lens would foster the development of multidimensional solutions to the problem of intimate partner violence.

Intimate partner violence is an economic problem, a public health problem, a community problem, and a human rights problem. And despite the fact that a strong argument can be made for decriminalizing intimate partner violence, intimate partner violence remains a criminal problem as well. Policies seeking to curb intimate partner violence must, therefore, address each of these areas (and more). Chapter 6 offers a vision of what a balanced policy approach to intimate partner violence would look like. Chapter 6 suggests new laws addressing economic abuse and programs designed to put financial power into the hands of people subjected to abuse. Using a public health framework, it argues for a shift in focus from punishment to prevention and considers the laws and policies that would undergird such a shift. Chapter 6 calls for the development of community-based alternatives both to prevent and confront intimate partner violence, reallocating responsibility for redressing violence from the state to the community. The chapter considers what tools will be necessary to inculcate human rights norms against intimate partner violence in the United States. It also advocates for a diminished role for the criminal legal system in responding to intimate partner violence, making the criminal system the response of last resort in those cases where no other measure can meet the justice needs of the person subjected to abuse and rejecting criminal policies that exacerbate intimate partner violence. Chapter 6 concludes with suggestions for starting the movement toward decriminalization.

Because intimate partner violence is a multifaceted problem, sometimes the strategies to respond to it will overlap. Economic and community-based solutions are important in and of themselves, but may also act as a form of primary prevention in the public health sense of that term. Strategies will also be mutually reinforcing. The existence of (more limited and less brutal) criminal legal interventions serves as a backstop for community accountability and community justice strategies; the criminal system should be available in situations where no other policy intervention will prevent further violence. Community-based strategies are unlikely to successfully stem intimate partner violence in low-income communities if persistent poverty and neighborhood disadvantage, which mitigate the impact of community interventions, are not addressed. Therefore, economic justice is an essential component of empowering communities. Moreover, the policy prescriptions for confronting intimate partner violence are not simple. Promising interventions will have downsides and drawbacks. Before embracing any policy initiative, we need to have a clear understanding of its benefits and detriments and assess who is helped and who is harmed by the policy.

There is no one-size-fits-all solution to the problem of intimate partner violence. Intimate partner violence law and policy should expand the range of options and solutions available to people subjected to abuse and to people who use violence, enabling them to access the supports and programs that meet their individual needs. The overreliance on criminalization tips the programmatic and policy scales in ways that are harmful to people subjected to abuse, their partners, their families, and their communities and prevents the development of a menu of options. A balanced policy approach, one that is attuned to the needs of the most marginalized people subjected to abuse and creates a range of alternatives, might achieve what criminalization has failed to provide—a meaningful reduction in intimate partner violence in the United States.

1. Intimate Partner Violence Is . . .

A Criminal Justice Problem?

Ensuring that the state treated intimate partner violence like any other crime was a cornerstone of the early antiviolence movement. When police and prosecutors were slow to exercise their power to protect women subjected to abuse, the antiviolence movement used litigation, research, and the political process to leverage state engagement via the criminal legal system. Criminalization brought tangible benefits to some people subjected to abuse. But the criminal legal system has failed to deter intimate partner violence, and the harms of criminalization are significant enough to justify abandoning the use of the criminal legal system in cases of intimate partner violence.

A BRIEF HISTORY OF CRIMINALIZATION

Although intimate partner violence was criminalized as early as 1641 in the Massachusetts Bay Colony, levels of state intervention have varied over time. By the 1970s the criminal legal system was loath to intervene into what it saw as private family disputes. Police officers were trained not to make arrests in intimate partner violence cases. Police instructional manuals suggested that officers tell men who had abused their partners to take a walk around the block to cool down. Even if police had probable cause to make an arrest, police officers in most states could not make a warrantless arrest in an intimate partner violence case. If an arrest was made, the likelihood of prosecution was low.

States received federal funding related to intimate partner violence in the 1970s, but that funding was not primarily intended to shore up the criminal legal response. Instead, the Law Enforcement Assistance Administration provided funding to a number of pilot projects intended to help law enforcement clarify their role in responding to intimate partner violence in relation to the efforts of community organizations and social services providers. That funding disappeared in 1980; new funding for the criminal legal system would not be authorized until the passage of VAWA in 1994. VAWA would, for the first time, express a clear federal preference for law enforcement to lead the response to intimate partner violence.

Beginning in the late 1970s, antiviolence advocates sought to shift the public perception of intimate partner violence, making the case that intimate partner violence should be treated like any other crime. New criminal laws were not, strictly speaking, necessary to realize this goal; those who used violence could have been arrested and prosecuted under existing assault laws, for example. The real problem was the failure of police and prosecutors to enforce the laws. Frustrated with police inaction, feminist lawyers sued police departments in New York City and Oakland, California, over their "arrest-avoidance" policies. As a result of *Bruno v. Codd,* police in New York City promised to respond swiftly to intimate partner violence calls, make an arrest whenever they had reasonable cause to believe that a felony had been committed or a protective order had been violated, and remain on the scene to prevent further violence against the person seeking protection. Laurie Woods, the lawyer who filed *Bruno v. Codd,* believed strongly that arrest and prosecution were necessary to challenge the social conditions that permitted intimate partner violence to flourish and saw criminalization as preferable to any other response to intimate partner violence. In response to a similar lawsuit filed in California, *Scott v. Hart,* the Oakland Police Department rescinded its arrest-avoidance policy and agreed to treat intimate partner violence like other crimes. Pauline Gee, who brought the California case, saw state intervention as neutralizing the power imbalances between men and women, making the criminal system a "path to women's liberation."[1]

The failure to protect women subjected to abuse was becoming increasingly expensive for cities. On June 10, 1983, Tracey Thurman's husband, Charles, stabbed Tracey repeatedly in the chest, neck, and throat; after police arrived at the scene, Charles dropped the bloody knife and kicked Tracey in the head. Charles ran away, returned, dropped their toddler son on top of Tracey, and kicked Tracey in the head a second time despite the presence of police. Charles continued to threaten Tracey while police looked on. Only after Charles approached Tracey while she was lying on a stretcher did police arrest him. Tracey had repeatedly called police for protection prior to the June 1983 assaults. In 1984 Tracey Thurman won a multimillion-dollar judgment against the city of Torrington, Connecticut. Concerned about similar litigation, jurisdictions throughout the United States looked for innovative police practices that would shield them from liability. They found a model in Oregon's 1977 law requiring police to make arrests in intimate partner violence cases when the officer had probable cause to believe that an assault had been committed or when a person holding a protective order feared imminent serious harm—the precursor to mandatory arrest laws.

Research seemed to support the intuition that changes to arrest policy in cases involving intimate partner violence would prevent further lawsuits. In studies in 1981 and 1982 in Minneapolis, researchers Lawrence Sherman and Richard Berk found that arrest was associated with lower rates of recidivism by men who abused their partners. Despite Sherman's warning that the research should be replicated before conclusions could be drawn about the effectiveness of mandatory arrest, antiviolence advocates lobbied hard for the adoption of such policies, and municipalities across the United States quickly adopted them.[2] Sherman's warning was prescient. Later research on the effects of arrest policies was mixed. Replication studies found that mandatory arrest laws had deterrent effects in some locations, no effect in other locations, and contributed to increases in violence in others. Nonetheless, mandatory arrest policies would be bolstered in 1994 by the passage of VAWA, which initially required that states enact mandatory arrest policies as a condition of receiving federal funding under the act.[3] As of 2014, twenty states and the District of Columbia had enacted mandatory arrest policies.

Antiviolence advocates next turned their attention to low prosecution rates. Prosecutors complained that they could not prove their cases without the cooperation of those who had been abused. Witnesses often refused to testify, however, citing fear of retaliation by their partners, concern about exposing their partners to criminal liability, or opposition to having their partners incarcerated, because incarceration would deprive them of economic, emotional, parenting, and other forms of support. Prosecutors, therefore, would not bring intimate partner violence cases to court. No-drop prosecution was among the policies designed to address this problem. In no-drop prosecution jurisdictions, lack of victim cooperation did not prevent prosecutors from filing cases. Instead, they pursued any case where the evidence was strong enough to litigate, with or without the willing assistance of the person subjected to abuse. In soft no-drop jurisdictions, prosecutors provided inducements (like support services) for people to testify but did not compel their participation. In hard no-drop jurisdictions, prosecutors used whatever means necessary to make their cases, including subpoenaing unwilling witnesses, asking that subpoenas be enforced by arresting witnesses to ensure their attendance at court, and, in extreme cases, imprisoning people subjected to abuse as material witnesses prior to trial. By 1996 two-thirds of prosecutors' offices had adopted (primarily soft) no-drop policies.

Antiviolence advocates did not advance this carceral agenda in a vacuum. Efforts to increase the criminalization of intimate partner violence paralleled the ascendancy of neoliberalism as the guiding philosophy for U.S. social policy. Neoliberalism, narrowly defined, is a system of economic ideas and policies that emphasizes small government and market-based solutions to social and economic problems. Neoliberalism has (perhaps counterintuitively) spurred the use of criminal law, with mass incarceration replacing social welfare policy as the response to structural economic and political issues. Antiviolence reformers took advantage of the growing interest in and money for carceral responses, advocating for increased funding and training for police, prosecutors, and courts, as well as for laws and policies that prioritized the criminal legal response to intimate partner violence.

By the time VAWA was adopted in 1994, the antiviolence movement's embrace of the criminalization agenda was clear. VAWA provided funding incentives that firmly entrenched that agenda. VAWA allocated hundreds of millions of dollars for training and support of courts, police, and prosecutors, creating a powerful motivation for law enforcement to take the helm of antiviolence efforts. VAWA also created monetary incentives for antiviolence advocates to collaborate with law enforcement, committing the antiviolence movement more firmly to the criminal legal response. By 2003 many in the antiviolence movement agreed with George W. Bush when he stated that "government has got a duty to treat domestic violence as a serious crime, as part of our duty. If you treat something as a serious crime, then there must be serious consequences, otherwise it's not very serious. . . . Our prosecutors are doing their job. They're finding the abusers, and they're throwing the book at them. And that's important."[4]

THE BENEFITS OF CRIMINALIZATION

Criminalizing intimate partner violence does offer benefits to some people subjected to abuse. Intervention by the criminal legal system can give people distance from abuse. Police intervention can interrupt a violent incident and remove the offender from the scene.[5] Courts can issue criminal stay-away orders to prevent unwanted contact between people subjected to abuse and their partners both before and after prosecution. Successful prosecution can ensure that those who use violence enter batterer intervention programs as a condition of their sentences, which may lead to changes in behavior. Prosecution can send the message that people are serious about ending the abuse; even the threat of prosecution can give people subjected to abuse some leverage with their partners. The criminal legal system can provide resources, including victim-witness advocates and crime victim compensation funds, to people subjected to abuse. Incarceration and other forms of monitoring can provide a respite that affords people subjected to abuse peace of mind and the ability to implement short- and long-term safety plans.

Ensuring accountability for illegal behavior is another goal of criminal interventions. Accountability—the belief that those who abuse should be held responsible for their behavior by experiencing negative consequences through punishment, preferably via the criminal legal system—is one of the central tenets of the antiviolence movement. Arrest, prosecution, conviction, and incarceration are all employed to that end. Using the criminal legal system to address intimate partner violence can also underscore the state's condemnation of intimate partner violence, a stance that both vindicates the experiences of the individual subjected to abuse and may help to change community attitudes about the acceptability of intimate partner violence.

Finally, criminalization can satisfy the desire for retribution among those who define justice through punishment. Retribution requires that a wrongdoer receive a punishment befitting the crime; wrongs are righted through the offender's suffering. Punishment expresses society's condemnation of the act being punished and reinforces societal norms repudiating such behavior. Retributive justice delivered through the state also prevents individuals from seeking revenge. If an offender is arrested, convicted, and given some punishment that the person subjected to abuse deems proportionate to the harm suffered, that person's justice needs may be met. Because the state has a monopoly on legal punishment in the United States, only the criminal legal system has the potential to meet the justice goals of those who define justice retributively.

CRITIQUES OF CRIMINALIZATION

But in the past several years the idea of regulating behavior through criminalization has been seriously questioned, both generally and in the specific context of intimate partner violence. Criminalization has been called a "remarkable" failure, "perhaps the greatest in American history."[6] Overcriminalization has driven disproportionately high incarceration rates in the United States, particularly for marginalized groups. Excessive criminalization renders criminal penalties meaningless. And criminalization cannot solve America's social problems.

Hyperincarceration is a relatively new phenomenon in America. Spurred by "tough on crime" rhetoric, legislators have significantly increased both the number of crimes and the duration of sentences over the past forty years. Between 1970 and 2010 the state and federal prison population grew from 196,000 to 1.4 million people. Between 2010 and 2016 that number increased to 2.3 million incarcerated Americans, and more than 8 million living under some form of state control (for example, in jail or prison, on probation or parole, or serving community sanctions). The United States incarcerates 730 of every 100,000 people, the highest rate in the world. One in three African American men, one in seven Latino men, and one in seventeen white men spend time in prison during their lifetimes. Lesbian, gay, bisexual, transgender, and gender-nonconforming people are also jailed at disproportionate rates.

Hyperincarceration is problematic not just because of the sheer number of people it affects, but also because of the problematic consequences of incarceration. The impact of hyperincarceration ripples out into families and communities, as political scientist Marie Gottschalk explains: "The carceral state directly shapes, and in some cases deforms, the lives of tens of millions of people who have never served a day in jail or prison or been arrested. An estimated eight million minors—or one in ten children—have had an incarcerated parent. . . . Millions of people reside in neighborhoods and communities that have been depopulated and upended as so many of their young men and women have been sent away to prison during what should be the prime of their lives."[7]

The excessive use of criminalization to address social problems has decreased the expressive and actual effectiveness of criminal punishment while at the same time shielding policymakers from having to confront the underlying issues driving criminality. Criminalization can make lawmakers feel as though they have done something to address a problem, but legislators do not, by and large, analyze the effectiveness of those actions in any meaningful way. Criminalization is a "one-way ratchet"—lawmakers are unlikely to revisit or rescind criminal laws that have already been enacted, regardless of their impact or lack thereof. As a result the United States is "criminalizing, recriminalizing, and overcriminalizing all forms of conduct, much of it innocuous, to the point of erasing the line between tolerable and intolerable behavior."[8] When everything is criminal, it is hard to know what is truly wrong, or how to prevent offending.

Finally, criminalization is an ineffective response to the intractable social problems faced by the United States. In recent years the political system has failed to allocate resources to pressing social problems like poverty, homelessness, and mental illness. The neoliberal turn in American public policy, and the resulting dismantling of the welfare state, left many communities struggling and underresourced. Rather than provide low-income communities with social services, the U.S. government has increasingly poured resources into the criminal legal system, using that system to address the consequences of unresolved social problems. As activist Angela Davis has observed, incarceration is like magic, making societal problems seem to disappear.[9] But criminal law is poorly suited to solve these types of problems, rooted as they are in both individual social circumstances and larger systemic contexts.

Critiques of the Criminalization of Intimate Partner Violence

At the first Incite! Women of Color Against Violence conference in 2000, Davis linked the general critique of criminalization with the specific critique of the criminalization of intimate partner violence. She stated, "The major strategy relied on by the women's anti-violence movement of criminalizing violence against women will not put an end to violence against women—just as imprisonment has not put an end to 'crime' in general."[10]

Social work professor Mimi Kim has described the attempts of antiviolence advocates to harness the power of the criminal system as "the carceral creep"—"a dance of contentious politics initially engaged, provocatively and boldly, by feminist social movement actors with clear intentions to dominate law enforcement, oft times by subversive means."[11] Some of those feminists understood that engaging the criminal system posed real dangers, particularly for communities of color, and were concerned that focusing on the criminal legal system would divert attention from other needs. Those concerns were outweighed, however, by the belief that advocates could control law enforcement's actions and use the criminal system to their own ends. But, Kim explains, those hopes were naïve: "As law enforcement targets engage in this dance, first as recalcitrant partners and eventually as more active participants, they begin to find confidence and legible roles in their position as law enforcement in this new dance of contention. . . . Social movement actors and institutions in civil society, once the lead in this dance of contention, eventually become the subordinate partner in a dance now directed and dominated by the goals, political logics and institutions of law enforcement."[12]

The critique of the criminalization of intimate partner violence tracks the general critique in a number of ways. Criminalizing intimate partner violence is one example of the increasing tendency to address social problems by "governing through crime." As law professor Jonathan Simon explains, "Domestic violence has emerged over the last three decades as one of the clearest cases where a civil rights movement has turned to criminalization as a primary tool of social justice."[13] Moreover, both critiques are concerned with the disproportionate impact of criminalization on men of color. Criminalization of social problems like intimate partner violence has contributed to the exponential growth in men of color's rates of involvement with the criminal legal system. In a study of Milwaukee County, Wisconsin, for example, men of color represented 24 percent of the population but 66 percent of the defendants in intimate partner violence cases, a disparity attributed in part to policing practices. Most intimate partner violence offenses are prosecuted as misdemeanors, and rates of misdemeanor prosecution are much higher among men of color. Arrest and conviction may have particularly negative consequences for men of color; finding employment after incarceration is difficult for all men, for example, but much more so for men of color.[14]

There are, additionally, a number of concerns that are specific to the criminalization of intimate partner violence. First, criminalization has harmed women, originally the intended beneficiaries of these policies. Since the inception of more stringent arrest policies, for example, arrest rates among women have increased significantly. At least part of that increase, writes criminologist Alesha Durfee, "is directly attributable to the implementation of mandatory arrest policies and not simply an increased use of violence by women in intimate relationships."[15] Dual arrests—the arrest of both a woman and her partner—have also increased substantially both in the United States and Canada, again without evidence that women's use of violence has increased. Women who are arrested are likely to have been subjected to abuse and to have been physically assaulted, injured, or threatened. If women were committing acts of violence at frequencies commensurate to the rates of arrest, these policies might be justified by formal equality arguments—women and men should face the same consequences for their use of violence. But the research instead suggests that it is women subjected to abuse who are being penalized by arrest policies without justification. Anecdotal evidence supports the research. A Baltimore woman called police to report that her husband had strangled her. One officer responded. Finding the husband asleep, the officer left without taking a report or making an arrest. Later that day the husband left the residence.

When he attempted to force his way back into the house, the woman pushed him away. A neighbor called 911. Several police officers responded and arrested the woman. She spent the night in jail, faced criminal charges, and almost lost her job. LGBT-identified people may also be at risk. Connie Burk, executive director of the NW Network of Bi, Trans, Lesbian and Gay Survivors of Abuse, an antiviolence advocacy organization in Seattle, notes that in one year, fully half of their clients who had contact with the police were arrested.[16]

Criminalization has also increased state control over women through the intervention of the child abuse and neglect system. Increased police involvement in families experiencing intimate partner violence leaves mothers who are subjected to abuse at greater risk of being reported to child protective services agencies for failing to protect their children from exposure to that violence. Some police departments require officers to make a report to child protective services whenever a child is present at the scene of an incident of intimate partner violence. Coupled with state laws and policies that hold mothers accountable for their inability to prevent their partners from being violent in the presence of their children, the increased involvement of the criminal legal system means greater scrutiny of women's parenting and an increased likelihood that mothers will lose their children.

Operationalizing criminalization through the use of policies like mandatory arrest and no-drop prosecution has been disempowering for some people subjected to abuse. Mandatory policies deprive people of the ability to determine whether and how the state will intervene in their relationships, shifting power from the individual to the state. Law professor Aya Gruber recounts her days as a public defender: "I observed government actors systematically ignore women's desires to stay out of court, express disdain for ambivalent victims, and even infantilize victims to justify mandatory policies while simultaneously prosecuting the victims in other contexts."[17] The unwanted intrusion by the criminal legal system, as well as the deployment of mandatory policies against the wishes of those affected, disempowers people subjected to abuse. As sociologist Laureen Snider recognized, criminalization "is a strategy that empowers officials and court systems rather than women."[18] Mandatory policies may also be counterproductive: mandatory arrest may reduce reporting of intimate partner violence among women subjected to abuse who oppose the policy.

Prosecutors misuse mandatory policies. In their zeal to secure convictions, prosecutors in Orleans Parish, Louisiana, allegedly issued illegal subpoenas compelling victims of crime, including people subjected to abuse, to meet with prosecutors. If recipients of the subpoenas, which were issued without judicial approval, failed to attend these meetings, they were threatened with fines, arrest, and imprisonment. Prosecutors followed up on these threats, seeking material witness arrest warrants for those who failed to comply with the fraudulent subpoenas, asking judges to set unreasonably high bonds, and delaying the court appearances at which people could ask to be released. Renata Singleton, for example, declined to talk to prosecutors after her former boyfriend was arrested for intimate partner violence. Prosecutors issued an allegedly fraudulent subpoena, and when Singleton failed to appear for an interview, asked the court to jail her and set bond at $100,000. During her court appearance, Singleton's hands and feet were shackled, and she was chained to other prisoners in the courtroom. Because she could not pay the bond, Singleton was held for five days before being released. Her former partner, by contrast, paid his $3,500 bond on the day of arraignment, pled guilty to two misdemeanors, and served no time in jail.[19]

Marginalized people are most harmed by this overreliance on the criminal legal system. Because women of color are less likely to voluntarily engage the criminal legal system, for example, a response that relies primarily on criminalization is more likely to exclude them. Stories of police violence in the community exacerbate that reluctance to engage with the police. Crime reports in African American neighborhoods decline substantially after high-profile cases of excessive use of force by police. These decreases continue for more than one year after such incidents.[20] The deaths of Mike Brown, Mya Hall, Freddie Gray, Korryn Gaines, Walter Smith, Sandra Bland, Eric Garner, Charleena Lyles, and Philando Castile at the hands of police are likely chilling reporting of intimate partner violence in their communities.

Criminalization has a disproportionately negative impact on women of color because it exposes them to greater risks of state violence and control. Arrest rates of women of color for intimate partner violence are higher in mandatory arrest jurisdictions.[21] Women of color frequently have negative, abusive, and even deadly experiences with police officers who are called to respond to intimate partner violence. In July 2016 Melissa Ventura was killed by police responding to an intimate partner violence call; in February 2015, after a fight with her girlfriend prompted a call to police, the responding officers shot and killed Janisha Fonville.[22] State intervention cannot guarantee safety for women of color so long as these women both fear and are actively harmed by engaging with the state.

Overreliance on the criminal legal system has larger societal consequences as well. Criminalization shifts the responsibility for policing intimate partner violence from the community to the state. While that initial move grew out of community failures to sufficiently protect people from abuse, the result has been to relieve communities of any responsibility for or ability to hold community members accountable without resorting to the criminal legal system. Criminologist Nils Christie has argued that conflicts provide the "*potential for activity, for participation.* Modern criminal control systems represent one of the many cases of lost opportunities for involving citizens in tasks that are of immediate importance to them."[23] The diversion of responsibility from community to state through criminalization has left community responses to intimate partner violence undertheorized and underdeveloped.

Criminalization also directs resources and attention away from people's other, sometimes more pressing, needs. Government funding is often a zero-sum game: money dedicated to policing, prosecution, and punishment cannot be used to provide other crucial services and supports for people subjected to abuse. Resources that are focused on the criminal legal system could be spent providing economic and housing support or civil legal assistance to people subjected to abuse. Criminalization also allows policymakers to ignore the larger structural economic, social, and political factors that contribute to intimate partner violence.

There are a number of potential responses to the criminalization critique. Abandoning mandatory policies would address some of the problems with criminalization. Channeling resources away from the criminal legal system or creating parallel community based systems without fundamentally changing the structure of the criminal legal response to intimate partner violence is another option. Prison abolitionists, for their part, argue for changing the punishment structure, replacing incarceration with other sanctions, but not necessarily for jettisoning the criminal legal response altogether. No theorist has proposed the complete decriminalization of intimate partner violence. But examining the leading theories of criminalization and decriminalization might provide support for such a proposal.

THE THEORETICAL BASIS FOR (DE)CRIMINALIZATION

Although much has been written about theoretical justifications for punishment, criminalization itself has been less comprehensively theorized. Motivated by concerns about overcriminalization, however, a number of scholars have grappled with the question of whether and under what conditions conduct should be deemed criminal. Over the past fifty years, Herbert Packer, Joel Feinberg, John Braithwaite and Philip Pettit, Jonathan

Schonsheck, and Douglas Husak have all developed theories of criminalization that are applicable to the criminalization of intimate partner violence.

The theorists share four concerns. First, only those acts that have the potential to cause harm should be criminalized. Second, there must be some reason to believe that criminalization will deter the harmful behavior. Third, criminalization of the behavior must do more good than harm. Finally, criminalization should occur only when less intrusive alternatives for preventing the behavior do not exist. The theorists all agree that assault (the primary crime charged in cases of intimate partner violence) should be criminalized. Nonetheless, their work supports the case for decriminalizing intimate partner violence.

APPLYING THE THEORIES

Harm

To justify the criminalization of intimate partner violence, the law must be either addressing or preventing a serious harm. The law of assault clearly does both. While not every assault actually causes serious harm, the types of behavior covered by assault law have the potential to inflict substantial damage. Moreover, whether prosecuted as misdemeanors or felonies, intimate partner assaults can in fact cause serious physical injuries ranging from bruising to broken bones to brain damage. New laws targeting specific forms of assault have been proposed and passed over the last several years as researchers have identified particularly harmful forms of intimate partner violence. States have increased penalties for strangulation, for example, as the medical evidence on the damage caused by strangulation and the dangerous role it plays in intimate partner violence has accumulated. Even when imperfectly or inconsistently enforced, the criminal laws targeting intimate partner violence are intended to prevent and address potentially serious harm.

Deterrence

Deterrence—the belief that criminalizing an act will decrease the likelihood that that act will be committed as a result—is central to a number of the theories. But simply citing deterrence as motivation should not be sufficient justification for criminalizing behavior. Instead, there must be some evidence that the law actually does or will deter the targeted conduct, even if the law serves other functions.

Notwithstanding the assumptions made by those who make and adjudicate the law, enacting criminal laws does not deter offenders from engaging in the behavior prohibited by those laws. The criminal law fails to deter in part because offenders are generally unaware of the legal rules designed to prevent them from engaging in criminal conduct. Moreover, even if they do know the rules, the cost-benefit analysis offenders engage in usually leads them to believe that violation of those rules is only minimally risky because the potential for punishment seems slight or remote. Finally, even if an offender both knows the rules and believes that the costs of violating those rules outweigh the benefits, that offender may still be unable to deploy that knowledge to refrain from criminal behavior. Because the evidence shows how unlikely it is that an offender will meet each of these requirements, "it will be the unusual instance in which the doctrine can ultimately influence conduct."[24]

The evidence that criminalizing intimate partner violence has had a deterrent effect is inconclusive. The last forty years have allowed for a kind of natural experiment testing the hypothesis that criminalization deters intimate partner violence. Prior to the late 1970s, police largely declined to charge assaults and other violations of the law involving intimate partners. Beginning in the 1980s, states began both to enforce existing criminal laws (like assault) and to pass statutes creating specific crimes of intimate partner violence. While rates of intimate partner violence dropped between 1994 and 2000, that decrease coincided with an overall decrease in the crime rate and cannot be specifically attributed to the more stringent policing of intimate partner violence. From 2000 to 2010 rates of intimate partner violence fell less than the decrease in the overall crime rate, suggesting that those who commit intimate partner violence were less deterred than criminals committing other types of crimes. Why rates have stayed high is unclear. It is certainly possible that reporting of intimate partner violence increased, for instance, leading to higher rates, though there is no research to support that proposition, and intimate partner violence remains one of the most underreported crimes.

Whatever the reason, studies have failed to find that the existence of laws specifically targeting intimate partner violence deters the behavior. Arrest in cases of intimate partner violence has effects on recidivism ranging from modest to nonexistent. For some groups of people, arrest can exacerbate violence. One study found that the relationship between arrest for intimate partner violence and future violence was attributable entirely to pre-arrest differences (for example, a prior criminal history) in risk of offending.[25]

Studies on the deterrent effect of prosecution on future violence are mixed. Conviction may have some effect on recidivism, but the deterrent value may disappear when ongoing monitoring and other provisions to ensure accountability are not part of the sentence. Some studies find that jail time and other sentencing options have no effect on recidivism; others suggest that the imposition of more severe sanctions (jail time plus continued monitoring postincarceration) may deter future violence. There is no evidence that longer sentences for violent crimes create any greater level of deterrence.

The failure to find a strong deterrent effect as a result of the criminalization of intimate partner violence could be attributed to a number of sources. First, inconsistent enforcement of intimate partner violence laws could make it difficult to detect deterrent effects. Even in jurisdictions that mandate arrest in intimate partner violence cases, for example, those laws are inconsistently enforced. Criminalization's lack of a deterrent effect has also been attributed to the combination of the low probability of arrest for intimate partner violence and the high probability that prosecutors will decline to bring the case forward. Without the credible threat of punishment as a result of violation of the law, deterrence is unlikely.

Second, the main measure of deterrence in cases of intimate partner violence is problematic. Deterrence and prevention have traditionally been measured through recidivism. Studies of recidivism generally ask whether an offender has been re-arrested rather than investigating whether intimate partner violence has recurred in the relationship. But these questions might yield very different results; one study found recidivism rates of 22 percent when using official reports and 49 percent when asking victims whether there had been any new violence.[26] Because criminal law defines intimate partner violence primarily as physical violence and threats of physical violence, new arrests for intimate partner violence may capture only a fraction of the violence within a relationship. Using re-arrest as a proxy for re-abuse misses noncriminal forms of violence like emotional abuse that may be as or more debilitating than physical violence. Moreover, people subjected to intimate partner violence may choose not to report new offenses to police or prosecutors if their initial interactions with the criminal legal system were negative. Although recidivism can also be measured through victim report, intimate partner violence is routinely underreported, particularly when the victim does not want further involvement with formal systems. Even in Quincy, Massachusetts, a jurisdiction that aggressively enforced intimate partner violence laws, recidivism rates were high in a 1999 study, in large measure because criminalization failed to deter serious, repeat criminals from engaging in abusive behavior.[27]

Finally, criminalization may not deter because criminal punishment fails to target the underlying causes of intimate partner violence and therefore cannot change the behavior of those who engage in it. This lack of understanding about why offenders engage in crime is a particular problem in the context of intimate partner violence. The antiviolence movement has long maintained that men abuse in order to exert power and control over their partners, building this belief into the intervention programs created to address men's use of violence. Criminal sentences for intimate partner violence often require offenders to participate in these programs. But as pioneering advocate Ellen Pence observed shortly before her death, whether men actually intend to exert power and control, or whether power and control is instead a byproduct of abuse, is an open question. Pence noted that neither the women nor the men with whom she worked identified power and control as the goal of abuse.[28] Assuming that obtaining power and control is the reason men engage in intimate partner violence has preempted serious study of other potential causes of that violence, leading to ineffective interventions.

Cost-Benefit Analysis

Although criminalization and incarceration are often conflated, criminalization has its own particular set of costs. Being labeled a criminal brings both social stigma and a host of restrictions, including denial of the right to vote, ineligibility for public housing, federal welfare benefits, military service, and education grants, and barriers to finding employment. For undocumented people, convictions can result in deportation. Just being arrested for intimate partner violence can create a record that the public can easily access through online court information systems. Criminalization invites surveillance of offenders through community monitoring and probation, even if offenders are not incarcerated—and sometimes even if they are not ultimately convicted. Diversion programs and other conditions imposed in lieu of adjudication allow the state to monitor offenders' behavior in exchange for a dismissal of charges if offenders meet enumerated conditions. But even minor infractions committed during the monitoring period can result in the imposition of more serious penalties, including incarceration.

When using incarceration as the benchmark, the costs of criminalization are exponentially higher. Not only does incarceration not deter future violence, time in prison may actually drive further offending. Incarceration creates or reinforces conditions that lead to greater recidivism: dehumanization of inmates, destruction of communities, and prevention of structural investment.

Penal facilities in the United States are dehumanizing institutions, relying upon practices of punishment and control abandoned by most developed nations. Law professor Jonathan Simon refers to U.S. penal facilities as "waste management prisons," arguing that such facilities are not intended to transform prisoners in any way, but are meant only to warehouse criminal offenders.[29] Incarceration in these kinds of facilities reinforces the bitterness of those subjected to such treatment and does nothing to decrease the odds of recidivism.

Incarceration helps to explain "why ex-prisoners earn less, are employed less, and toil at 'bad jobs characterized by high turnover and little chance of moving up the income ladder.'"[30] Prior to being jailed, two-thirds of male inmates are employed, and half of them serve as the primary source of support for their families.[31] When fathers are incarcerated, family income declines by as much as 22 percent, and 65 percent of families cannot meet all of their needs.[32] The children of incarcerated fathers are more likely to experience homelessness; their mothers are more likely to receive public assistance[33]; and the families are more likely to live in unsupportive neighborhoods.[34] Upon release, formerly imprisoned men both work and earn less. Sixty percent of former prisoners experience long-term unemployment, and employed former prisoners earn 40 percent less than those who have not been incarcerated.[35] Having been incarcerated poses a significant impediment to finding employment for white men and a "nearly insurmountable barrier" for men of color; as few as 5 percent of African American applicants for employment with criminal records receive callbacks for interviews.[36] Incarceration depresses both the wages and annual income of former inmates. As criminologist Elliott Currie concludes, "[T]he experience of incarceration, especially in a society that already suffers from a hollowed opportunity structure and thin social supports, is often a disabling one that sharply reduces the number of prospects of a good job and decent earnings—and thus serves in practice to cement great numbers of former offenders into a condition of permanent marginality."[37]

Former inmates are frequently released into neighborhoods whose stability is undermined by the loss of their members to prison. In communities already weakened by poverty and high unemployment rates, social networks are essential in providing support. But the disappearance of significant numbers of individuals who should be raising children and contributing to the local economy saps community strength. "[T]hese ongoing removals, isolations and relocations can prove a formidable barrier to building a stable, close community in which people look out for their neighbors."[38] When members of communities know less about each other, their capacity for understanding each other's behavior decreases. Given this lack of familiarity, the community is less able to address conflicts when they occur. The state, however, is ready and willing to take these conflicts out of the community's hands; when community relationships are frayed, the community is open to allowing the state to assume responsibility. In such communities, informal social controls are undercut, creating conditions that are ripe for violence. By ceding responsibility for conflict resolution, communities lose the opportunity to discuss and recalibrate the norms by which members of the community should live—including norms around nonviolence.

Moreover, investment in prisons diverts resources away from the economically disadvantaged communities that many offenders are released into, depriving those communities of funding for education, health care, employment assistance, housing, and other services that could benefit ex-offenders and stabilize communities. Such services are more likely to prevent further violence than doing time in a "waste management" prison.

The costs of incarceration are similarly high in the specific context of intimate partner violence. Incarceration depresses employment opportunities for former offenders. Rates of intimate partner violence correlate with male unemployment; the more often a man is unemployed, the higher the rate of violence.[39] Both subjective reports and objective measures of economic strain correlate with intimate partner violence.[40] Moreover, rates of intimate partner violence increase in economically disadvantaged neighborhoods, possibly as "a product of the loss of social controls in a community and the weakening of social ties. When residents have weak ties with their neighbors, they are unlikely to effectively shape social norms in the neighborhood."[41] The intersections of economics and community characteristics with intimate partner violence will be more thoroughly explored in chapters 2 and 4.

Finally, the violence that offenders experience in prison is recycled in their interpersonal relationships. The irony of incarceration is that individuals being punished for violence are sent to places where they are likely to be perpetrators or victims of, or witnesses to, violence. Up to 20 percent of prisoners have been physically abused in prison. Ten percent of state prisoners report being sexually abused. The trauma of victimization has serious consequences, including posttraumatic stress disorder (PTSD) and other mental health issues. Witnessing violence in prison can also trigger symptoms of trauma. Former prisoners bring this trauma with them into their relationships in the community, with harmful consequences; perpetration of intimate partner violence and PTSD are strongly correlated.

Moreover, as law professor Angela Harris has argued, "relying on criminal justice to punish the perpetrators of violence against women and sexual minorities in the long run perpetuates more gender violence."[42] Prisons reinforce and magnify the destructive ideologies that drive intimate partner violence. Prison culture reflects the values and norms of the outside society, including norms around masculinity. Inmates, like other men, often construct masculinity in opposition to the feminine or feminized. The need to be seen as powerful (and therefore not feminine) is an essential component of hegemonic masculinity. Violence against women, or those perceived as feminine, reinforces the hegemonic masculine identity. Prison violence, particularly sexual violence, is an assertion of masculinity; sexual assault demarcates the victim as "female" within the prison ecosystem. Prisoners bring problematic notions of masculinity into the prison, have experiences that further shape, warp, and reproduce those norms, and return to their communities with those ideas—a process that law professor SpearIt has called "the cycle of destructive masculinity."[43] Those notions of masculinity, in turn, poison the relationships that former prisoners have in the community.

Incarceration does not help offenders to value others or create empathy—the necessary preconditions to preventing further harm. Instead, offenders report that prisons create an atmosphere where they can ignore or repress the effects of their actions on others, making future violence more likely. Decreases in empathy continue after an offender's release from incarceration; African American men who have been incarcerated are less likely to feel empathy for family members who were currently incarcerated, suggesting that "empathetic inurement," which may help men to survive incarceration, "follows these men back into the community."[44]

Weighed against these costs are the actual and potential benefits of criminalization. Criminalization brought significant resources to the antiviolence movement. In 1980 federal funding for programs designed to improve the legal system's response to intimate partner violence was eliminated. The Family Violence Prevention and Services Act continued to allocate funding for shelter and social services programs, but that funding did not benefit law enforcement. With the recasting of intimate partner violence as a criminal problem through VAWA, however, millions of dollars became available to police, prosecutors, courts, and community advocacy agencies—a total of $430 million in 2015. The majority of that funding flows to the criminal legal system, primarily through VAWA's two largest grant programs: the STOP Program and the Improving the Criminal Justice Response to Sexual Assault, Domestic Violence, Dating Violence, and Stalking

Program (formerly known as the Grants to Encourage Arrests and Enforcement of Protection Orders Program). Additional funding is allocated to law enforcement through other VAWA programs (for example, through grants funding services for rural victims, college students, and marginalized communities). Antiviolence advocates receive significant amounts of funding through the criminal system provisions of VAWA as well. Encouraging collaboration between antiviolence advocates and law enforcement is an explicit goal of VAWA, and many of VAWA's grants require the participation (and funding) of community partners. Prioritizing the criminal legal response to intimate partner violence is directly responsible for bringing millions of dollars in funding into the antiviolence movement.

The other benefits of criminalization are less tangible. Criminalization could deter an individual offender from engaging in future violence (a claim addressed above) or serve as a general deterrent by sending the message that society will not condone intimate partner violence. On the individual level, criminal laws forbidding intimate partner violence validate the experiences of people subjected to abuse by clearly and unequivocally stating that what has been done to them is wrong. Moreover, criminalization provides a process through which individuals (through the state) can pursue retributive justice and the possibility of vindication, if their claims of abuse are believed.

Criminalization could also increase safety for people subjected to abuse. To the extent that arrest incapacitates their partners, prosecution and conviction result in incarceration, or the criminal court issues an order for the offender to stay away from a person subjected to abuse, that person's immediate safety could increase. Some people subjected to abuse believe that intervention by the criminal legal system will provide them with protection, reporting that punishments like jail time and probation give them the opportunity to put short- and long-term safety measures into place. Regardless of the sentence imposed, some people experience less fear after their partners are convicted. Although it may have no broader societal impact, individuals' safety may be enhanced through criminalization.

If accountability is defined as ensuring that those who abuse face the prospect of punishment through the legal system, criminalization can also provide accountability. Prosecution and conviction rates for intimate partner violence have increased significantly over the last twenty years. Between 60 percent and 70 percent of arrests lead to charges, and between 25 percent and 50 percent of offenders are convicted of those charges. If convicted, somewhere between two-thirds and three-quarters of offenders are imprisoned. Those numbers are slightly misleading, because they do not include cases in which no arrest was made; when those numbers are included, the overall rates of charging, conviction, and incarceration are significantly lower. But to the extent that accountability correlates with prosecution and conviction, criminalization increases accountability, at least when police make arrests.[45]

Finally, criminalizing intimate partner violence has expressive value. As law professor Danielle Citron writes,

> Law creates a public set of meanings and shared understandings between the state and the public. It clarifies, and draws attention to, the behavior it prohibits. Law's expressed meaning serves mutually reinforcing purposes. Law educates the public about what is socially harmful. This legitimates harms, allowing the harmed party to see herself as harmed. It signals appropriate behavior. In drawing attention to socially appropriate behavior, law permits individuals to take these social meanings into account when deciding on their actions. Because law creates and shapes social mores, it has an important cultural impact that differs from its more direct coercive effects.[46]

The early efforts of antiviolence advocates to increase awareness and condemnation of intimate partner violence were meant to ensure that intimate partner violence would be treated as a crime like any other. Enacting new laws against intimate partner violence was an important component of that strategy. For better or worse, the social importance of intimate partner violence is measured by the level of punishment meted out for the crime; recall the widespread condemnation of the six-month sentence handed down to Brock Turner, the Stanford University student convicted of raping an unconscious woman behind a dumpster on campus in 2015. Moving away from criminalization, some fear, would signal tacit acceptance of intimate partner violence and a waning of the state's commitment to protecting people subjected to abuse.

This analysis should also take into account how the costs and benefits of criminalization are allocated. Those who commit crimes of intimate partner violence most obviously, but not exclusively, shoulder the costs of criminalization. Those costs disproportionately fall on people of color and low-income people, who are more likely to become enmeshed in the criminal legal system and lack the resources to secure private representation or engage services that might prevent them from being incarcerated. The partners of those who abuse also bear the costs, particularly when intervention by the criminal legal system is not what the person subjected to abuse would have chosen or when they themselves are arrested and prosecuted. Children are both emotionally and economically harmed by parental involvement in the criminal legal system. Communities lose economic contributions and struggle with the weakening of societal bonds. Taxpayers subsidize the costs of arresting, prosecuting, monitoring, and incarcerating those who are subject to the criminal legal system.

Criminalization most benefits those who feel safer as a result of interventions but are immune from most of its costs: people who don't share children with their partners, people who are no longer in relationships with those partners, people who don't rely on their partners in any way, higher-income people. For those who equate justice with punishment by the criminal legal system, criminalization is the only means of achieving justice. Incapacitation of a violent offender (assuming conviction and incarceration) is a benefit in cases where the safety of a person subjected to abuse is imperiled by an offender who is undeterred by civil protection orders and other noncriminal interventions. Given the funding priorities in this area, criminalization also benefits law enforcement and the nonprofits who collaborate with law enforcement.

Alternatives to Criminalization

All of the theories of criminalization require proponents of criminal legislation to consider whether the state could reduce the incidence of undesirable conduct through means short of criminalization. Alternatives to criminalization are underdeveloped, making criminalization the default response to bad behavior. But given that the majority of people subjected to abuse do not seek assistance from the criminal legal system, developing alternatives to that system should be a priority for policymakers.

Currently available programs and legal solutions could partially replicate the role of criminalization—to control or deter abusive behavior. People subjected to abuse can seek civil protective orders requiring that their partners refrain from abuse or stay away and providing other forms of relief. Those who abuse may be able to access batterer intervention counseling without being ordered to do so in a criminal case, although many such programs are court affiliated.

In terms of programs designed to replace state control with community or other forms of informal social control, however, both policymakers and antiviolence advocates have been leery of experimentation. Antiviolence advocates have opposed the idea of using alternative dispute resolution in cases involving intimate partner violence. Concerns have been raised about whether such processes can be made sufficiently safe and whether they will actually hold offenders accountable for their actions. Moreover, having worked for forty years to have intimate partner violence treated as a crime, advocates are unwilling to risk diluting the power of the criminal legal response by creating parallel or alternative justice systems.

Nonetheless, alternatives to prevent and address the harms of intimate partner violence do exist. Economic interventions could relieve some of the conditions that spur intimate partner violence. If prevention is the goal, public health initiatives might serve that function more effectively than criminalization. Community-based alternatives, like restorative justice, transformative justice, community accountability, and male peer support interventions, are being used successfully in some communities and could be expanded. But criminalization hampers the development, implementation, and evaluation of these alternatives. Criminalization is the default response that policymakers and some antiviolence advocates are loath, even afraid, to abandon. And so long as funding for antiviolence efforts remains focused on the criminal legal system, criminalization will deprive efforts to develop alternatives of needed resources.

The United States has developed a robust response to intimate partner violence. That response relies heavily on the effective operation of the criminal legal system. But intervention by the criminal legal system does not deter intimate partner violence. Moreover, the costs of criminalization, particularly when intervention results in incarceration, significantly outweigh its benefits. Given those realities, a persuasive argument could be made for decriminalizing intimate partner violence.

The U.S. policy experiment with criminalization as a primary response to intimate partner violence is neither an unqualified success nor a total failure. What it has revealed is the need for a multidimensional response to intimate partner violence. Policies grounded in economics, public health, community, and human rights should all be part of that response.

2. Intimate Partner Violence Is . . .

An Economic Problem

Intimate partner violence imposes huge costs on the U.S. economy. Poverty and intimate partner violence are strongly correlated. Low-income women are much more likely to experience intimate partner violence, and under- and unemployed men more likely to perpetrate it. Economic instability prevents women from leaving abusive relationships. Economic abuse is a widely recognized form of intimate partner violence, experienced by the majority of people subjected to abuse. Intimate partner violence is affected and exacerbated by structural economic forces. A strong case can be made for confronting intimate partner violence as an economic problem.

THE COSTS OF INTIMATE PARTNER VIOLENCE

While it is impossible to pinpoint an exact amount, intimate partner violence costs the U.S. economy as much as $67 billion annually. That figure includes expenditures by local government (in payments for police, medical, and social services) and losses to individuals (for decreased productivity, health care, destruction of and damage to property, and diminished quality of life). Injuries resulting from intimate partner violence total approximately $5 billion per year in medical expenses and lost productivity.

People subjected to abuse, not surprisingly, bear the majority of the economic burden. Health-care costs are 19 percent higher for women subjected to intimate partner violence; people subjected to abuse spend as much as $1,775 more yearly on health care than those who have not been abused.[1] Each time an employed woman is assaulted, she averages seven days of absence from work and needs $800 in medical and mental health care.[2] Women subjected to abuse report significantly worse physical health than other women and are three times as likely to experience a mental health disorder.[3] People subjected to abuse also earn less. Women may lose as much as $18 million annually in earnings as a result of intimate partner violence.[4] Intimate partner violence contributes to structural economic inequality as well; violence against women may contribute to the gender pay gap, for example.

Seeking protection from intimate partner violence results in economic penalties and contributes to income instability. Contact with police can lead to loss of housing, employment, and welfare benefits. Participating in prosecution imposes economic harm on those who are forced to miss work for court dates. Women lose up to $1,018 in income the year after they petition civil courts for protection from abuse and never recoup that income.[5] Studies likely underestimate the true costs of intimate partner violence for people subjected to abuse. A comprehensive estimate of the costs would have to include "reduced wages, work hours, job experience, employment stability, and earnings; increased food insecurity and trouble paying rent or utility bills; chronic individual and intergenerational cycling between work and welfare and in and out of abusive relationships; and what researchers term 'dangerous dependencies' on abusive men for job supports such as childcare and transportation."[6]

Employers also incur significant expenses as a result of intimate partner violence. The U.S. Centers for Disease Control and Prevention estimates that intimate partner violence costs employers $5.8 billion annually in health care and lost productivity. Women subjected to abuse use approximately $2,000 more in benefits than others enrolled in health plans.[7] Offenders' tardiness and absenteeism also impose economic burdens on employers. Seventy-five percent of men convicted of intimate partner violence reported missing at least one day of work as a result of intimate partner violence. Forty-six percent were late, 39 percent left early, and 17 percent attributed mistakes on the job to abuse. Offenders also use work equipment to stalk and harass their partners, expenses borne by employers. Seventy-eight percent of the men used workplace resources either to monitor or to threaten their partners; 48 percent reported trouble concentrating at work.[8] Men who use violence were more likely to make mistakes at work and to report bad health.

THE RELATIONSHIP BETWEEN ECONOMICS AND INTIMATE PARTNER VIOLENCE

The early antiviolence movement described intimate partner violence as a problem that plagued women without regard to race, ethnicity, or socioeconomic class. But low-income women are disproportionately represented among people subjected to abuse. As many as two-thirds of low-income women are subjected to intimate partner violence.[9] The lower a woman's income, the more likely she is to experience intimate partner violence: women who are at or below the poverty level are subjected to abuse almost twice as often as women at 101 percent to 200 percent of the poverty level.[10] Women with household incomes of less than $10,000 per year experience intimate partner violence four times more often than women with annual household incomes of $50,000 or more.[11] Women with household incomes of $7,500 or less annually are subjected to intimate partner violence nearly seven times as often as women with household incomes of $75,000.[12] Debt is also related to rates of intimate partner violence. Women with significant debt are 75 percent more likely to be abused than women with little debt.[13] According to researchers Lisa Goodman, Katya Fels Smyth, Angela M. Borges, and Rachel Singer, "[H]ousehold income level is one of the most, if not *the* most, significant correlates of partner violence."[14] Intimate partner violence is particularly prevalent among women on welfare. Between 40 percent and 60 percent of the welfare population has been subjected to intimate partner violence at some time.[15]

Intimate partner violence is also associated with indicators of material deprivation: food insufficiency, lack of stable housing, and utility disconnection, for example. Women subjected to abuse are more likely to be materially deprived than women who have not been abused. Upon leaving abusive relationships, some women struggle financially, finding it difficult to meet their basic needs; material deprivation may continue for as long as three years after the abuse has ended. Sophie's story is illustrative. After Sophie obtained a protective order, her partner, Henry, "emptied the entire apartment, turned off the utilities, cancelled the lease (which was only in his name), and moved to another state. 'So there I was," Sophie recalled, "'in an empty apartment, eight months pregnant, with a toddler, with no job." Over time, Sophie's economic status deteriorated. "I couldn't keep a job. I'd try to get a job and I'd lose it because I couldn't handle myself at work. . . . I had no money, I had no food, I had no brain, I had no time, I had no friends, I had no church." Court appearances cost Sophie job after job, and her inability to keep a job prevented her from seeking full custody of her children after losing them to Henry.[16]

Women subjected to abuse earn less than other women, with those effects beginning as early as adolescence. Being abused in a teen dating relationship depresses women's adult earnings, a deficit attributable to their lower educational attainment. Women subjected to abuse earn $3,900 less annually than women who had not experienced violence[17] and are paid 76 cents per hour less than nonabused women.[18] Women who sought protective orders saw their wages decrease 53 cents per hour after doing so.[19] The more severe the violence to which they are subjected, the less women earn. Women may also experience material deprivation because programs for women subjected to abuse are sometimes reluctant to provide services to very poor women, particularly if they are considered deviant in some way (for example, if they are homeless or substance users).[20]

Intimate partner violence is more frequent and more severe for low-income women and is particularly acute among low-income women of color, for reasons that may be tied to neighborhood disadvantage. A number of studies have found that intimate partner violence is more prevalent and more serious among couples who live in low-income neighborhoods, with rates of intimate partner violence highest among those in the lowest-income locations. Women who live in economically disadvantaged communities and are struggling financially are at greatest risk of intimate partner violence.[21] The overrepresentation of people of color in economically stressed neighborhoods likely accounts for the high rates of intimate partner violence among low-income women of color.

There is a reciprocal relationship between intimate partner violence and neighborhood disadvantage. Intimate partner violence is more prevalent in low-income neighborhoods, and couples experiencing intimate partner violence are more likely to be economically vulnerable and to live in disadvantaged neighborhoods. Both couples who are financially overextended and those who believe themselves to be financially strained are at greater risk for intimate partner violence. Moving to a better resourced neighborhood does not eliminate the risk. Economically vulnerable couples always have higher rates of intimate partner violence than those with fewer economic constraints (as much as three times higher, according to one study), regardless of where they reside. The combination of neighborhood disadvantage and subjective feelings of economic strain is particularly problematic, however; 14 percent of couples living in low-income neighborhoods and reporting acute economic stress experience intimate partner violence, as opposed to 7 percent of high-strain couples living in advantaged neighborhoods. The relationship between community income levels and intimate partner violence is not a function of who lives in low-income neighborhoods or the individual characteristics of the men living in those neighborhoods. The relationship is instead a result of the neighborhood context—living in a low-income neighborhood in and of itself increases the risk of intimate partner violence.[22]

ECONOMIC ABUSE

Economic abuse is defined as "behaviors that control a woman's ability to acquire, use, and maintain economic resources, thus threatening her economic security and potential for self-sufficiency."[23] Economic abuse includes economic control (blocking the acquisition of assets, controlling how resources are distributed, and monitoring how they are used), economic exploitation (depleting women's resources), and employment sabotage.

Most women who are subjected to other forms of abuse are also economically abused. Estimates of the prevalence of economic abuse range from 68 percent in a 2004 study of a shelter-based population[24] to 100 percent of women receiving services from a community-based antiviolence organization in a 2015 study.[25] Ninety-four percent of participants in a financial literacy program for women subjected to abuse had experienced economic abuse.[26] Between 79 percent and 92 percent reported economic control, 79 percent experienced economic exploitation, and between 78 percent and 88 percent had their employment sabotaged. Most women report that their partners are responsible for their economic problems.[27]

Economic abuse takes a number of forms. Economic control includes restricting or preventing access to joint bank accounts or other sources of income, refusing to contribute financially, forcing a person to make deposits into an abusive partner's bank account, withholding funds or providing a strict allowance, denying access to financial information, demanding to know how money is spent, or making economic decisions without consulting a partner. When Darlene asked her husband for money to buy shoes for her children and grandchildren, for example, her husband responded, "I've decided that this is my money. I'll do what I want to do with my money. I don't have to give you any money, spend money on you, I don't have to pay the bills 'cause I don't live here. . . . And by the way, I took your name off the checking account and the savings account. So that's it. If you want some money . . . if you think you need some money, then you need to ask me for some money. And if I have it I'll give you half of what you ask for."[28] Increases in economic control often correlate with decreases in the self-sufficiency of the person subjected to abuse.

Economic exploitation includes paying bills late, spending money intended to pay rent or bills, stealing money, creating costs by destroying property, failing to pay taxes or putting tax liability in a partner's name, or generating debt. Kara was forced to declare bankruptcy when her partner ruined her credit; Louise lost her home after her partner insisted that she add him to the title, then took out a second mortgage on the home, which he failed to pay.[29] Sixteen percent of the women living in Humboldt Park, Chicago, reported economic control and exploitation in a 1999 study: their partners withheld money from them, made them ask for money, or took their money.[30] Note that this study surveyed all women living in the area—not solely those who reported intimate partner violence.

Coerced debt—amassing and using consumer debt to exercise control over a partner—is a particularly pernicious type of economic abuse with long-term consequences for people subjected to abuse. Coerced debt can take a number of forms: obtaining credit through the use of fraud or duress; secretly taking out credit cards using a partner's name; pressuring or forcing a partner to sign loan documents; tricking a partner into relinquishing rights to property, such as a family home; refusing to allow a partner access to credit; and borrowing knowing the partner will be liable for the debt. Coerced debt may not be discovered until after people subjected to abuse have left their relationships, when the debt is already delinquent or is close to being delinquent. Bankruptcy filings provide an interesting perspective on this problem. Data from the 2007 Consumer Bankruptcy Project indicate that 18 percent of the married or cohabiting women who filed for bankruptcy were subjected to intimate partner abuse in the year prior to filing, suggesting that coerced debt plays a significant role in bankruptcy filings for women with partners. Coerced debt is problematic not just because of the immediate financial hardship it imposes on people subjected to abuse (which can include losing assets, like homes, that are used for collateral), but also because those debts are recorded on credit reports, which are used by everyone from employers to landlords and utility companies to determine creditworthiness. The inability to secure employment, housing, or utilities because of a poor credit rating can mean longer stays in shelter, returning to abusive relationships, or not leaving those relationships at all.[31]

Abuse can significantly impair a woman's ability to work. Although women subjected to abuse are no less likely to be currently employed than other women, they are more likely to have experienced past unemployment and high job turnover. Women subjected to intimate partner violence are much less likely to maintain work over time than other women. Intimate partner violence decreases women's annual hours worked by more than 10 percent.[32]

Women subjected to abuse report being late and absent from work more often and have greater difficulty maintaining long-term employment.[33] Intimate partner violence reduces women's job stability by an average of three months. This lack of job stability can hamper a woman's ability to accrue enough time in a job to earn employment-related benefits, including retirement accounts, health insurance, sick days, and vacation time. The effects of intimate partner violence on employment stability can last for up to three years after the abuse has ended. Fifty-two percent of women in a support group for intimate partner violence said that they were not able to positively change their employment status after the abuse ended.[34] Postseparation abuse, stalking, and harassment, which can continue long after women leave abusive relationships, also negatively affect women's ability to work.

Between 24 percent and 52 percent of women subjected to abuse have lost a job as a result of intimate partner violence; between 44 percent and 60 percent have been reprimanded at work for behavior related to intimate partner violence.[35] Intimate partner violence can also cause women to scale down their employment aspirations; about half of the women in one survey reported more modest hopes for employment after separating from their abusive partners.[36] Abuse deters some women from working altogether. "I want to work, but I'm afraid. I have gotten messages from my girlfriends. They said he said if he sees me he's going to kill me. You had better watch your back and all other kinds of stuff, and believe me he'll do it."[37]

Abusive partners prevent people from getting the education they need to qualify for work, finding work, and actually working. People who abuse may damage or destroy work clothes, employment related documents, and other needed items. They inflict visible injuries that make it impossible to go to work. Women are stalked or harassed before, during, and after work. People who abuse fail to provide promised transportation or child care, interfere with a partner's education and training, and spread lies about their partners to their employers (that they are using drugs or experiencing mental illness, for example). Welfare recipients regularly report being harassed by their partners at work. The majority of welfare recipients have been late to work, left early, or missed work as a result of intimate partner violence. Georgia's partner was so jealous that he "didn't want me to work or meet people outside the home. . . . He would call or come to the job or be there when I got off. He would demand that I come over, would call and threaten the boss where I worked. . . . He stole a VCR from [the place] where I was working." Georgia was fired as a result of her partner's behavior.[38] Although some employers have workplace policies to assist employees subjected to abuse, others are unable or unwilling to provide workers with the job adaptations they need to be safe. Fear of her abusive partner prompted Rachel to resign from her job as a systems analyst. Rachel's shift ended at night, and "[t]here's no way I was going to walk through the parking lot at 10:00 at night," particularly given that the security guards were not willing to walk with her.[39]

Economic abuse "is the ultimate anti-response to female financial autonomy."[40] It prevents people subjected to abuse from establishing economic security and self-sufficiency. Anxiety about financial instability looms larger than safety concerns for some people subjected to abuse. As Yolanda explained, her fear of losing her only asset, her home, kept her in an abusive relationship for years: "I thought about our property . . . the house we were living in . . . if I left I would lose the property. . . . And I always wanted it for my kids, so they could have it. . . . I thought at least I would have that for retirement."[41] Economic dependency traps some people in abusive relationships. Others leave their relationships without access to money, "unbanked," with damaged credit, large debts, and few material resources.

HOUSING

The inability to find and keep housing is among the most significant economic problems associated with intimate partner violence. Without stable housing, people are more vulnerable to intimate partner violence. Women subjected to abuse make up a substantial percentage of the homeless population, in part because of the barriers they face in obtaining and maintaining housing.

The difficulty of securing stable housing has long been recognized as a critical problem for people subjected to abuse. In VAWA's legislative history, lawmakers noted that women subjected to abuse "often lack steady income, credit history, landlord references, and a current address, all of which are necessary to obtain long-term permanent housing."[42]

People who have been subjected to economic abuse may lack sufficient resources to cover the up-front costs associated with renting. Although some public housing complexes prioritize housing for people subjected to abuse, most have long wait-lists, making them impractical solutions for people needing immediate housing. Moreover, while waiting for a property to become available, people may relocate or change their phone numbers, making them difficult to contact; if the housing agency can't reach them when a spot opens up, the agency will move on to the next person seeking housing. Leaving rental housing unexpectedly in response to a crisis has serious financial ramifications and can result in financial penalties for early lease termination, loss of security deposit, or eviction proceedings.

Having an eviction on one's record creates tremendous barriers to finding new housing. People subjected to abuse may have been evicted as a result of excessive noise, criminal activity on the property, or because a partner has leased the apartment in the person's name but refused to pay the rent. Landlords routinely screen the credit and eviction histories and criminal records of potential renters. Broken leases and past evictions hurt the credit and rental histories of people subjected to abuse, making it much more difficult to qualify for both private and public housing. A 2008 study found that applicants for housing in Washington, DC, who had been subjected to abuse or were seeking housing on behalf of someone subjected to abuse were given harsher lease terms and conditions than other applicants (56 percent) or denied housing outright (9 percent).[43]

Once people subjected to abuse have found housing, they face a number of barriers to keeping that housing. One particularly problematic practice is the use of nuisance property laws against people subjected to abuse. Nuisance property laws allow police to penalize landlords for their tenants' behavior. Imagine that the police have received multiple calls from a tenant for assistance with intimate partner violence. Nuisance property laws permit police and prosecutors to require landlords to self-police their properties to keep law enforcement from having to repeatedly respond to calls, using the threat of fines and license revocations to compel landlords to act. In Saint Louis, for example, prosecutors threatened to fine landlords between one hundred dollars and five hundred dollars for each violation of the nuisance property law, and, if that failed to stop calls to 911, to board up the property. Landlords who aid law enforcement must provide police or prosecutors with plans for abating the nuisance to avoid being penalized. Landlords often include evictions or the threat of eviction in those plans and use those threats to prevent tenants from continuing to seek assistance from the police.[44]

Nearly a third of the nuisance citations issued to landlords in Milwaukee, Wisconsin, in 2008 and 2009 involved intimate partner violence. That abuse included hitting, strangling, beating, and throwing bleach in a partner's face. Forty-four percent of the incidents involved physical abuse, and 14 percent involved a weapon. For those two years, a Milwaukee landlord received a nuisance citation involving intimate partner violence every five days; those citations disproportionately involved female victims, male offenders, and African American neighborhoods. Eighty-three percent of landlords responded to the nuisance citations with either threats to evict or formal and informal evictions. After a woman called 911 when her abusive boyfriend appeared on her porch, for example, her landlord sent her the following letter: "Because the numerous calls from this address, the police has [*sic*] identified the property as a nuisance property. . . . This is your notice to cease this behavior and to cure these problems. . . . If these activities continue, your lease will be terminated." The landlord informed police of his intention to terminate the resident's lease should she make another call to law enforcement. The Milwaukee Police Department accepted that plan. Four months later Milwaukee police informed the landlord that the problems with the tenant had continued; the landlord evicted the tenant. The landlord submitted the eviction letter to police, who responded, "Plan Accepted! Please ensure eviction takes place." Another landlord sent a letter to Milwaukee police explaining that "we are evicting Sheila M. . . . She has been beaten by her 'man' who kicks in doors and goes to jail for 1 or 2 days. . . . We suggested she obtain a gun and kill him in self-defense, but evidently she hasn't. Therefore, we are evicting her."

Landlords see claims of intimate partner violence as unimportant and petty. As one landlord explained, "Like I tell my tenants: You can't be calling the police because your boyfriend hit you again. They're not your big babysitter." Landlords hold abused tenants responsible not just for controlling their partners, but for doing so without involving the police. Landlords discouraged tenants from calling 911 and threatened tenants that calling 911 could result in eviction. For example, a landlord wrote a tenant, "[P] olice are not to be used to solve disputes and family problems. . . . The police are to notify me immediately if 911 is called [again]. . . . If the situation they are called for is deemed to be *non-life threatening*, I will immediately start the eviction process for the tenant or tenants where the problem originates from."[45]

Nuisance laws create what women's and gender studies professor Gretchen Arnold has called a double bind for tenants: "[I]f their abusers showed up at their apartments again, they would be evicted, but the women had no way to keep their abusers away without calling 911, which would itself trigger eviction under the nuisance ordinance." One woman explained, "Well, it seem like with the nuisance thing, you have to deal with, you know, the situation like my ex-boyfriend, or whatever. [The landlord] come over and tell me I have to deal with that. Or just pray he don't kill me or anything because if I call the police, they're going to contact my landlord and then I'll probably be homeless."[46] Notably, the vast majority of the tenants evicted for intimate partner violence in Milwaukee were not living with the partners who abused them. Only nine of the seventy-one cases in which landlords threatened or carried out evictions involved cohabiting couples.[47]

Sociologists Matthew Desmond and Nicol Valdez conclude, "*The nuisance property ordinance has the effect of forcing abused women to choose between calling the police on their abusers (only to risk eviction) or staying in their apartments (only to risk more abuse).* Women from black neighborhoods disproportionately face this devil's bargain."[48] About half of the women in Arnold's Saint Louis study were forced to move as a result of the laws—either because they had already been evicted or in order to avoid eviction.[49]

Eviction brings with it a host of other problems. Eviction is correlated with homelessness, material hardship, residential instability, job loss, depression, and suicide. Eviction keeps tenants from qualifying for public housing and from finding affordable housing in desirable neighborhoods. As one woman told Arnold, "[A] couple of people, when I tried to get an apartment, told me, 'We see that there are some things in here about you calling the police.' And they didn't want to rent to me."[50] Women reported to Arnold that they had lost all of their personal possessions as a result of eviction and that eviction exacerbated preexisting physical and mental illnesses. The consequences of eviction can be so dire that Desmond and Valdez question whether reported declines in intimate partner violence owe more to the effectiveness of increased enforcement of the criminal law or to the unwillingness of people to report lest they lose their housing.

Protecting people subjected to abuse from housing instability using the law has had mixed results. The American Civil Liberties Union has sued a number of jurisdictions for misuse of their nuisance property laws in cases involving intimate partner violence, but those ordinances persist in many places. Lawyers have also argued that targeting women subjected to abuse violates the gender discrimination provisions of the Fair Housing Act. VAWA prohibits housing authorities, landlords, and owners of federally subsidized housing from using intimate partner violence as a justification for denial of housing, termination from a federally subsidized housing program, or eviction. There are few reported cases brought under VAWA, although one federal judge found that a woman could bring a claim based on VAWA's housing provisions where the Zanesville Metropolitan Housing Authority allegedly failed to appreciate that the damage done to her housing unit was a result of intimate partner violence, made unfounded accusations that the woman herself caused the damage, attempted to evict her and her children, and provided inaccurate information about her to other potential landlords.[51] A number of states have passed laws preventing private landlords from discriminating on the basis of intimate partner violence. But it is likely that people subjected to abuse continue to face adverse housing actions as a result of intimate partner violence, and it is impossible to know how often such actions occur. Moreover, such protections do not prevent landlords from using other justifications for barring residents from housing, even when those conditions (past history of eviction, poor credit history, criminal record) stem from intimate partner violence.[52] People subjected to abuse could easily become "unhouseable" as a result.[53]

ECONOMIC POWER FOR PEOPLE SUBJECTED TO ABUSE

Women subjected to abuse want economic security: the ability to pay their monthly bills, meet their basic needs, and have money left over for entertainment or savings. As one woman explained, "I just want to be able to breathe."[54] Recognizing this desire for economic empowerment, antiviolence advocates have developed programs designed to improve women's financial literacy, self-efficacy (the belief that a woman can be economically stable), and self-sufficiency. Most programs focus on teaching women basic financial skills, including goal setting and financial planning, managing cash flow, banking, and credit, and investing, as well as confronting the complex financial problems that come with intimate partner violence, including repairing damage to credit done by a partner. These programs are generally successful in improving women's basic financial literacy and sense of economic self-efficacy and self-sufficiency. Most of the women participating in the Allstate Foundation's Moving Ahead Through Financial Management program, for example, set financial goals, created a budget, and paid off debt; around a quarter of them started a retirement account.[55] A similar financial literacy program, Redevelopment Opportunities for Women's Economic Action Program (REAP), improved women's confidence in handling financial issues, but their financial knowledge did not significantly increase. After completing REAP, women reported that they used their money differently, kept to a budget, tracked their spending, sought to repair their credit, attempted to reduce their debt, and saved more.

Individual Development Accounts (IDAs) were an essential component of REAP. Low-income families often lack access to employer-sponsored retirement plans or 401(k) plans; IDAs match the money that low-income families are able to save, enabling them to purchase a home, start a business, or finance a family member's education. Matching funds for REAP IDAs came from a combination of government and private sector sources, and match incentives ranged from one dollar to two dollars for each one dollar saved, depending upon a woman's household income. REAP IDA funds could be used to buy or repair a home, pay for education, start or support a small business, save for retirement, or purchase a car (something that most IDAs do not permit but that is essential for women attempting to leave violent relationships and establish economic independence). Participants were also permitted to access their own (but not matching) funds in case of emergencies. Monthly deposits of as little as $10 were required to participate in the program, and women could accumulate as much as $2,000 in savings and $4,000 in matching funds. Women involved in REAP saved an average of $87 per month, accruing an average total savings of $1,310. African American women, who started the program with much lower incomes than other participants, saved significantly less than other women enrolled in the program. The average woman reached her savings goal in nineteen months. Most participants used their accounts to purchase a car or pay for education. Participants in the IDA program reported improved financial management and restraint, which included making and following a budget, consistently saving money, and changing their spending behavior. Saving increased participants' self-confidence and gave them greater hope for the future; participants believed that saving might even prevent future violence. Knowing that their partners would not be able to withdraw money from their IDAs made women feel that they had options if their relationships turned violent. As Ella explained, "It makes me feel strong enough to have something that somebody cannot take away from me . . . where I can stand up and walk away."[56] Moreover, having savings made women feel more stable because they would not need to rely on their partners economically and would be able to secure housing and other necessities.

At least one financial literacy program puts resources directly into the hands of women subjected to abuse. The Kentucky Coalition against Domestic Violence's Economic Empowerment program coupled financial education and IDAs with credit counseling and microloans. Upon completion of the program, participants were more likely to use a budget, check their credit score, save money, and decrease household debts. Homelessness declined significantly among participants in the program, and women reported being better able to meet their basic living and health-care needs. Average monthly income and savings also increased among participants.[57]

It seems, then, that "financial literacy and economic empowerment programs are indeed effective in assisting survivors to improve their financial knowledge, increase their confidence about managing their financial affairs, and enhance financial behaviors that will improve their financial safety and security."[58] But existing financial literacy programs are grounded in the very specific context of corporate capitalism. The programs assume that what women need is to learn financial management rather than giving women access to and control over resources or redistributing wealth in any significant way. Moreover, the programs fail to challenge structural inequalities based on class and race, ignoring harmful practices like predatory lending, which people subjected to abuse have identified as an obstacle to financial stability, and payday loan centers. Law professor Deborah Weissman concludes, "Financial literacy is driven by the interests of the financial industry whose purpose differs from the goal of social justice movements to further the well-being of victims. These curricula depoliticize the understanding of the financialization of daily life and obscure the consequences of the transformation of economic systems now dominated by financial markets at the expense of industrial and agricultural communities. No critique of the consumer-consumption culture in the United States is offered."[59]

ECONOMICS AND PEOPLE WHO ABUSE

Economic pressures may also help to explain why people abuse their partners. Masculinity, work, and violence may be intertwined in ways that explain why intimate partner violence is more prevalent among low-income couples, particularly when men are under- and unemployed.

It is hard to overstate the damage done by economic instability and job loss, which many compare to the traumas of combat or the death of a loved one. Studies link loss of work to headaches, stomach ailments, insomnia, anxiety disorders, depression, alcoholism, drug abuse, and admission to mental health hospitals. Suicide and homicide rates increase among the unemployed.[60]

Economic success through work is one of the hallmarks of masculinity in American society. While work provides self-worth and meaning for most individuals, it may be particularly important for men, whose sense of self may be predicated on their ability to provide for themselves and their families. As Deborah Weissman explains, "Unemployed Americans, especially unemployed American men, are often considered failures or otherwise defective for their inability or unwillingness to support themselves and their families through productive economic means."[61]

Economic insecurity increases stress and anxiety within the family. Weissman notes that workers fighting to retain economic stability often work longer hours or cobble together part-time work and "experience the disappointment of unmet aspirations and diminished hopes of career development," exacerbating anger and strain within the home. Those who remain employed may nonetheless lose the benefits and protections traditionally associated with employment as full-time work disappears, agreeing to or being forced to accept cuts in pay and hours to retain their jobs. In addition to experiencing significant anxiety, they may be vulnerable to abusive workplace practices because they lack bargaining power.[62]

The symbolic aspects of losing a job can be as distressing as the economic impact. The masculine ideal requires that men exercise economic control over their partners and within their families. Although low-income men may be relatively powerless in terms of access to resources, retaining control of even limited finances allows them to exercise masculine privilege within the family. Job loss may make that exercise of privilege impossible, especially when men's partners continue to work and earn.

The shame and powerlessness associated with job loss and economic instability may lead to intimate partner violence. Based on years of working with incarcerated men, psychologist James Gilligan theorizes that the root of violent behavior is the desire to dampen feelings of shame and humiliation, feelings that can be provoked by economic instability. Gilligan writes, "[I]t is not unemployment as such that causes violence; what causes violence, rather, is the loss of self-esteem and feelings of self-worth, the blow especially to one's sense of adequacy as a man . . . and the shame brought on by rejection and enforced passivity and dependency, which can all be precipitated by being fired from one's job."[63] Violence becomes the vehicle for eradicating shame and reestablishing masculinity.

Whatever the cause, male under- and unemployment is strongly correlated with intimate partner violence. Men who are unemployed are more likely to abuse their partners, and men's poor work history predicts a greater risk for intimate partner violence. In ethnographic research, men have repeatedly made the connection between their loss of work, the deterioration of their relationships with their partners, increased stress, and intimate partner violence. As periods of male unemployment increase, rates of intimate partner violence increase. Women whose partners experienced two or more periods of unemployment over a five-year period were almost three times as likely to be subjected to intimate partner violence as women whose partners' employment was stable.[64] Male unemployment is also strongly correlated with—is, in fact, the "most important demographic risk factor for"—intimate partner homicide.[65] Rates of intimate partner violence, particularly severe intimate partner violence, are highest among women in disadvantaged neighborhoods whose male partners have high levels of job instability.[66] Men who commit intimate partner violence are more likely to recidivate when living in neighborhoods experiencing high rates of unemployment.[67] In periods of significant job loss, like the 2009 U.S. recession, spiking male unemployment and increases in rates of intimate partner violence coincide.

Women recognize that male unemployment drives intimate partner violence. Jill associated her partner's sporadic work with his abuse of her, explaining, "I think he felt inferior and wanted to beat the hell out of me because of the way he felt about himself because he wasn't doing what he was supposed to be doing. He wasn't pulling his weight."[68] Kara described how her partner's adherence to traditional norms of masculinity increased his violence against her: "He was out of work or we were struggling. It seemed to cause the physical abuse more, you know, his worrying and his blaming me or . . . he didn't want me working."[69]

STRUCTURAL ECONOMIC FACTORS AND ABUSE

Most discussions of the relationship between economics and abuse focus on individuals. But to confine the discussion to the micro level ignores the impact of macroeconomic factors and policies on intimate partner violence.[70] The uptick in intimate partner violence during economic recessions is not a coincidence. Macroeconomic policies profoundly affect workers, particularly workers at the lower socioeconomic end of the labor market, and those policies can create and reinforce the conditions in which intimate partner violence flourishes. Structural issues involving work, deindustrialization, and neoliberal economic policy are all linked to intimate partner violence.

Work provides women with the economic stability that can protect them from intimate partner violence. But structural labor market factors operate to keep women in jobs that pay less and lack security and power. Women continue to be paid less than men for the same work. While the gender pay gap has decreased over time, as of 2017 in the United States, Latinas earned sixty-two cents on every dollar earned by male workers, African-American women sixty-eight cents, white women eighty-two cents, and Asian American women ninety-three cents.[71] Women are segregated in the labor market both horizontally (by being limited to specific kinds of work) and vertically (through the inability to rise within hierarchies). Most women work in sales or service (including care work), the lowest paid jobs in the labor force. The United Nations reports that even those women who hold professional jobs are not nearly as likely to hold positions of authority or influence within their professions as men.[72] Women in flexible, low-wage jobs and women who lack power and authority within their institutions are less likely to be protected from economic downturns or adverse employment actions, making them more vulnerable to intimate partner violence.

Deindustrialization in the United States exacerbates the inability of low-income workers to achieve economic stability. The availability of cheaper imports and decreased labor costs overseas contributed to the significant decline of the U.S. manufacturing sector. As manufacturing jobs moved overseas, a service-dominated market featuring low-paying, insecure jobs replaced American's once-robust manufacturing sector, which offered secure jobs with high wages and generous benefits to less educated workers. The manufacturing jobs that remain no longer promise economic security. Manufacturing production workers make less than the median U.S. wage, particularly if those workers are placed in jobs through intermediary staffing agencies. As a result of low wages (rather than, for example, insufficient hours), a third of manufacturing workers rely on government benefits like the Supplemental Nutrition Assistance Program, Temporary Assistance to Needy Families, and Medicaid to support their families.[73] Sociologist Lisa Brush notes, "The old expectations about job security, benefits, and other rewards to seniority and loyalty to a specific firm have eroded. . . . These changes have distinctly different consequences for people employed in different parts of the labor market. . . . At the low end of the labor market, workers now face stagnant or sinking wages, irregular work schedules, and no affordable health insurance, paid sick time, paid vacation, or paid family leave."[74]

Women have been disproportionately affected by deindustrialization in the United States. Women laid off after plant closings are twice as likely to experience long-term unemployment as men, and depending upon how they are classified by employers, some of those women are ineligible for unemployment benefits. Deindustrialization is linked to economic disadvantage and community instability—conditions within which intimate partner violence flourishes.[75]

Neoliberal economic policy magnifies the economic instability of low-income workers. The goal of neoliberal economic policies is to achieve economic efficiency and rapid economic growth by decreasing the role of the state in the economy while encouraging private enterprise, social organizations, and individuals to assume responsibility for those services that the state no longer provides. In the neoliberal state, growth is the predominant economic concern; redistribution can only happen after economic growth is achieved. Market regulation is eased to allow for faster and easier movement of goods and services. Neoliberal economic policy addresses poverty through increased market participation by the poor, limited government redistribution (to the extent that such efforts do not slow growth), and, primarily, private efforts. Monies previously devoted to social services are redirected into policies and programs (like mass incarceration) that benefit economic elites. Moreover, the state's ability to regulate and tax is constrained in the neoliberal state, depriving the state of revenue with which to address pressing social problems like intimate partner violence.

Neoliberal policies have had a disproportionate impact upon poor women. Women have lost employment through recessions and financial crises, as cheaper imports displace the need for their labor and governments focus on the needs of poor men, to women's disadvantage. The jobs that do exist are less likely to have any form of employment security or meaningful benefits, including protection against wrongful termination, pensions, health insurance, or maternity benefits. When poor women lose their jobs, there are few government services or supports available to help them meet their basic economic needs, leaving them more vulnerable to violence and entrapping them within violent relationships as a result of economic dependence. As early as 2009, Yakin Ertürk, then the United Nations special rapporteur on violence against women, argued, "[E]conomic destabilization brought about by globalization processes and neoliberal policies . . . [is] heightening the conditions for, and increasing the extent of, violence against women."[76] Neoliberal policies have been problematic for low-income men as well, fueling the cycle of job instability and job loss that contributes to intimate partner violence.

The global recession made visible the impact of structural factors impeding economic stability for low-income men and women. Rates of intimate partner violence increased during the recession of the late 2000s. Eighty percent of U.S. shelters reported an increase in requests for services between 2008 and 2011; 73 percent of that need was attributed to "financial issues," including unemployment.[77] Sixty-five percent of the women in shelters could not find employment as a result of the economic downturn. Anecdotally, two murder suicides in the Washington, D.C., area "were linked to severe financial stress, debts, and depression caused by the recession. Most alarming was that neither family had a known history of domestic abuse."[78] Government policies enacted in response to the recession compounded the economic impact on low-income workers, particularly women. After passing a stimulus package to stabilize the economy, political scientist Jacqui True explains, the United States, like other nations, significantly limited public expenditures. "These austerity policies have set back women's economic and social status relative to men, putting more women than before in precarious situations with respect to housing, employment, and livelihoods where they are more vulnerable to violence and less able to protect themselves."[79]

Both individually and structurally, economics affects and is affected by intimate partner violence. A balanced policy must pay close, careful, and comprehensive attention to intimate partner violence as an economic problem.

3. Intimate Partner Violence Is . . .

A Public Health Problem

In 1994, the United States House of Representatives held a hearing on "Domestic Violence as a Public Health Issue." In his opening statement, Representative Ed Towns noted, "Until recently, domestic violence has been viewed primarily and predominately as a criminal justice issue. Therefore, proponents for a solution to the domestic violence problem urged state legislatures" to pass a variety of criminal laws addressing the problem. But, Towns noted, "those measures did not decrease the incidence or severity of domestic violence."[1] Towns argued that rather than relying on the legal system, intimate partner violence should be viewed as a public health issue.

The World Health Organization designated intimate partner violence one of the world's most pressing public health problems in 1996; by 2003, intimate partner violence was also at the top of the research agenda of the U.S. Centers for Disease Control and Prevention National Center for Injury Prevention and Control. The recognition that intimate partner violence poses a public health problem stems from the host of adverse health-related consequences associated with that violence. For instance, intimate partners are responsible for over half of the femicides in the United States.[2] In addition, intimate partner violence results in injuries ranging from scratches and bruises to deep cuts, broken bones and teeth, and head trauma. It is also tied to severe and chronic illnesses, including irritable bowel syndrome and other gastrointestinal conditions, depressed immune system function, type 2 diabetes, asthma, migraines, sexually transmitted infections, pregnancy complications, and chronic pain. The risk of stroke, heart disease, and asthma are greater for people subjected to abuse. Moreover, the mental health consequences of intimate partner violence include anxiety, depression, posttraumatic stress disorder, eating and sleeping disorders, self-harm, and suicide. Intimate partner violence is also linked with a number of unhealthy behaviors and conditions, including smoking and substance use. The impact of abuse on health is long lasting and cumulative over time. The more severe the abuse, the more destructive it is to a person's health.

Physicians have always treated people subjected to intimate partner violence for these conditions; intimate partner violence is responsible for approximately 486,000 visits to hospital emergency rooms annually.[3] But public health interventions center on "[p]revention, not treatment," as Dr. Mark Rosenberg, the director of the CDC's National Center for Injury Prevention and Control, told Congress in 1994.[4] In 2010, the World Health Organization lamented that despite the provision of direct services to people subjected to abuse throughout the world, "there have been remarkably few efforts to prevent intimate partner or sexual violence from occurring in the first place."[5] Intimate partner violence has long been understood as a public health problem. But declaring that intimate partner violence is a public health problem has done little, it seems, to convince policymakers to prioritize public health-based law and policy solutions.

THE PUBLIC HEALTH APPROACH

Most of the current law and policy responses to intimate partner violence in the United States, particularly those associated with the criminal legal system, are reactive, addressing violence after the fact through punishment and monitoring. By contrast, taking a public health approach means believing that violence can be prevented, an idea that the World Health Organization calls "not an article of faith, but a statement based on evidence."[6]

The public health conception of prevention is complex. Prevention can occur on multiple levels: primary, secondary, and tertiary. The meanings of these terms are fluid, but primary prevention generally refers to efforts to stop a problem before it occurs. Primary prevention interventions are "upstream" interventions, addressing risk factors and raising awareness of the problem.[7] Once a problem is evident, secondary prevention is meant to keep that problem from recurring or increasing in frequency or severity. Tertiary prevention reduces or minimizes the harm that is caused after the problem has already occurred.

In the context of intimate partner violence, primary prevention might involve fostering healthy relationships, increasing gender equality, and addressing structural social and economic factors that are correlated with or cause intimate partner violence. Moving public housing residents to areas with greater amounts of green space has been associated with decreased intimate partner violence, for example; increasing green space in low-income neighborhoods, then, might constitute a primary prevention effort. Secondary prevention could include screening for intimate partner violence, enabling providers to identify violence in its early stages and mitigate the harms (although screening operates on all three levels of prevention depending upon whether the person being screened has been or is currently being subjected to abuse).[8] Most of the policy responses to intimate partner violence in the United States involve tertiary prevention: the provision of medical and mental health care to people subjected to abuse, abuser intervention programs, and legal system interventions, for example. Although responding to the needs of people subjected to abuse (and the behavior of their partners) is crucial, those efforts are individually focused, expensive, and have shown little evidence of effectiveness in preventing further violence or fostering societal change.

With the belief that violence is preventable as its foundation, a public health campaign against intimate partner violence would involve four essential components:

1. collecting data on the prevalence, magnitude, and impact of the problem;
2. investigating the causes and correlates of the problem;
3. designing, implementing, and evaluating interventions based on that evidence; and
4. widely disseminating and implementing the most promising approaches.

A public health approach engages affected communities in understanding the problem and developing solutions and invites representatives from a variety of sectors into the effort. Legal solutions have been influenced by a feminist understanding of intimate partner violence as rooted in the patriarchy, with interventions designed to decrease individual men's power and control over their partners. By contrast, a public health approach is focused on decreasing morbidity and mortality and improving health outcomes for people subjected to abuse.

Investigating the prevalence and causes of violence means understanding not just the immediate contributors to the problem, but also "the causes of the causes": the social conditions that give rise to public health issues like intimate partner violence, called social determinants.[9] Social determinants are factors in the social, economic, and environmental strata that create and reinforce health disparities. These determinants include economic stability, access to education, community and social supports, physical environment, access to food, residential segregation, and racism. Social determinants work on a variety of levels, from societal to community to individual, and can be situational as well. The impact of social stressors on health is cumulative: "The longer people live in stressful economic and social circumstances, the greater the physiological wear and tear they suffer."[10] A growing body of research suggests that social determinants have as great an impact on health as genetic factors or the availability of health care; social factors may account for over a third of U.S. deaths. Understanding the social determinants of health is essential in crafting public health responses. As Michael Marmot, the chairman of the World Health Organization's Commission on Social Determinants of Health, wrote, "If the major determinants of health are social, so must be the remedies."[11]

Designing effective public health interventions also requires identifying the multiple, intersecting risk factors for intimate partner violence. Public health researcher Lori Heise explains that the early research on the causes of intimate partner violence promoted "single-factor theories" influenced heavily by the discipline of the researcher. Not surprisingly, criminologists, sociologists, psychologists, and feminist theorists saw the primary causes of intimate partner violence quite differently and argued about the one true cause of intimate partner violence. By the mid-1990s, however, some researchers were looking beyond those single-factor theories to develop more nuanced and complex understandings of the causes, recognizing that "violence is more or less likely to occur as factors interact at different levels of the social ecology."[12] The ecological model is rooted in the belief that no single factor is either necessary or sufficient to cause intimate partner violence; instead "[t]here are likely to be different constellations of factors and pathways that may converge to cause abuse under different circumstances."[13]

The ecological model scrutinizes contributing factors on the individual, relationship, community, and societal levels. On the individual level, researchers study biological and personal histories for attributes that make a person more likely to perpetrate or be subjected to intimate partner violence. The relationship level examines interactions with peers, intimate partners, and family members. The community level looks at the wider contexts (like schools, workplaces, and neighborhoods) within which intimate relationships occur in order to pinpoint the characteristics of these settings associated with intimate partner violence. Finally, public health research surveys the broader economic, social, and cultural factors that have an impact upon intimate partner violence. Risk factors can have effects on multiple levels; for example, gender inequities and conceptions of masculinity that exist on the societal level can influence individual beliefs and interpersonal relationships, contributing to intimate partner violence. Public health interventions, then, must work across the levels of the ecological model to prevent violence.

PUBLIC HEALTH STRATEGIES TO COMBAT INTIMATE PARTNER VIOLENCE

Although the policy response to intimate partner violence in the United States has been primarily reactive, there are promising attempts both in the United States and in other parts of the world to develop preventative interventions. Those strategies target individuals across various stages of life, address risk factors for violence throughout the social ecology, and seek to engage communities in creative ways. A few of the more promising strategies are outlined below.

Working with Men

The following exchange between Representative Ed Towns and Dr. Mark Rosenberg of the CDC took place during the 1994 House of Representatives hearing on "Domestic Violence as a Public Health Issue":

MR. TOWNS: You are stressing in terms of women and treatment for women . . . are we making a mistake here when we keep emphasizing women? What are we doing with the men? They are part of this problem, too. . . .

DR. ROSENBERG: You are absolutely right. The men play a critical role, and I agree, it is not until men take responsibility for their actions, and it is not until men take responsibility for what other men do that we will be able to really change the problem.

Towns and Rosenberg agreed that a substantial part of the problem they were discussing was men, and more specifically, men's use of violence against their partners. Federal statistics confirm that women comprise 76 percent of the victims of intimate partner violence,[14] and since only about 1 percent of women in the United States self-identify as lesbian,[15] the vast majority of these women are partnered with men. It stands to reason, then, that if most victims of violence are heterosexual women, most of those doing the violence must be heterosexual men. Not everyone concurs, however, that men are more likely to perpetrate violence than women. As noted in the introduction, the claim that men and women use violence against their intimate partners at comparable rates has been the subject of tremendous debate among scholars and advocates. While men make up the majority of those who use violence in crime statistics and arrest rates, some studies suggest that women may be as likely to perpetrate intimate partner violence as men. Critics have noted that those claims are based on studies that count individual acts of physical violence without contextualizing that violence and equate minimal physical violence (a push) with serious injury (a stabbing or shooting). Regardless of one's take on these studies, it is clear that men do a substantial amount of violence to their intimate partners. As activist Michael Flood argues, "Most violence is men's violence."[16] Preventing men from using violence must be part of a comprehensive public health strategy to address intimate partner violence.

Men's use of violence is likely related to the ways in which masculinity is understood and practiced. Although most men do not use violence, violence and masculinity are inextricably bound. Violence, particularly violence against women, is a way of proving one's manhood by distinguishing oneself from the feminine. Michael Kaufman, the cofounder of the White Ribbon Campaign, explains that violence is a "compensatory mechanism" for men who cannot attain idealized, or hegemonic, masculinity; violence "is a way of re-establishing the masculine equilibrium, of asserting to oneself and others one's masculine credentials."[17] Not surprisingly, men with rigid beliefs about appropriate gender roles are more likely to use violence. This need to establish traditionally masculine dominance through violence is exacerbated by economic instability. As anthropologist Philippe Bourgois writes of the men he studied in New York, "[T]he unemployed . . . man lashes out at the women and children he can no longer support or control effectively."[18]

Preventing intimate partner violence means changing the behavior of abusive men. The United States has relied on the criminal legal system to spur behavioral change. The legal system has, by and large, failed in that task. But confronting toxic beliefs about masculinity, tying the concept of masculinity to the actions of individual men, and delinking masculinity from violence could prompt that change.

The relationship between attitudinal change and behavioral change is complex. While much prevention work has centered on changing attitudes and hoping behavioral change will follow, there is little evidence to support that approach. The relationship between attitudes and behavior is "complex and bidirectional."[19] Interventions that attempt to reconfigure gender roles and promote equitable relationships between men and women—known as gender-transformative approaches—may prevent violence against women.

But interventions that embrace a simplistic view of men who use violence are ineffective. Men who use violence are complex, sitting at the intersection of identities that both create and mitigate risk. Programs "that view men mainly as oppressors—self-centered, disinterested, or violent—instead of as complex subjects whose behaviors are influenced by gender and sexual norms" are unlikely to effectuate behavioral change.[20]

The best-known and most widely available programs seeking to change men's behavior are abuser intervention programs. These programs vary in length and philosophy, though the Duluth model, a feminist cognitive-behavioral program, is probably the most popular. The evidence for the effectiveness of abuser intervention programs is mixed at best. Few programs have been properly evaluated; of those that have been evaluated, even fewer show positive results, and many of the studies have methodological problems. Abuser intervention programs are, however, taking creative approaches to engaging men in treatment and addressing both the individual and societal factors that prompt and prevent abuse.

The Men Stopping Violence Program in Atlanta, Georgia, for example, requires that men enrolled in its abuser intervention program "bring men from their own microsystems (e.g., workplace, peer group, or family) to witness some of the work they are doing in the program,"[21] giving those who attend a snapshot of the behavior that brought the man to the program and the effort that will be necessary to sustain positive change. These community partners provide support and can hold participants accountable for maintaining the change they begin through the program. Witnesses may be motivated to examine their own behaviors and to become involved in other efforts to combat intimate partner violence. Men and their families can also participate in Men Stopping Violence's Community Restoration Program, a community education and advocacy effort open to those who have completed the twenty-four-week abuser intervention program. Members of the Community Restoration Program make presentations to community groups and write editorials on men's role in stopping violence against women. Participants have worked with legislators to craft and testified on legislation related to violence against women. Programs like Men Stopping Violence work on both the tertiary and primary prevention levels, offering direct services to those who have already been abusive and reaching out to other audiences and communities (including the men who provide support to participants in the abuser intervention program) to prevent intimate partner violence.

As Men Stopping Violence and other programs have recognized, engaging men must involve more than working with those who have already been abusive. Including nonviolent men in antiviolence work is important not only because men are the primary offenders, but also because nonviolent men and boys can have a positive impact on violent men. Both groups benefit from their involvement in the work. Men's silence in the face of intimate partner violence allows that violence to flourish. Abusive men and boys may be more likely to listen to other men than they are to women or the media, and, when confronted by other men, to change their behavior. Moreover, the toxic conceptions of masculinity that are at the core of men's violence against women are unlikely to change without the active engagement of men in redefining those norms.

Partnering with nonviolent men in antiviolence work has both philosophical and practical dimensions. Being an ally involves "working to end the system of oppression that gives [members of dominant social groups, like men] greater privilege and power based on their social group membership."[22] Ally development is more than simply acknowledging the existence of a problem; it also requires critical self-reflection skills and real world chances to take action. In the context of intimate partner violence, men seeking to be allies must recognize how prevailing conceptions of masculinity empower men to use violence against their partners and must work to change both the behavior and the belief structure underlying the behavior. As allies, men must recognize that their silence in the face of misogynistic and abusive behavior makes them complicit, and they must commit to intervening when necessary to address such behaviors. All of this, of course, presupposes that men can change the way that they relate to women in the world, that they have "an inherent capacity to relate to women as equals and as leaders worthy of love and respect."[23] Men report that they are interested in doing this work and believe that they can personally help to prevent intimate partner violence. They are more likely to engage in antiviolence work "when they are invited by people they know, in contexts that are familiar to them, and through topics or discussions that facilitate a personal connection with the issue of gender-based violence."[24]

Public education programs are often the first step in involving men in antiviolence work. Such programs seek to raise the visibility of the issue and prompt men to affirmatively pledge "never to commit, condone, or remain silent about violence against women."[25] The White Ribbon Campaign, for example, was created in the aftermath of the December 6, 1989, Montreal Massacre, during which Marc Lépine, after declaring his hatred for feminists, shot, stabbed, and killed fourteen women in an engineering class at L'École Polytechnique at the University of Montréal. Recognizing that their silence had allowed violence against women in

Canada to flourish, Canadian men donned a white ribbon not "as an act of contrition, nor a symbol of misplaced collective guilt" but as "a catalyst for discussion and soul-searching . . . a public challenge to those men who may use violence against a wife, girlfriend, family member, or stranger. . . . From the beginning, the primary goal of the WRC has been to encourage men to look at their own attitudes and behavior and to learn to challenge other men to stop all forms of violence against women."[26]

The White Ribbon Campaign offers men concrete examples of opportunities for intervention, from pointing out the sexism in a joke to confronting a friend about his abusive behavior and urging him to seek help. The White Ribbon Campaign partners with schools, corporations, and trade unions and organizes an annual White Ribbon Week, during which white ribbons are widely distributed and public service announcements appear in print and broadcast media. The campaign also distributes posters reading, "These men want to end violence against women," with a hundred empty lines available for men to sign. Having spread to more than sixty countries, the White Ribbon Campaign owes its success partly to its narrow focus. It does not require men who join to agree on all issues of concern to feminists (for example, abortion); it demands only a commitment to the core issue of ending violence against women.

Other public education campaigns strike a similar tone. In 2014, the United Nations announced its HeforShe campaign, designed to encourage men and boys to speak out about intimate partner violence and other gender-based inequities. Signers "commit to taking action against gender discrimination and violence in order to build a more just and equal world." As of May 2017, over a million men, including former Vice President Joe Biden, comedian Trevor Noah, and Canadian Prime Minister Justin Trudeau, have signed the HeforShe pledge. Other national campaigns rely upon athletes to spread their message. In 2010, the Springboks South African Rugby Union joined Brothers for Life, the South African national men's campaign, to mobilize support for the Sixteen Days of Activism against Violence against Women and Children; in 2011, the B.C. Lions football team and the Ending Violence Association of British Columbia partnered on the Be More Than a Bystander Campaign. SafeIreland's Man Up campaign features UFC fighter Cathal Pendred, who states, "As a man, and as a fighter, domestic violence appalls me. It's something I'm proud to stand up against—and do whatever I can to prevent it happening."

Public education campaigns exhort men to intervene against violence but don't necessarily give them the tools to do so. Bystander intervention training is designed to address that gap. In 1991, Jackson Katz piloted the first bystander intervention project; that project, which later became known as Mentors in Violence Prevention, urged male college athletes to use their status among other men to speak out about intimate partner violence and other forms of violence against women. Bystander intervention programs couple antiviolence education with training on the concrete skills needed to safely and effectively interrupt potentially violent situations.

Although some bystander intervention programs include women as well as men, the approach grew out of the idea of motivating men to use their masculinity in a positive way to prevent gender-based violence. Bystander intervention programs admonish men "to actively intervene on the street, at a frat party, in a bar" to prevent violence against women. Bystander intervention programs for men often stress that "good men" take action to prevent violence and may appeal to "men's sense of responsibility to the male group; intervening . . . preserves the integrity of the team, the frat, or the military unit by preventing men in the group from getting into trouble."[27] The converse, however, is also possible. Bystander intervention programs could prompt men to see violence as the problem of other (bad) men, immunizing them from responsibility for examining their own potentially problematic behavior.

The research on the effectiveness of bystander intervention programs is mixed. Those who receive bystander training express a greater willingness to intervene in violent situations. Rates of violence are lower on campuses that have received bystander intervention training through the Green Dot program. Such change may not be sustained over time, however.

Engaging men in the antiviolence movement seems like a logical strategy to combat intimate partner violence. But anti-violence advocates—both male and female—have raised concerns about shifting the focus to men, bringing men into the movement at all, and the methods used to involve them. First, working with men means devoting attention and resources to men—sometimes to the exclusion of women subjected to abuse. Organizations that had previously provided services solely to women have expanded their work to include men, a move that some advocates fear has fragmented their efforts and diminished the amount of time, money, and attention the women receive. Engaging men may be seen as an end in and of itself, rather than a project in service of ending violence against women. Highlighting the role of men in antiviolence work also risks further empowering men by entrenching social norms casting men as the protectors of women.

Second, there are concerns about who engages men. Although a few men have been involved since its inception, women have always led the antiviolence movement. But because of the belief that men are more effective in confronting their peers, men head up most of these efforts. Some antiviolence advocates are uncomfortable with men assuming leadership roles in the movement or with increasing the influence of men's voices in the conversation, thereby risking silencing women. As antiviolence advocates Michael Messner, Max Greenberg, and Tal Peretz note, "Men, because of their privileged social positions as men, are more likely than women to be listened to when they speak in opposition to violence against women."[28] Women in the movement may also resent the excessive praise men receive for doing the antiviolence work that women have been doing, with much less acclaim, for decades. Bringing men in as allies has the potential to create conflict, to displace women from positions of power, and to prioritize men's voices in the creation of policy and programming.

Finally, the tactics used in efforts to engage men are sometimes seen as problematic. Because men may be uncomfortable with having their privilege challenged, some programs shy away from confronting men about their use of power directly or from infusing the work with the insights provided by masculinities theory. Instead, "[t]he current standard curriculum . . . strategically sidesteps the off-putting guilt of previous curricula—so often experienced as 'anti-male'—by instead appealing to boys' and men's sense of masculine honor. In effect, today's antiviolence pedagogy *deploys* dominant forms of masculinity, rather than arguing for masculinity's eradication or radical transformation."[29] This elision prevents these programs from challenging the hypermasculine norms at the root of violence against women, a challenge that some advocates believe is the central to the work of engaging men. Similarly, the failure of some programs to confront men's homophobia and transphobia, and the general lack of an intersectional analysis in work with men, have drawn criticism. Programs that engage men may provide little more than public relations cover for the institutions (like universities) hosting those programs, enabling them to "gloss over, rather than directly confront, the root causes of gender-based violence."[30]

Preventing Adverse Childhood Experiences

Risk is a complicated concept. As criminologist Michael Salter explains, "Risk factors may be statistically robust in research studies but slippery at the level of individual cases and practice. Risk is dynamic and influenced by context and situation factors that shift over time."[31] Nonetheless, being exposed to and experiencing violence as a child correlate strongly with both using and being subjected to intimate partner violence. Witnessing intimate partner violence in one's family of origin, being physically abused or maltreated, and being harshly disciplined are all predictors of perpetration of intimate partner violence. Being physically or sexually abused as a child and being exposed to intimate partner violence increase the risk of victimization. The Adverse Childhood Experiences study, a survey of approximately nine thousand Southern California Kaiser Permanente patients, asked participants about their exposure to psychological, physical, and sexual abuse, and other forms of household dysfunction (substance use, mental illness, criminal behavior in the household, and intimate partner violence). The study found that a child's own victimization or exposure to a mother's abuse created twice the risk for perpetration or victimization. Those risks are cumulative: the greater the number of adverse experiences in a child's life, the greater the likelihood of perpetration or victimization in intimate relationships.[32] Exposure to four or more adverse childhood experiences increased the risk of perpetrating intimate partner violence five times. Lax supervision and negative communication within the family are also associated with perpetration of intimate partner violence.

Although it is not entirely clear why childhood abuse and exposure to violence are linked to later perpetration of intimate partner violence, a number of theories exist. Violence and trauma may affect a child's neurological development, impairing a child's ability "to empathize, to trust, and to build healthy relationships."[33] The violence and trauma that boys experience as children may make it difficult for them to regulate and interpret their own and others' feelings or shape their understanding of the relationship between violence and masculinity. Violence is learned behavior; experiencing and being exposed to violence as children may teach children that violence is an acceptable and appropriate way to resolve issues in relationships. Two caveats are important here. First, understanding the impact of early violence on later perpetration of intimate partner violence helps to explain, understand, and address the behavior, but not to excuse it. Linking adverse childhood experiences to later perpetration of intimate partner violence can aid in the development of services that deal with the root causes of that violence, allowing offenders to see their adult behaviors in the context of their violent childhoods and offering them motivation to address their childhood trauma. Secondly, not all of the substantial cohort of children who are abused, exposed to violence, or both, commit acts of intimate partner violence; "only a minority go on to become perpetrators themselves."[34] But while not all children who are exposed to or experience violence become offenders, most who use violence did experience childhood trauma.

Preventing adverse childhood experiences could substantially reduce rates of intimate partner violence. Interventions targeting parents during pregnancy, just after childbirth, or when children are quite young are promising prevention strategies. Parenting programs can reduce child abuse and neglect and harsh discipline and improve interactions between parents and children. Parenting interventions can be offered at home or in the community and often involve some form of counseling (individual or group), role playing and other exercises to model positive parenting behaviors, and monitored play between parents and children. Home visitation programs like the Nurse Family Partnership, in which a public health nurse is paired with a low-income, first-time pregnant mother, have had a significant impact on child maltreatment. Over the last thirty years, leveraging a combination of public and private funds, Nurse Family Partnership programs have served more than 270,000 families in 42 states.[35] Ideally, the nurse and expectant mother begin meeting one-on-one no later than twenty-eight weeks into the pregnancy. Using professional judgment and skills as well as assessments and screening tools, the nurse creates individualized interventions for the family based on the family's strengths and risks. Visits continue until the child is two years old. Over fifteen years of evaluation, the Nurse Family Partnership lowered rates of child abuse by 48 percent. Home visitation has been called "the most effective child maltreatment prevention program to date."[36]

Lauren Biser's story demonstrates how home visitation can benefit people subjected to abuse. Biser was being physically and emotionally abused by her partner when she learned she was pregnant. Concerned about whether the violence would increase during her pregnancy and what that would mean for her and her child, Biser began working with nurse Julie Goodrich through the Nurse Family Partnership Program. With Goodrich's support, Biser decided that while she wanted her child's father to be involved in the child's life, continuing the relationship would not be healthy for either her or the child. Biser says that Goodrich offered her a different way of looking at her situation; her desire for the father to be involved in the child's life did not mean that the couple had to stay together. Biser left the relationship and set boundaries with her child's father. With those boundaries, Biser found, she and her former partner could successfully coparent their child and she and her child could be safe.[37]

Home visitation programs have been linked to decreases in intimate partner violence. Families enrolled in the Hawaii Healthy Start Home Visitation Program experienced fewer injuries as a result of intimate partner violence, although the effects diminished over time.[38] These programs do not need to be staffed by professionals. An Australian program pairing trained mentor-mothers and new mothers for a year of home visitation found decreases in intimate partner violence (as well as increases in physical and mental well-being) among the mothers receiving visits.[39] The effectiveness of home visitation programs may be impaired by chronic violence, however. Home visitation failed to reduce rates of child maltreatment in families where mothers reported multiple incidents of intimate partner violence over time.[40]

Prevention efforts can also target men in their roles as fathers. A significant percentage of the men arrested for intimate partner violence are fathers, and fathers who commit intimate partner violence are often very involved with their children. Becoming a father can be stressful for men, who may have unrealistic expectations of what the experience will be or lack role models from whom they can learn positive parenting skills. Some men become jealous of the relationship between the child and mother, which can create strain within the adults' relationship. Fatherhood programs can help to alleviate the stresses that accompany new parenthood and teach men to develop positive, nonviolent relationships with their current or former partners and their children. Fatherhood is a powerful motivator for violent men to stop their abusive behavior. When men who have committed intimate partner violence recognize the impact of that violence on their children, they frequently express a desire to change.

Fatherhood programs can help to prevent intimate partner violence on a number of levels. Some programs, like the MenCare program, target all fathers in an effort to "promote men's involvement as equitable, responsive and non-violent fathers."[41] Such programs prevent intimate partner violence by encouraging men to treat their partners with respect and care, to refrain from using corporal punishment or abusing or neglecting their children, and by asking fathers to provide boys with examples of peaceful and progressive masculinity, potentially making those boys less likely to commit intimate partner violence as adults. Other programs specifically target fathers with a history of intimate partner violence. Fathers for Change, for example, focuses on men with a history of intimate partner violence and substance abuse. Ninety percent of Fathers for Change participants were abused, neglected, or witnessed intimate partner violence as children, significantly increasing the risk that they would commit intimate partner violence. Zane, for example, had been exposed to emotional, physical, and community violence. Although he was a committed father, Zane was arrested twice for assaulting his partner and was abusing alcohol before entering the Fathers for Change program. Zane attended individual therapy sessions focused on the impact of his behavior on his child; once he understood the harm done by his violence and anger, Zane committed to changing his attitude toward his partner. Zane participated in coparenting sessions with his former partner and father-child sessions with his son, designed to help Zane understand the impact of the parents' separation on the child. Zane reported that without Fathers for Change, he would certainly have assaulted his partner again.[42] Preliminary studies of the program show substantial decreases in both violence and substance use upon completion of the program. Fatherhood programs are also deploying technology to improve men's parenting. Dads to Kids (Dad2K) uses an interactive web-based curriculum to explain and model positive parenting skills for fathers; home visitors show fathers the content, then provide opportunities for fathers to practice those skills and provide feedback.

Adverse childhood experiences—child abuse and neglect and exposure to intimate partner violence—predict both perpetration of intimate partner violence and victimization. Shielding children from those experiences should be an essential component of any public health strategy to prevent intimate partner violence.

Interventions with Adolescents

In arenas ranging from fashion to music to language, adolescents are profoundly affected by the beliefs, attitudes, and biases of their peers. Adolescents' perceptions of intimate partner violence are no different. Young men who abuse their partners are more likely to associate with friends or peers who adopt sexist beliefs about male dominance and who support or perpetrate intimate partner violence. Reaching adolescents before those views become entrenched and changing their perceptions of masculinity and acceptable behavior within relationships could prevent later intimate partner violence.

Adolescents can be reached in a number of settings. Coaches, for example, may have a significant impact upon their players; "their role as influential, nonparental role models renders them uniquely poised to positively impact how young men think and behave."[43] Coaching Boys Into Men takes advantage of those relationships, training coaches to have brief weekly conversations with their athletes about intimate partner violence throughout the course of an athletic season. Participants in the program initially reported that they would be likelier to intervene to prevent abuse and showed a better understanding of intimate partner violence. Over time, athletes who participated in Coaching Boys In to Men were significantly less likely to abuse their dating partners or to support violent peers.[44]

Schools are another obvious place to reach adolescents. Effective school-based prevention programs share a number of attributes: They give students the opportunity to learn and test conflict management and problem-solving skills, provide information about the risks and consequences of intimate partner violence as well as how to seek help, and attempt to change the attitudes and beliefs associated with intimate partner violence through awareness raising and empathy building. Some of these programs take a "whole school approach": rather than confining antiviolence messages to one class or one lesson, antiviolence teaching is integrated into the larger curriculum and supported by other initiatives. The Shifting Boundaries program, which targets middle-school students, involves both a classroom component and other interventions throughout the school, including "Respecting Boundaries Agreements" (temporary restraining orders effective on school grounds), posters with antiviolence messages, the identification of safe and unsafe spaces within the school, and the assignment of staff and faculty to the spaces deemed unsafe by students. These interventions are designed to reinforce the concepts of boundaries and personal space the students have learned through the antiviolence classroom curriculum. The whole school approach underscores the idea that gender-based violence "is reflected in gendered power relations in society and that the school space itself, as a microcosm of society, needs to reflect the challenge to [intimate partner and other forms of gender-based violence]."[45]

Safe Dates takes the whole school approach out into the community. The goal of the Safe Dates program is to help students understand the features of healthy and abusive relationships, raise awareness of and change social norms regarding dating violence, and enable students to help themselves or their friends who are experiencing dating violence by providing students with skills and information. At school, students attend a student-led theater production on dating violence, participate in a poster contest, and complete a ten-session dating violence curriculum. The community component involves delivering services to students experiencing or perpetrating violence in dating relationships and offering training for community service providers. The results of the Safe Dates program have been significant and lasting. Students who participated in Safe Dates were less likely to experience psychological abuse and were much less likely to experience sexual and physical violence.[46] The program sought to change students' perceptions of the norms of dating violence, challenged gender stereotypes, and made students more aware of the availability of services, which may account for the significant decreases in violent behavior. These effects were seen both among students who reported having been abused in the past and students who had been abusive in previous relationships, but its greatest impact was in the primary prevention subgroup—students who had never been abusive before. Safe Dates' positive effects on perpetration of psychological, physical, and sexual violence were sustained throughout four years of follow-up.

Technology provides additional opportunities to reach students. Teen Choices, for example, is a web-based program for high school students. The program uses information about a student's risk factors and relationship status to create an individual, three-session multimedia intervention. An evaluation of Teen Choices found that participation in the program reduced both victimization and perpetration of emotional and physical violence among both teens who had previously used or been subjected to violence and those who had not.[47]

While all students can benefit from antiviolence education, adolescents who have been maltreated at home or witnessed abuse have the most acute needs. A Canadian program, Fourth R: Strategies for Healthy Youth Relationships, targets these teens. The curriculum covers dating violence, bullying, sexuality, and substance abuse and teaches social action, conflict resolution, and communication skills. The Fourth R significantly reduced both perpetration of and being subjected to physical and emotional abuse and signs of emotional distress; effects were more pronounced for male students.[48]

While the data on interventions with adolescents are promising, some studies fail to disaggregate their data by gender or offender status, making it difficult to know exactly who is benefiting. Other studies suggest that these programs are more effective in preventing perpetration of dating violence than in reducing victimization. Who is actually being helped by these programs, why some programs are more effective than others in reaching teens subjected to abuse, and how to craft interventions that better reach those teens are all questions that these programs should address.

Edutainment

Popular culture can have a profound impact on the way a community views a problem. The popular BBC Radio 4 drama *The Archers*, for example, featured a storyline on intimate partner violence. For more than two years, viewers listened as Rob Titchener emotionally (and possibly physically) abused and controlled his wife, Helen. Rob's constant belittling and isolation left Helen questioning her sanity, but in an April 2016 episode, Helen finally told Rob that she was leaving him. Rob responded by forcing a knife into her hand and telling her to stab herself, because it was the only way he would let her go. Rob was stabbed in the confrontation that followed. After the broadcast, thousands of listeners in the United Kingdom sought help and information through the BBC's website and helpline, and newspapers drew parallels between the experiences of Helen and women in local communities. *The Archers* raised community awareness of intimate partner violence and provided an impetus for those experiencing violence to seek assistance.

Antiviolence activists are harnessing the power of entertainment to increase community knowledge of social problems and shift community norms. Such efforts are often dubbed edutainment, defined as "the process of purposely designing and implementing a media message to both entertain and educate, in order to increase audience members' knowledge about an educational issue, create favorable attitudes, shift social norms, and change overt behavior."[49]

Antiviolence activists in South Africa and Central America, for instance, have used the audience's connection with the characters and issues featured in radio and television broadcasts to challenge the audience's preconceptions about intimate partner violence. In South Africa, *Soul City* uses radio, television, and print media campaigns as vehicles for social change. In its fourth season, partnering with the National Network on Violence against Women, *Soul City* took on intimate partner violence through a prime-time television drama, a radio drama broadcast in nine languages, and three information booklets. The program's goals were individual, interpersonal, and systemic: to shift attitudes about intimate partner violence, spur dialogue within communities, and create support for collective action such as implementing national legislation on intimate partner violence. The campaign reached approximately sixteen million South Africans, including residents of rural and marginalized communities.

Soul City 4 achieved a number of its goals, including enhancing the understanding of intimate partner violence and shifting attitudes on the acceptability of violence. Moreover, *Soul City* spurred the community to act, prompting women to march in support of national legislation and building a sense of community efficacy. As one viewer noted, "At the end [of *Soul City* 4] we too decided that when a man is beating his wife we should all wake up and try to help that woman."[50] Community members adopted behaviors used in *Soul City* 4 to interrupt violence; patrons began banging their bottles, for example, when a man in a pub physically assaulted his girlfriend, just as characters in season four had done. *Soul City* 4 has been credited with contributing to the implementation of national legislation on intimate partner violence; the series pressured politicians to act and changed the attitudes of government officials.

Programs like *Soul City* 4 and Nicaragua's Puntos de Encuentro—a feminist media organization that features a soap opera (titled *Sexto Sentido*), radio show, magazine, and training for activists—use storytelling to change attitudes and behaviors on intimate partner violence. By reaching those who have never used or been subjected to violence as well as those who have, edutainment works on all three levels of prevention.

POPULATION LEVEL INTERVENTIONS

Individual interventions through education and edutainment show promise, but some prevention initiatives require "population-level interventions"[51]—like restricting access to the substances and products that make intimate partner violence more likely and more lethal.

Alcohol

As many as 70 percent of men who use violence also abuse alcohol.[52] Men are eleven times more likely to use violence on days when they have been drinking.[53] Drinking alcohol has a number of effects that make the correlation between drinking and increased risk of intimate partner violence unsurprising. Drinking is associated with loss of inhibition, impaired problem solving, aggression, increased risk taking behavior, and decreased awareness of the consequences of actions. While drinking, men may feel freer to embrace archaic and problematic notions of a man's entitlement to use violence against his partner, misinterpret a partner's actions, lack the ability to communicate or problem solve, and fail to appreciate the consequences of violent or abusive behavior. Intimate partner violence is more severe and more likely to cause injury when the offender has been drinking, particularly when binge drinking.[54]

Making alcohol less available, then, could have an appreciable impact on rates of intimate partner violence. Using data from the 1985 National Family Violence Survey, studies have suggested that raising the cost of an ounce of pure alcohol by 1 percent could decrease rates of intimate partner violence by as much as 5 percent.[55] Similarly, econometric analyses suggest that increasing the price of beer by 10 percent could reduce intimate partner violence among college students by 4 percent yearly.[56] Raising alcohol taxes could also depress intimate partner violence. Increasing alcohol taxes decreases drinking; decreased drinking has been associated with reduced rates of violence in other contexts but studies have thus far failed to find a link between increased alcohol taxes and reduced intimate partner violence.[57] "Outlet density" and intimate partner violence are also related; the presence of an additional location in which a person can buy, but not drink, alcohol increases intimate partner violence-related calls for assistance to police by 4 percent and reports of intimate partner violence by 3 percent.[58]

Closely monitoring those known to abuse alcohol can decrease intimate partner violence as well. South Dakota's 24/7 Program required participants to undergo breathalyzer tests twice a day (morning and evening) as a condition of receiving bail for various offenses. Arrests for domestic violence decreased by 9 percent among those subjected to the testing.[59]

Firearms

Restricting access to firearms is a second population-level intervention likely to prevent serious intimate partner violence. During the 1994 congressional hearings, Representative Towns expressed his concern about how law enforcement was handling firearms associated with intimate partner violence. Indeed, "for more than a generation" researchers have been aware of the risks that guns pose to people subjected to abuse.[60] Over the past thirty years, guns have been involved in about half of intimate partner homicides.[61] The risk of intimate partner homicide is five times greater for women when their partners have access to a firearm.[62] An intimate partner assault involving a firearm is twelve times more likely to result in death.[63] Women who are killed by intimate partners are more likely to be victims of gun violence than to be killed by all other methods combined.[64] Offenders with access to firearms are more likely to engage in more serious intimate partner violence and are more likely to report engaging in other dangerous behaviors, including attempted homicides and threatening their partners with guns.[65]

Firearms are also used in nonfatal incidents of intimate partner violence. Although the nonfatal use of guns is relatively rare, the number of people harmed by those incidents is substantial. Approximately 4.5 million women in the United States have been threatened with guns by intimate partners, and nearly a million have had guns used to harm them in some way; "a gun does not need to be shot for there to be a negative outcome."[66] Threats of gun violence can be terrifying for people subjected to abuse. Just the knowledge that a gun is present in the home may be sufficient to control a partner's behavior or prevent her from seeking help.

Restricting access to firearms could prevent serious intimate partner violence. Recognizing the enormous danger created by firearms in the context of intimate partner violence, both the federal government and state legislators have enacted laws to block offenders' access to guns. In 1994, VAWA amended the federal Gun Control Act to prohibit gun possession or purchase by a person subject to a domestic violence protective order. In 1996, New Jersey Senator Frank Lautenberg sponsored another amendment to the Gun Control Act, prohibiting anyone convicted of a misdemeanor crime of domestic violence from possessing or purchasing a firearm (the Gun Control Act already prohibited persons convicted of felonies from possessing or purchasing firearms). The Lautenberg Amendment is notable for its refusal to exempt police and military from its reach, as other parts of the Gun Control Act do.

State laws implement, and in some cases fill the gaps left by, the federal law. At least eighteen states have passed laws allowing or requiring law enforcement to confiscate firearms at the scene of an incident of intimate partner violence. Those laws vary considerably on details including whether removal of firearms is mandatory or discretionary; whether police can search for guns or confiscate only those weapons that are in plain view; whether the firearm must have been used in the incident to be eligible for removal; and whether ammunition can also be seized. At least twelve states have laws mirroring the Lautenberg Amendment, preventing those who have been convicted of misdemeanor domestic violence from purchasing or possessing a firearm. Those statutes often define intimate partner violence more broadly than the Lautenberg Amendment does, allowing states to reach behavior that the federal law does not. At least thirty-five states and the District of Columbia prohibit individuals who are subject to final protective orders from possessing firearms. In at least thirteen states, the prohibition extends to temporary orders as well.

Evidence of the effectiveness of these measures is mixed. Most studies have found that the Lautenberg Amendment has had no significant impact on rates of intimate partner violence, although public policy professor Kerri Raissian has recently argued that the misdemeanor gun ban has reduced intimate partner femicides by 17 percent.[67] Laws that require (rather than allow) police to remove firearms also decrease intimate partner homicides.[68] Restricting the possession and purchase of firearms by those subject to restraining orders correlates with a decrease in intimate partner homicide, but only state laws that ban both the possession and purchase of firearms (as opposed to just possession) have the desired impact.[69]

Purchase restrictions are effective only when gun sellers and law enforcement have access to accurate information about whether an individual is prohibited from owning or purchasing a gun as a result of a conviction or the issuance of a protective order. The United States Air Force, for example, failed to report Devin Kelley's 2014 conviction for assaulting his wife and stepson to the FBI for inclusion in the federal database used to clear gun purchases. Kelley later killed more than two dozen people at his mother-in-law's church in Sutherland Springs, Texas, with guns that he bought after his conviction. The Air Force has since found a number of other cases that should have been reported and were not.

Laws denying access to firearms to people who abuse can only prevent violence when they are enforced. But judges routinely fail to ask people subjected to abuse whether they want their partners to surrender firearms as a condition of protective orders. When people do ask for guns to be seized, judges sometimes refuse to enter those orders, often at the partner's attorney's request.[70] Court-ordered surrender is more likely when the gun is used in the incident before the court or if the abuse is deemed more serious. Moreover, judges sometimes refuse to enter protective orders into state protective order databases, depriving law enforcement and gun dealers of information that could keep offenders from purchasing firearms. Even when judges do order the surrender of firearms, those orders often go unenforced. One study found that guns were seized in only 24 percent of the cases in which surrender was ordered.[71] Men are less likely than women to believe that guns should be removed from those who use violence[72], an obvious problem in a system that disproportionately employs men as judges and police officers. And a variety of system actors, including judges, law enforcement, and victim advocates, have expressed skepticism about law enforcement's ability to actually retrieve the firearms, calling the central premise of firearm removal laws into question.

CHALLENGES TO THE PUBLIC HEALTH RESPONSE

Crafting primary prevention interventions in the context of intimate partner violence poses significant challenges. Intimate partner violence ranges in seriousness from pushing to homicide, making it difficult to target specific behaviors for prevention. Determining "when, and with whom, to intervene" may be problematic as well, particularly when gearing efforts toward adolescents, who may experience the trauma associated with increased risk of intimate partner violence long before they themselves become involved in intimate relationships.[73] Moreover, intimate partner violence is a complex, multifaceted problem with numerous intersecting risk factors; finding interventions that address those factors singly and in combination is a huge task. Finally, primary prevention efforts often begin and end with raising awareness of the problem, which does not always lead to tangible, long-term, sustainable change. Primary prevention efforts must do more than educate. Changing social norms about the acceptability of intimate partner violence is essential.

Assessing the effectiveness of public health interventions is difficult in the absence of evaluation. Programs should have "a clear rationale at the outset of *why* the work is being done, *how,* and what achievements are sought—what it is that you are going to do that is going to make a change," and should measure those achievements to determine whether the desired change actually occurs.[74] Although some prevention programs have been rigorously evaluated, many others have not, making their value questionable. Without reason to believe that programs will actually prevent intimate partner violence, investing in taking such programs to scale is at best risky, at worst foolish, notwithstanding their innate appeal. But asking for rigorous evaluation can be problematic as well. Determining whether programming has actually resulted in long-term change can be difficult, particularly for programs that work to educate the wider public, shift community norms, or build community efficacy. Evaluations could, instead, measure mobilization, visibility, and community presence—but none of those variables captures the impact that programs have on rates of intimate partner violence or provides data on whether they are changing the attitudes and behaviors of those at risk of using violence.

Adopting a public health perspective on intimate partner violence is a strategic choice, one that some advocates fear will depoliticize the work to end intimate partner violence. But the public health approach can also provide opportunities for organizing, creating space for a "strategy that 'draws away from working victim by victim by victim and moves towards the community by community by community.'"[75] Employing a public health frame, law professor Linda Hamilton Krieger has argued, would reveal the complex web of individual and environmental determinants that contribute to intimate partner violence and refocus efforts on therapeutic interventions and harm reduction strategies.[76]

Antiviolence advocates have long recognized the importance of efforts to prevent intimate partner violence. Despite that recognition, public health solutions have taken a backseat to other approaches to intimate partner violence. What Dr. Mark Rosenberg recognized in 1994 is still true today: "To move beyond locking up offenders will require a radical shift in the way we think about violence in our society. We should not be surprised if this simple idea—the importance of thinking about prevention—takes a long time to take hold."[77]

4. Intimate Partner Violence Is . . .

A Community Problem

Criminalization of intimate partner violence is often justified by the need to "do justice." Doing justice, in turn, is usually defined as criminally punishing the partners of people subjected to abuse. But a growing body of research suggests that punishment generally, and incarceration specifically, may not be the foremost concern of victims of violence. In a recent report by the Alliance for Safety and Justice, crime victims stressed their preference for prevention and rehabilitation over punishment and for holding offenders meaningfully accountable outside of penal institutions.[1] Other studies suggest that victims of violence want offenders to experience and express remorse, develop empathy, and, most importantly, stop hurting others. That desire to find options beyond the criminal legal system extends to people subjected to intimate partner violence. As Jacquie Marroquin of the California Partnership to End Domestic Violence explained, "We keep hearing from survivors that criminal legal sanctions are not necessarily what they want. . . . They tell us: 'We don't want to break apart our families. We want the abuse to stop.'"[2]

Moreover, few victims of violence, including people subjected to intimate partner violence, turn to state-based systems like the criminal legal system. Two-thirds of the people surveyed by the Alliance for Safety and Justice received no help at all after being victimized. Those who did were much likelier to get assistance from family and friends than from the criminal legal system. State systems tend not to be involved in part because intimate partner violence is chronically underreported to law enforcement. Between 2006 and 2015, 44 percent of crimes involving intimate partner violence were not reported to police.[3] Like victims of violence generally, people subjected to abuse who do not report to police are likely receiving assistance from families, friends, and other informal sources of support. We see, then, that communities are already playing a central role in responding to intimate partner violence.

Investing in community-based responses to intimate partner violence would be consistent with the historical underpinnings of the antiviolence movement, whose roots are in communities, not the state. The first collective responses to intimate partner violence were community-based shelters and support groups for women. Not until the 1980s, when government money (with its attendant requirements for professionalization of services) became available to the antiviolence movement, did the state response to intimate partner violence eclipse the grassroots service-provision work done by volunteers, many of whom had been subjected to abuse themselves. While organizations in communities continue to provide crucial services to people subjected to abuse, many of those organizations are so enmeshed with the state by virtue of funding and collaboration with law enforcement that they operate more as an arm (however attenuated) of the state than an authentic community-based response.

There is, of course, potential danger in turning to community to respond to intimate partner violence. As Radhika Coomaraswamy, the former United Nations special rapporteur on violence against women, writes, "[T]he community may be the site for brutality, violence and discrimination against women." But, she continues, "the community is often a nurturing space, which provides women with social support and solidarity. . . . The community is often the buffer, the support which gives solidarity and strength to women victims of violence during their times of crisis."[4] Thinking through how to minimize the threat of and maximize the support available through the community is essential, given that so many people subjected to abuse will turn first to the community (and often nowhere else) for assistance.

Intimate partner violence is, without question, a community problem The characteristics of a community, the supports available, and the willingness of residents to intervene to stop violence all shape the experience of intimate partner violence. Community problems require community-based solutions, and communities across the country are already experimenting with those solutions.

THE RELATIONSHIP BETWEEN COMMUNITY AND INTIMATE PARTNER VIOLENCE

The development of community-based responses to violence relies on two core intuitions: (1) developing relationships deters violence; and (2), with support, communities have the capacity to intervene. One example of the power of neighbors joining together to prevent violence comes from Chicago's Englewood neighborhood. Tamar Manasseh asked local women to patrol the streets after the 2015 murder of a woman in their community. Members of Manasseh's organization, Mothers against Senseless Killings, or MASK, were on the streets during the afternoons and evenings of the summer of 2016, and their presence deterred gun violence in their community. Throughout that summer, despite rampant gun violence in Chicago, police did not record a single shooting on the block. Manasseh sees her work as about more than stopping violence—she's building community. As she explained, "You want to know your neighbors. When you know your neighbors people don't die. That's how that works."[5]

Using a similar logic, in the 1990s Washington state created Family Policy Councils, community-based programs designed to curtail youth violence. City officials talked individually with community members to identify and prioritize their goals, helped communities form networks and neighborhood associations, and supported those associations in finding funds to create infrastructure and develop leadership. Communities that developed partnerships and coalitions focused on responding to violence reduced the social, emotional, and physical consequences of abuse, neglect, and other forms of childhood trauma.[6] More recently, police in Longview, Washington, have pointed to community involvement as an essential component of crime reduction. As Captain Debbie Johnson of the Longview Police Department observed, "[T]here's just less opportunity for crime when neighbors watch out for each other."[7] These same principles can be applied to intimate partner violence.

The relationship between intimate partner violence and community is complex. A number of community-level factors are associated with increased rates of intimate partner violence: living in a neighborhood with high unemployment, low average incomes, and low male literacy rates; lack of social cohesion within the community; the perception of high levels of neighborhood disorder; and community cynicism with respect to the power of law. Community-level factors also protect against intimate partner violence. Communities where women are empowered have lower rates of violence. Moreover, the existence of community spaces, like churches, playgrounds, and shelters, and access to resources like public health centers, community centers, and women's groups within the community positively affect violence. Research has yet to explore how other facets of the built environment of a community, like the architecture of a neighborhood or the number of vacant houses and lots, affect rates of intimate partner violence, but studies of gun violence suggest that such violence decreases when dilapidated and abandoned housing stock is rehabilitated.

Social supports within the community color the experience of intimate partner violence as well. Violence decreases where social ties within neighborhoods are strong and residents are willing to intervene. Interacting with social networks can increase the scrutiny of a couple's relationship, prompting others to step in to protect the abused partner, bring cultural and religious proscriptions against violence to bear, or confront abusive partners about their behavior. Family and friends often provide material and emotional support to people subjected to abuse. Social support from family members is linked to both a lower likelihood of being subjected to intimate partner violence and a lower frequency of abuse. Social ties with friends may also deter intimate partner violence.

Membership in a particular social group may protect against intimate partner violence. Immigrants, for example, sometimes create informal networks that make them less susceptible to crime. Intimate partner violence is less prevalent among recent immigrants than it is among those who have spent longer in the United States. The strong family ties and interaction among families in immigrant communities may reduce opportunities for intimate partner violence. Concentrated immigration can actually reduce levels of intimate partner violence within neighborhoods if the immigrant community embraces cultural norms supporting intervention—where violence is seen as a community, rather than a private, problem.[8]

But concentrated poverty can interfere with the benefits of social support. Neighborhood disadvantage may undercut social support by decreasing the number and quality of the social ties that people develop and by fostering isolation, which makes intervention less likely. Neither social ties nor interventionist cultural norms can overcome the impact of neighborhood disadvantage, and the cumulative effect of neighborhood disadvantage and isolation can be devastating. Women who live in underresourced neighborhoods and have low levels of social support are most at risk of being subjected to abuse.

Collective efficacy is central to community interventions to interrupt violence. In neighborhoods with higher levels of disruption (like poverty and high residential mobility), community members may be less able to prevent violence because they lack social connections and trust. Those deficits can be overcome, however, in neighborhoods with greater collective efficacy. Collective efficacy reflects a community's belief in its capacity to act to end violence and a resulting active engagement by community residents. To exercise collective efficacy, residents must have mutual trust and the willingness to intervene to exercise social control. Strong preexisting personal ties among community residents are not necessary. Collective efficacy relies on the capacity for social action—a shared commitment to intervening to stop violence and the readiness to act on that commitment—not the interpersonal relationships of the actors. The existence of both cohesion and willingness to intervene are essential in decreasing violence. While social ties make the exercise of control possible, violence abates only when control is exercised. Collective efficacy also contributes to the prevention of intimate partner violence. Studies have repeatedly shown that communities with less collective efficacy experience more intimate partner violence. And inversely, intimate partner violence decreases in communities with greater collective efficacy. Similarly, increasing social capital (a measure including collective efficacy, psychological sense of community, and neighborhood cohesion) can decrease domestic violence. Each 1 percent increase in social capital was associated with a 30 percent decrease in intimate partner violence among families in a study in North and South Carolina.[9]

This relationship might exist for a number of reasons. First, in neighborhoods with higher collective efficacy, people who might otherwise abuse their partners could be deterred by the knowledge that their neighbors are likely to intervene. Collective efficacy could also make people subjected to abuse more likely to confide in or seek assistance from their neighbors, who are more willing to provide that assistance. Even if neighbors do not directly intervene, people who abuse might be loath to risk the stigma and shame resulting from their neighbors' awareness of their actions. Whatever the reason, the relationship between collective efficacy and intimate partner violence is significant enough to bolster the case for approaching intimate partner violence as a community problem.

Poverty, however, complicates the relationship between collective efficacy and intimate partner violence. Collective efficacy mitigated the strong positive relationship between community disadvantage and intimate partner homicides in one study.[10] In a later study, however, although higher collective efficacy correlated with lower rates of intimate partner violence, collective efficacy did not mediate the relationship between neighborhood disadvantage and intimate partner violence.[11] Collective efficacy has been credited with lowering the risk of dating violence victimization regardless of neighborhood disadvantage. Collective efficacy depressed male perpetration of dating violence in neighborhoods experiencing low- and mid-level poverty but actually increased the risk of male perpetration of dating violence in the highest poverty neighborhoods.[12]

STRATEGIES FOR COMMUNITY INTERVENTION

Developing and exercising informal social controls and fostering stronger community ties can disrupt intimate partner violence. Linking community members, who may bring different perspectives to the problem, can help create a broader vision for intervention, corral a wider array of resources, and generate innovative strategies for community involvement. Those strategies could take a number of forms, all of which require community buy-in and labor to effectuate, as well as the development of formal or informal community-based structures through which to operate. Community organizing, community accountability strategies, and community-based justice projects can all provide outlets for community engagement in response to intimate partner violence.

Community Organizing

The noncriminal response to intimate partner violence revolves largely around service provision. Shelters and agencies (community based and not) provide emergency and transitional housing, counseling, civil legal services, financial literacy and employment training, parenting classes, and other concrete forms of assistance that may be invaluable to people subjected to intimate partner violence. But few of these organizations engage in the kind of community building that could be protective for people subjected to abuse. Empowering the community to act requires more than simply dropping services into a community. Community-building strategies strengthen the community's capacity to respond to violence without the intervention of professionals. As social worker Paul Kivel explains, community building requires "identifying common goals, figuring out how to work together and support one another, and coming up with strategies for forcing organizational and institutional change. When people get together, they build community by establishing projects, organizations, friendships, connections, coalitions, alliances, and an understanding of differences."[13] Community building is hard work in the best of circumstances and can be more difficult in communities beset by poverty and violence, where social ties are already frayed. But given the importance of social supports and collective efficacy in decreasing intimate partner violence, community building must be a component of antiviolence policy.

Community building can take a number of forms. Given the relationship between neighborhood demographics and intimate partner violence, organizing geographic communities to respond to intimate partner violence is essential. But community can be defined in a number of other ways as well:

through religion, culture, or common interest. At Xavier University, for example, community members organized around their shared religious culture to combat gender violence on campus. At the core of Xavier's efforts was the concept of *cura personalis,* understood by the Jesuit community to encompass care for a person's mind, body, and spirit. Using cura personalis as an organizing principle, the campus community discussed the pervasiveness of gender violence and considered what Xavier's response to that violence should be. Xavier's president set the tone for those deliberations: "It is impossible for us to imagine advancing efforts to truly care for the whole person when gender-based violence affects individuals every day. It is therefore of primary importance that an institution dedicated to caring for the whole person place the elimination of gender-based violence at the forefront of our efforts."[14] While gender violence hasn't been eradicated at Xavier, "[b]y harnessing a locally meaningful cultural concept, leaders and members in the community mobilized their culture as an asset in a larger movement against gender violence."[15]

Cultural communities provide fertile ground for organizing. The Shanti ("harmony" or "peace") Project created a social marketing campaign targeting intimate partner violence the Gujarati Indian community in a Midwestern city. The project first surveyed the community (via focus groups and individual interviews) to ascertain the community's knowledge of intimate partner violence. Using that data, project staff and members of a community action team (a group of community residents diverse in age, immigration status, and education) identified a number of issues that could be addressed through community-based participatory social marketing. Those issues included the community's limited definition of intimate partner violence, community norms about privacy and the prevalence of gossip about intimate partner violence, the importance of family, and the link between patriarchy within the community and intimate partner violence. The project found that community members considered emotional and verbal (as opposed to physical) abuse acceptable. They felt uncomfortable talking about intimate partner violence openly or intervening to prevent violence but would gossip about it. In response, the social marketing campaign sought to raise awareness of the scope of intimate partner violence. The Shanti Project developed community-based seminars, radio announcements, articles for ethnic, religious, and cultural publications in the community, and brochures disseminated at ethnic grocery and video stores, featuring the slogan "How peaceful is your home?" and stressing the importance of communication and respect. The project found that community engagement was essential in challenging traditions and values (like patriarchy within the community) that were important to community members but created a context within which violence could occur, and it used the concept of "respect" to "bridge the two seemingly different agendas."[16]

Community building can also entail creating spaces where people can organize to share their experiences of and develop strategies to address intimate partner violence. Community organizing was a central component of the nascent battered women's movement. Because no government funding was allocated for domestic violence services in the early years of the antiviolence movement, women turned instead to their communities for support. They organized into collectives and created and ran shelters, hotlines, and coalitions. Women subjected to abuse were seen as "participants in a joint struggle," explains social work professor Susan Schechter, a founding member of the movement.[17] The emphasis on organizing people subjected to abuse, all but lost in the movement's transition from a grassroots-led effort to a government-funded social service provision system, has been revived in a number of communities.

People subjected to intimate partner violence are once again organizing around intimate partner violence, and through those efforts, building community. Gather Together, for example, is a Baltimore, Maryland, based "collective of survivors of sexual and domestic violence. We believe that as survivors, we should lead the conversation about prevention and healing." A project of FORCE: Upsetting Rape Culture, Gather Together uses art and performance to tell survivor stories and reach out to the larger community. Gather Together and FORCE coordinated Not Alone Baltimore, a month-long public awareness campaign designed to build support for survivors of sexual and domestic violence using public art, including advertisements on buses and billboards. Gather Together also participated in a series of town hall meetings for survivors, one focused on developing community accountability strategies and another inviting local government representatives and service providers to a listening session on the needs and concerns of people subjected to abuse. Led by FORCE staff, members of Gather Together also organized a public comment session on the United States Department of Justice's investigation into gender-biased policing in Baltimore, enabling people subjected to abuse to tell representatives from the Department of Justice directly about the Baltimore Police Department's shoddy handling of gender violence cases. As Hannah Brancato, the organizer of Gather Together, explains:

> People most impacted by any issue have to be at the table deciding on solutions. When survivors of rape and abuse are at the table, people who

> don't see themselves as impacted by this issue can first of all learn to listen to stories from survivors and second, see how, most likely, this is an issue that does have a personal impact on their life. Survivors of sexual and domestic violence becoming more visible as a political constituency is the only way to make a significant impact on reducing stigma, ending rape culture, and decreasing statistics of rape and abuse.[18]

COMMUNITY-BASED JUSTICE

Offender accountability and the safety of people subjected to abuse are the oft-cited cornerstones of the conventional justice response to intimate partner violence. But people subjected to abuse have multiple justice needs: information, participation, voice, validation, vindication, material reparation, and offender accountability beyond criminal punishment. To meet these multifaceted justice goals, people subjected to abuse need a menu of options, some centered in formal legal systems and some available outside of those systems.[19] Frustrated with the limited and problematic options available through the legal system, some people subjected to abuse are searching for justice outside of formal systems they see as repressive and immune to reform. People subjected to abuse, advocates, and activists are collaborating to develop a range of community justice strategies, including community accountability and restorative justice.

Community Accountability

Community-based transformative justice efforts empower communities to develop responses to violence that ensure safety without police intervention. Transformative justice is more a conceptual framework than a specific process or practice. Generation Five, a collaborative dedicated to ending child sexual abuse within five generations using transformative justice principles, defines transformative justice as "a liberatory approach to violence . . . which seeks safety and accountability without relying on alienation, punishment, or State or systemic violence, including incarceration or policing."[20] Appreciating how intersectionality functions in the lives of people subjected to harm and those who do harm is central to transformative justice efforts. While transformative justice believes in the community's capacity to foster safety for people subjected to abuse, it also acknowledges the need to hold communities accountable for their role in failing to prevent or actively promoting intimate partner and other forms of violence. Transformative justice views "individual justice and collective liberation" as "equally important, mutually supportive, and fundamentally intertwined" and recognizes that state responses to violence often spur, rather than reduce, violence.[21] Transformative justice efforts therefore work on multiple levels, redressing individual acts of violence while attempting to remedy the social conditions or systems of oppression that create the environments within which violence flourishes.

Community accountability puts the principles of transformative justice into action. People subjected to abuse often turn to friends, family, and other supporters when they experience violence, but those "first responders" frequently lack the skills and capacity necessary to provide assistance. Organizations like Creative Interventions provide those tools, enlisting community members in confronting and responding to intimate partner violence. Creative Interventions' Community-Based Interventions Project was designed to "develop, pilot test, evaluate, document and distribute a replicable comprehensive alternative community-based approach to violence intervention" that would expand the capacity of "family, friends, neighbors, co-workers and others toward whom persons in need first turn . . . with the model and tools to effectively intervene."[22] Creative Interventions' materials include tools to use in identifying and understanding violence, thinking about how to stay safe and reduce harm during an intervention, finding allies, identifying barriers to addressing violence, determining goals or outcomes, supporting people subjected to abuse, helping abusers accept accountability, and forging strong collaborations. Using those tools, communities can craft individualized interventions that meet the needs of people subjected to abuse. Similarly, the Chrysalis Collective has developed an eight-step program for addressing violence through transformative justice, including forming survivor support and accountability teams and defining the relationship between those teams; creating a transformative justice plan; planning for and holding a meeting to establish accountability; following up with the accountability team for as long as is necessary to implement the plan; and debriefing when the process is completed.

Conceptualizing what community accountability looks like in practice can be challenging. Creative Interventions provides a concrete example in its materials. The Creative Interventions toolkit describes a woman subjected to abuse who was married to a police officer. She felt that she could not turn to the criminal legal system for protection when her partner's verbal abuse and stalking made her feel unsafe. Instead, she brought together a number of friends and supporters to help her brainstorm options. Her friends worked with her to identify her goals and thought about ways to help her feel safe in her home. Her friends set up a schedule to ensure that she was not home alone, which helped to restore her feeling of security. The group sought to identify people who could talk with her partner in an attempt to calm him down; her mother took on that role. They created a phone list so that she always had someone to call for assistance. The group approached the abuse as a collective, rather than an individual, problem, taking responsibility for ensuring that further harm did not occur in their community.

Community accountability efforts must be grounded in achieving accountability as defined by the person subjected to abuse. Some transformative justice–based organizations have found, though, that distinguishing accountability from retribution, revenge, or punitive justice can be difficult. Organizations like Generation Five and Support New York, a collective founded to confront sexual abuse in communities, ask people to develop comprehensive lists of accountability options, then review those lists to see whether and how the needs expressed can be met in ways that are consistent with a transformative justice framework. As Support New York explains, "Our focus on transformation means that we strive to move beyond a 'guilty or not guilty' and 'what really happened' dynamic, and instead seek acts of accountability that redress the individualized effects of abuse and heal the [offender's] relationship to the community."[23]

Successful community accountability strategies depend upon the development of a network of community actors willing to intervene when violence occurs. The NW Network's Friends Are Reaching Out (FAR Out) program starts from the premise that those who commit acts of intimate partner violence are more likely to listen to the people they love and that people subjected to abuse are more likely to disclose to a friend or family member than anyone else. But the antiviolence movement has failed to mobilize friends and families to hold offenders accountable for their actions and has not offered supporters concrete strategies for helping people subjected to abuse. FAR Out provides this kind of guidance, enabling friends and family to lend that assistance. The FAR Out website includes tools to help people subjected to abuse repair relationships with friends and family, identify and set appropriate boundaries in relationships, and work with family and friends to pair the support needed by the person subjected to abuse with the resources friends and family are able to offer. The NW Network also conducts relationship skills classes in the community. The goal of those classes is both to help people think about how they want their relationships to be and encourage them to reach out if their relationships are not meeting those expectations.

Knowing how to intervene in a way that aids rather than endangers the person subjected to abuse is essential. To provide that information, the

Neighbors, Friends, Families campaign, a project of the Ontario, Canada, government, the Ontario Women's Directorate, and the Centre for Research and Education on Violence against Women and Children, developed a pamphlet titled *How to Talk to Men Who Are Abusive.* The pamphlet lists warning signs for those who are concerned that a neighbor, friend, or family member is being abused and suggests strategies for initiating a conversation with the person they suspect is being abusive. Those strategies include:

- Choose the right time and place to have a full discussion.
- Approach him when he is calm.
- Be direct and clear about what you have seen.
- Tell him that his behavior is his responsibility.
- Avoid making judgmental comments about him as a person.
- Don't validate his attempt to blame others for his behavior.
- Inform him that the behavior needs to stop.
- Don't force him to change or to seek help.

The pamphlet warns interveners that arguing with the person about their behavior might make the situation worse for the person being abused. The pamphlet also suggests responses in the event that the person denies the abuse. Finally, some common concerns about whether to intervene are covered, including the fear that the intervener won't know what to say, will anger the person, or will make things worse. What the pamphlet fails to do, though, is to suggest that the intervener first talk with the person subjected to abuse to get her assessment of the impact of intervening on her behalf.

Neighborhood violence prevention programs are also confronting intimate partner violence. Safe Streets Baltimore deploys community outreach workers to interrupt potentially violent situations. Safe Streets workers come from the communities they canvass, and most have interacted with the criminal legal system. Workers report that many of the potentially violent incidents they disrupt begin as or involve intimate partner violence. Safe Streets works with both offenders and victims to intervene before violence occurs and connect those involved with services and supports, including employment training, mental health care, and substance abuse treatment.

Community-based accountability mechanisms can have a profound impact on those who abuse. As one Tlingit man who experienced community accountability explained, "First one must deal with the shock and then the dismay on your neighbors' faces. One must live with the daily humiliation, and at the same time seek forgiveness not just from victims, but from the community as a whole. . . . [A prison sentence] removes the offender from the daily accountability, and may not do anything towards rehabilitation, and for many may actually be an easier disposition than staying in the community."[24]

But relying on community accountability strategies to prevent violence poses a number of challenges. Margaret Hobart of the NW Network notes that programs like FAR Out are most effective before the violence becomes acute; the more dangerous the relationship, the harder it may be to develop effective community-based solutions. Community accountability strategies often require that those who use violence be engaged in the process and willing to accept responsibility for their actions. Securing that buy-in through the exercise of moral (as opposed to legal) authority may be difficult. And community accountability strategies require responsive communities that embrace nonviolence as a norm, which can be hard to find.

Restorative Justice

The shortcomings of the legal system's response to intimate partner violence have led scholars, advocates, and people subjected to abuse to seek justice processes that do not disempower people subjected to abuse or further alienate and exacerbate the anger of those who use violence. Restorative justice is frequently cited as having the potential to achieve these goals. Definitions of restorative justice vary, but all center on the concept of harm: what harm was done, the impact of that harm, and how the harm can be redressed. Restorative justice has both a values and a process dimension; absent either dimension, the understanding of restorative justice is incomplete. As criminologist John Braithwaite writes, "Restorative justice is a process in which all the stakeholders affected by an injustice have the opportunity to discuss the consequences of the injustice and what might be done to put them right."[25]

Braithwaite argues that the overarching value of restorative justice is healing: "because injustice hurts, justice should heal."[26] Restorative justice relies on the exercise of moral authority and the belief that moral authority can have a greater impact on offenders' actions than legal sanctions. Restorative justice is not a morally neutral practice. Injustice, sometimes defined as domination of another, is seen as immoral and therefore requiring remedy. Restorative justice's moral authority derives from the establishment of relationships between those who have been harmed, those who do harm, and members of the community; the grounding in connections that comes through the development of these relationships gives restorative justice its moral force.[27] Restorative justice is victim-centered, and empowerment is central to restorative processes. In the restorative justice context, empowerment is defined as enabling people who have been harmed to keep control of their conflicts, rather than having the state take them over, and work through those conflicts in the way that best meets their justice needs.

Holding those who do harm accountable is a cornerstone of restorative justice. Punishment in the criminal legal system is a passive process, requiring only that "people sustain the suffering imposed upon them for their transgression."[28] The desire to escape punishment prevents offenders from accepting responsibility for what they have done. At the time of criminal punishment (sentencing), offenders are unlikely to admit responsibility or acknowledge the injury that their actions have caused. As Jeremiah Bourgeois, an inmate at Stafford Creek Corrections Center in Washington writes of his own experience at sentencing, "His mind is not in the right state. He has not given up on his cause, not just yet."[29] During incarceration, prisoners are still not asked to grapple with the implications of the harm they have done. Punishment does not require that offenders meet face-to-face with the people they have harmed or work to remedy that harm in any way. Punishment does not help offenders develop empathy for their victims.

Restorative justice, by contrast, involves active accountability, requiring offenders to accept responsibility for and acknowledge the impact of their actions, have face-to-face meetings with their victims or victim surrogates, listen to the victim's account of that harm, hear how the offender's actions affected the lives of the victim and the victim's community of support, and work actively to repair that harm. Restorative justice demands more of the offender than criminal punishment and may be more difficult to endure. But that direct engagement is essential if offenders are to develop empathy, which can act as a safeguard against further harms. Neuroscientist Daniel Reisel explains that through restorative justice, "[t]he perpetrator can see, perhaps for the first time, the victim as a real person with thoughts and feelings and a genuine emotional response. And [that] may be a more effective rehabilitative practice than simple incarceration."[30]

Accountability and the appropriate use of shame are intertwined in restorative justice. Restorative justice rejects the idea of stigmatizing offenders for their transgressions, believing that stigma only spurs further criminality. Instead, restorative justice embraces the idea of reintegrative shaming—separating disapproval of the act from condemnation of offenders—and welcomes offenders back into community once they are willing to accept responsibility for their actions. Restorative practitioner Danielle Sered explains, "They deserve to pay in a meaningful and dignified way for what they have done. They deserve the difficulty of that reckoning, and even the fear and pain it may cause. But they also deserve an opportunity to repair harm that will allow them an avenue out of shame and its associated violence."[31] The goal of restorative justice is to engender remorse rather than the anger, shame, guilt, and regret generated by traditional criminal punishment. Without remorse, the offender cannot be held truly accountable, and the victim of harm may be unable to achieve some measure of justice.

Community engagement is another key component of restorative justice. Community serves a number of functions in restorative practice—as the location where restorative practices are centered, the source of supporters for victims of harm, a secondary set of victims of harm, a locus of accountability for offenders, and, through connection to community members, a bulwark against future harms. Restorative justice can be transformative for the community as well. Engaging community members in restorative practices can help to shift norms that permit, and even facilitate, harm.

Restorative processes share a number of elements, including the opportunity for dialogue among victims, offenders, and supporters and consensus development of a plan for addressing harm. But the umbrella term restorative justice covers a variety of different opportunities for interaction between victims and offenders, some of which are channeled through the criminal legal system. Victim-offender mediation, for example, involves conversations between those who have been harmed and those who have done harm, facilitated by a trained mediator. The goals of those conversations vary. In some sessions, the intent is to develop a restitution agreement to remediate the harm; in others, the person who has been harmed simply wants an opportunity to ask questions and obtain information from the person who has done harm. Victim-offender mediation usually occurs within the context of a legal proceeding and can take place at multiple points within the life of a criminal case, with the potential to influence charging, disposition, and sentencing decisions. Victim-offender dialogues, by contrast, are facilitated conversations that generally take place postconviction, after a sentence has already been handed down. Postconviction dialogues are held at the behest of and are driven by the needs of the person subjected to harm. Participants engage in the process in order to seek answers or information, give the offender a sense of the impact of the crime, voice their own feelings about the harm and promote healing, and engage offenders on a human level. Victim-offender dialogues are often run through state departments of corrections and are subject to the rules of the correctional system. At least thirty-one states offer victim-offender dialogue programs.

Restorative conferences engage a wider range of participants in the conversation. In addition to the person who has been harmed and the person who has done harm (and accepted responsibility for the harm, a crucial component of restorative processes), conferencing can also involve supporters for both the victim and offender and members of the wider community. Conferencing focuses on the central questions of restorative justice: what was the harm, what was the impact of the harm, and how can that harm be addressed. Successful conferences end with tangible agreements outlining what the offender will do to mitigate the harm, as well as concrete commitments from supporters and community members to hold the offender accountable for following the agreement. Conferencing provides the opportunity to craft agreements that are individualized, contextual, and culturally appropriate and engages the community in the kind of regular monitoring necessary to ensure compliance. Conferencing widens the net of social control, "except it is nets of community rather than state control that are widened."[32]

Restorative processes can be used preventatively as well. Restorative circles are deliberative processes that sit at "the intersection of information sharing, education, reflection, and community building."[33] The circle process involves bringing community members together to create connections, discuss an issue of concern, and develop both shared norms around the issue and an action plan for addressing it. The circle process has also been used to support offenders' reintegration into the community and to prevent reoffending.

When given the option, both victims and offenders are likely to opt in to restorative processes, despite the requirement that offenders admit culpability as a condition of participation. Participating in restorative justice processes gives victims more information and an enhanced understanding of what motivated the offender's behavior. Victims feel greater control over restorative processes, and that control both empowers them and makes them feel safer. After restorative conferences, victims are less afraid of, experience less anger at, and are more empathetic toward offenders. Victims feel that they get more "justice," as they define the term, from restorative alternatives. Offenders, in turn, are more likely to understand the impact of their actions, be held accountable in meaningful ways, and provide the kinds of redress requested by victims. Offenders who opt for restorative justice are much more likely to accept responsibility for their actions and develop greater empathy for their victims. Both victims and offenders report high levels of satisfaction with restorative processes and outcomes.[34] Society benefits from restorative justice as well. When offenders accept responsibility for their actions and engage in restorative processes, they are much less likely to recidivate. Those reductions are greater for serious crimes. "[T]he higher levels of emotional engagement by victims and offenders in these kinds of encounters is the 'engine' leading to the emotions of empathy and remorse which may be the essential ingredients for reduced reoffending."[35]

Restorative processes have been used in a number of contexts—including as a response to gender-based harms. In December 2014, for example, female students at the Dalhousie University Faculty of Dentistry in Nova Scotia, Canada, learned that a number of male dental students had started a private "Gentlemen's Club" on Facebook, where they posted sexist, misogynistic, and homophobic material about female dental students. The women filed a claim under the university's sexual harassment policy and opted to have the claim resolved through a restorative process. Twenty-nine students (twelve of the men involved in the Facebook group, fourteen female students, and three other male students) participated. The women students explained their decision to opt for a restorative process:

> Restorative justice provided us with a different sort of justice than the punitive type most of the loudest public voices seemed to want. We were clear from the beginning, to the people who most needed to hear it, that we were not looking to have our classmates expelled as 13 angry men who understood no more than they did the day the posts were uncovered. Nor did we want simply to forgive and forget. Rather, we were looking for a resolution that would allow us to graduate alongside men who understood the harms they caused, owned these harms, and would carry with them a responsibility and obligation to do better.[36]

Over five months, the process examined the specific events that gave rise to the complaint as well as the culture within the Faculty of Dentistry and the wider society that allowed destructive sexist attitudes to flourish. Members of the faculty of the dental school, the university community, the Nova Scotia Dental Association, and the wider community joined in the process.[37] The restorative process involved a thorough investigation of the claims, regular meetings between facilitators and participants in the process, restorative circles with various groups of participants, and participation in a day of learning at the end of the process, during which the male students presented their insights gained from the process.[38]

At the outset of the process, the male students noted, "when we realized the hurt and harm our comments caused for our classmates, faculty and staff we wanted to convey our overwhelming regret." During the restorative process, however, "we learned that saying sorry is too easy. Being sorry, we have come to see, is much harder. It takes a commitment to hear and learn about the effects of your actions and an ongoing and lasting commitment to act differently in the future. We have hurt many of those closest to us. We do not ask for our actions to be excused. They are not excusable."[39]

By the end of the process, the male students involved in the Facebook group stated that they "[saw] the world through a different lens now. We recognize more clearly the prejudice and discrimination that exists inside and outside of dentistry. We understand we have contributed to this through our actions and by failing to stand up when we saw it happening. It may be impossible to undo the harms but, we commit, individually and collectively to work day by day to make positive changes in the world. The problems extend far beyond us, and we will work to ensure the lessons we have learned will as well."[40]

These men took responsibility for their actions, understood how their actions created and reinforced gender-based harms and stereotypes, and committed to addressing those harms. The learning and change that occurred at Dalhousie would most likely not have happened in a punitive process. Rather than achieving some understanding of the harm that they caused, the men would have been bitter and angry about being expelled from school and denied the chance to practice dentistry. Nothing would have been learned and no insight gained. The justice goals of the female students who had been harmed were met because the process was deliberately designed to help the male students understand the damage they caused and to change their future behavior rather than simply punishing them.

There has been significant resistance to using restorative justice in matters involving intimate partner violence, and the laws of some states explicitly forbid the use of restorative practices in those cases. That resistance reflects concerns about reprivatizing violence against women, women's safety, and entrusting justice to the community.

The efforts of early antiviolence advocates to ensure that intimate partner violence was treated as a crime like any other brought cases of intimate partner violence into the public sphere. Since that time, significant resources have been dedicated to the law enforcement response to intimate partner violence. Implementing community-based restorative practices could be used to justify diverting those resources away from law enforcement efforts to combat intimate partner violence. Such a move would allow the government to sidestep responsibility for adjudicating these crimes, essentially reprivatizing intimate partner violence.

Resistance to community-based restorative practices often emerges from concerns about safety. Community-based restorative processes are "informal" in that they take place outside of the confines of the legal system, which is thought to have the knowledge and expertise needed to handle such matters safely. Restorative facilitators, however, may be unfamiliar with the dynamics of intimate partner violence and fail to take precautionary measures to protect people subjected to abuse. Because restorative processes often involve face-to-face encounters, people who abuse could have unrestricted access to their partners. Offenders might use the opportunity provided by restorative processes to exert control over or physically or emotionally harm their partners.

Relying on the community to hold offenders accountable is another concern. The restorative justice literature often references community without defining the term, but the actual implementation of restorative practices requires the identification of specific communities to be tasked with doing the work. Given the fragmentation and lack of connection within communities in the United States, one could question whether sufficient community structure exists to support restorative justice programs. Moreover, in order to ensure that offenders are held accountable for their violence, restorative justice efforts must be embedded in communities with strong antiviolence norms. But those norms are weak or absent in some communities, and there is reason to question whether such communities will, in fact, hold those who abuse accountable for their actions. An offender is often situated within a community that "legitimizes, condones, and even supports his use of violence."[41] Even in communities with strong antiviolence norms, resources are often scarce. Although resources could be redirected from the criminal legal system into restorative efforts, the criticisms of the justice reinvestment movement make it clear that diverting resources from the criminal legal system into communities is no easy task.

Finally, there are questions about whether restorative processes are well suited to cases involving intimate partner violence. Law professor Julie Stubbs, for example, contends that the restorative justice literature assumes that restorative practices will be used in response to discrete incidents between victims and offenders previously unknown to each other, which is not true of intimate partner violence. Moreover, Stubbs explains, women subjected to abuse make choices about how to respond to violence under conditions of constraint, most notably the need to consider how responses will affect their children. The restorative justice literature, she argues, has yet to grapple with the involvement of participants lacking unfettered agency.[42] Stubbs also questions whether the timing of restorative processes can accommodate the different needs, ranging from safety and survival to justice, which people subjected to abuse may have over time.[43]

Notwithstanding these criticisms, there are many—including some antiviolence advocates—who believe that community-based restorative justice processes can meet the justice needs of people subjected to abuse. Disillusionment with the legal system's response to intimate partner violence, the desire to provide people subjected to abuse with options that are empowering, and the belief that communities are essential to antiviolence efforts drive that support.

For some advocates, the willingness to consider restorative justice is linked to the realization that the criminal legal system does not serve some people subjected to abuse well. The criminal legal system is ideal for those who seek a retributive response; indeed, the state is the only body legally sanctioned to mete out punishment for crime. But for those whose justice needs revolve around something other than punishment, the criminal legal system has little to offer. People subjected to abuse may instead be seeking individualized responses that provide opportunities for voice, validation, and vindication. Voice involves both the opportunity to actively participate in a justice process and the ability to speak out. Simply having the opportunity to tell one's story, unmediated by the rules and norms of the legal system and in whatever form one chooses, is an essential element of justice for some who have been harmed. Voice is important on a number of levels: to enable people subjected to abuse to reclaim power through participation, establish the facts, frame the facts as they see fit, and be recognized as valid and trustworthy sources of information, thus restoring their dignity. As law professor Quince Hopkins explains, "Truth-telling about the traumatic events is central to any process of recovery."[44]

Validation—an acknowledgement of the harm done—is a second concern of some people subjected to abuse. Women subjected to abuse seek "a mechanism to communicate loudly and clearly that they were serious, and a public record of the abuse and their effort to stop it."[45] If validation is an acknowledgment of harm, vindication is "a clear and unequivocal stand in condemnation of the offense."[46] Vindication requires the community to publicly stand with the victim of harm and to hold offenders accountable for their actions.

These justice needs can be met through both retributive and restorative justice processes. In the retributive system, people subjected to abuse can testify, though that testimony is filtered through the rules of evidence and the structure of a criminal trial, and can provide victim impact statements after a guilty verdict has been rendered. The power of such statements was evident in the Michigan courtroom where more than 150 women gave victim impact statements at the sentencing of former U.S. gymnastics team doctor Larry Nassar, who sexually abused the women. In her statement, gymnast Aly Raisman declared, "I have both power and voice, and I am only beginning to just use them." Restorative processes provide forums in which people subjected to abuse can share their stories, but those stories might be mediated by what an individual feels comfortable disclosing to community members. A criminal conviction and sentence can serve as validation and vindication when the sentence is commensurate with the victim's assessment of the harm; a community's understanding and condemnation of wrongdoing and provision of support can serve the same function. Determining whether justice has been done in cases involving intimate partner abuse turns on the individual's experience of both the process and the outcome.

Making restorative processes available could ensure that justice is done in a wider array of situations. For those uninterested in having their justice needs met through punishment-based state systems, or who are afraid of exposing themselves to the state, community-based restorative justice processes may prove a more palatable alternative. Although fears about the reprivatization of intimate partner violence are used to justify opposition to restorative justice, some people subjected to abuse, particularly low-income women, suffer from too little privacy, not too much.[47] For women whose housing, financial status, and parenting are frequently subjected to state scrutiny, sometimes with destructive results, a private, community-based process might be preferable. Moreover, restorative justice can respond to harms that the criminal legal system does not reach. Emotional and verbal abuse are rarely prosecuted criminally; in many places, they are not crimes. Similarly, isolation and control tactics are not illegal. But all of these forms of abuse can do as much damage as the physical abuse that is actionable under the law. Restorative justice could provide redress for those harms.

Restorative processes can be empowering for people subjected to abuse. Victims of harm control the process, deciding whether to engage in the first instance, selecting support people, and playing whatever role they choose in the proceedings. After engaging in a restorative process with her former partner, one woman subjected to abuse "felt as if I could knock out Mike Tyson. I could have taken on anything or anyone. In the days and weeks afterwards, it was as if a massive weight had been lifted off my shoulders. I had been carrying it for so long that I did not even notice it anymore, so when it disappeared it was amazing. I felt completely empowered."[48]

One of many motivations for criminalization was the belief that changing the law could shift the cultural norms supporting intimate partner violence. But beefing up the legal system's response to intimate partner violence has not shifted community norms as much as antiviolence advocates had hoped. Intimate partner violence is still alarmingly common, and whatever expressive value law has may be insufficient to change culture. Introducing restorative practices and engaging community members in those processes provide another avenue for attempting to create the culture change necessary to prevent intimate partner violence. Restorative justice expands the circle of those who are aware of intimate partner violence in the abstract and who might view the issue differently in the concrete context of friends and family members. Bringing community members into restorative practices creates a setting within which community norms on intimate partner violence are aired and can be challenged; as criminologists John Braithwaite and Kathleen Daly argue, "exploitation and brutality flourish more in secretive settings, when they go unchallenged and unnoticed."[49] Restorative justice works on the individual and community levels, offering support to people subjected to abuse and engaging offenders in repairing harm, but also challenging the broader community to consider its role in tacitly or overtly condoning intimate partner violence. Restorative justice can prompt communities to actively embrace and articulate nonviolent norms and develop new services and supports for those who are harmed and who do harm.

Another advantage of restorative justice is the ability of engaged communities to better monitor offender accountability. Reliance on the legal system as the sole accountability mechanism has enabled communities to avoid their role in policing intimate partner violence. But communities are best placed to ensure compliance with accountability plans and reinforce nonviolent norms on a daily basis. Community members are able " to exercise periodic surveillance of family violence or abuse, to talk with family members to ensure they are enjoying freedom from violence, to shame family members when abuse of power does occur, to enforce agreements such as not drinking alcohol, to negotiate understandings that an abused person has a safe harbor nearby to stay, and to negotiate the circumstances of the abuser's removal from the household until there is satisfactory assurance of violence-free family life."[50] Restorative justice engages community members in supporting people subjected to abuse and developing solutions that hold offenders accountable, making intimate partner violence more visible within the community.

If the criminal legal system were meeting the justice needs of people subjected to abuse and achieving meaningful offender accountability, there would be little need for alternative processes. But the criminal legal system often fails to achieve these goals. It is adversarial by design, and its due process requirements and evidentiary rules make it a difficult, and often hostile, space for people subjected to abuse to negotiate. In the criminal legal system, people subjected to abuse are frequently silenced or blamed for their victimization. Engaging with that system "risk[s] further degradation and disappointment with very little chance of a so-called successful outcome, for example, a conviction."[51] Although victims' justice needs are multifaceted, the criminal legal system can deliver only punishment, which does not provide some people with the reparation they seek. The criminal legal system discourages offenders from accepting responsibility for their actions in the hope of escaping criminal culpability. Prosecution hardens offenders' attitudes toward their victims, making the development of empathy and behavior change unlikely at best. Incarceration does nothing to change offenders' attitudes toward their partner or about their use of violence. And although restorative justice is, without doubt, resource intensive, those resources pale in comparison to the funding dedicated to the criminal legal system in the United States.

The debate about the use of restorative practices in the context of intimate partner violence is, at this point, based largely on ideology and conjecture rather than data. The opposition to the use of restorative justice to respond to intimate partner violence has meant that a limited number of programs are doing that work; few of those programs have been evaluated. This situation has created a vicious cycle: because very few programs exist, there is no data, and without data, opponents of restorative justice remain unconvinced of its utility and concerned about its safety. But the studies that do exist support the expansion of these fledgling efforts.

Although the United States has largely rejected the use of restorative justice in situations involving intimate partner violence, the rest of the world has not been as hesitant. A number of countries, including Austria, Finland, Denmark, Greece, the Netherlands, Australia, New Zealand, Canada, and South Africa, offer various restorative options in cases of intimate partner violence. Most countries offer victim-offender mediation; some also use conferencing. Most of these projects are linked to the criminal legal system in some way, with police administering, making referrals to, and attending sessions. In the Netherlands, for example, conferences might be called by police to help people subjected to abuse stop violence while continuing the relationship, separate safely from an abusive partner, or ensure that the partner stays engaged as a parent despite the end of the relationship.

While relatively little research on these programs has been published, the existing data, which is largely drawn from restorative conferencing projects, is promising. Joan Pennell and Gale Burford piloted a restorative justice project with families in the Canadian child welfare system that experienced domestic violence. Pennell and Burford used family group decision-making, a form of restorative justice conferencing, to help participants create plans to address the abuse in the family, drawing upon the support and input of community resources. Pennell and Burford found that no new violence occurred either during or as a result of the conferences, both adult abuse and child maltreatment declined in the participant families, and two-thirds of the families reported being better off following the conference.[52] The Daybreak Dove Program in Hampshire, England, held conferences with fifteen families referred as a result of domestic violence between 2006 and 2007; eleven of the fifteen families were not seen by police again during the six-month follow-up period. Participants in South Africa's victim-offender conferencing program who stayed with their partners told researchers that conferencing led to positive behavior change and improved relationships and communication postconference. In New Zealand, researchers found that most people subjected to abuse who chose restorative practices were satisfied with the process, were glad that they took part, felt positive about their partners taking responsibility for their actions, believed their relationships with their (former) partners had improved, and would recommend the process to others. Of the nineteen people surveyed, six said the violence stopped completely after the process, five said the violence either stopped partially or changed (from physical to psychological), five had no further contact with their partners, and one ended the relationship because the violence did not stop. All of those surveyed said they would recommend restorative justice to others experiencing intimate partner violence.[53] Eighty-seven percent of the offenders in a presentencing restorative justice process in New Zealand who entered into accountability plans with their partners completed all of the tasks in those plans; those who did not complete restorative justice agreements all recidivated. Sixty-two percent of those surveyed in an Australian study of women subjected to abuse whose cases went through the criminal legal system reported that they would have liked a restorative option, either before or after a finding of criminal responsibility. That interest largely grew out of their "desire to convey something to the violent person": "the harm to them, the consequences to others, the wrongfulness of the assault, and the desire for a different person or a different relationship."[54]

While some advocate for the inclusion of restorative processes within the criminal legal system, such programs are ripe for misuse. In parts of England, Wales, and Northern Ireland, for example, police pressure women to participate in "what they call restorative justice or community resolutions in cases of domestic abuse, but the majority of those are street-level disposals [informal resolution by police]."[55] Such programs rightly give rise to fears of a return to the bad old days when police failed to take intimate partner violence seriously or safeguard the legal rights of those people subjected to abuse who wanted to use the criminal system to hold their partners accountable. Moreover, when restorative justice becomes part of the criminal legal system, the incentives for participation change drastically. Offenders may feign accountability in return for a lighter sentence but never truly engage in the process. Embedding restorative practices in the criminal legal system also raises structural issues; the racism endemic in the criminal legal system, for example, could similarly infect restorative practices housed there. Systematizing restorative justice creates a number of risks, including reliance on unskilled facilitators and the elimination of certain participation requirements now considered essential (like the acceptance of responsibility by those who do harm), a problem emerging in New Zealand as restorative justice programs are brought to scale.

Rather than incorporating restorative justice into the criminal legal system, then, restorative processes should be community-based, with the criminal legal system as a backdrop. John Braithwaite explains: "Where punishment is thrust into the foreground even by implied threats, other-regarding deliberation is made difficult because the offender is invited to deliberate in a self-regarding way—out of concern to protect the self from punishment. This is not the way to engender empathy with the victim, internalization of the values of the law and the values of restorative justice . . . that I will argue can transform lives in permanent ways."[56]

Not every case will be appropriate for community-based restorative resolution. But restorative justice has the potential to reach those who will not voluntarily interact with the criminal legal system, to encourage people subjected to abuse to confront their offenders in empowering settings, to provide the tools offenders need to change their behavior, and to engage the community in reparation, both on the individual and societal levels.

"Crime," Lois Presser and Emily Gaarder write, "is neither 'just personal' nor 'just political.' It is an acutely personal experience that at the same time reflects larger societal structures. Although broadly based, these structures are not remote or untouchable. They are found in our own communities—in everyday norms and narratives—and we can affect them there."[57] Intimate partner violence is both a crime and a community problem. It requires community-based solutions.

5. Intimate Partner Violence Is . . .

A Human Rights Problem

In 2011, the Cincinnati, Ohio, City Council declared freedom from domestic violence a fundamental human right. In the wake of Cincinnati's resolution, more than thirty additional cities and counties in the United States have made similar declarations, all condemning intimate partner violence as a human rights violation and committing to various forms of redress. International conventions recognize that intimate partner violence is a human rights issue, but the United States has failed to ratify many of those agreements. Nonetheless, the United States can be—and has been—held accountable for violating the human rights of people subjected to abuse. Moreover, by "bringing human rights home"—applying human rights standards and norms to domestic law—states and localities have expanded human rights protections for those subjected to abuse. Conventions, case law, and grassroots efforts all bolster the argument that even in the United States, intimate partner violence is a human rights problem.

THE LEGAL FRAMEWORK

Human rights, broadly defined, are "internationally-recognized and accepted norms and values that promote dignity, fairness and opportunity for all people and enable individuals to meet their basic needs," including the rights to life and safety.[1] Human rights are universal, afforded to each individual by virtue of being alive. National governments (and their constituent parts) are responsible for safeguarding those rights. The concept of human rights provides a language and a framework for holding states accountable when they fail to do so.

Human rights include civil, political, social, and economic rights. Intimate partner violence, particularly intimate partner violence against women, implicates all of those rights.[2] As the former United Nations special rapporteur on violence against women, Rashida Manjoo, noted, "Violence against women impairs and nullifies women's realization of all human rights, it prevents women from participating in their communities as full and equal citizens, it reinforces male dominance and control, it supports discriminatory gender norms and it maintains systemic inequalities between women and men."[3]

But intimate partner violence has not always been recognized as a violation of human rights. Notwithstanding Manjoo's statement, some might argue that a clear human rights norm against intimate partner violence does not exist. No international convention explicitly prohibits intimate partner violence or violence against women. Few of the foundational human rights documents even mention women or gender. The reluctance to condemn intimate partner violence as a violation of human rights stems from the "private" context within which intimate partner violence occurs. Historically, violations of human rights required some action by the state; human rights conventions did not apply to the behavior of private actors. In addition, early efforts to expand the human rights system to address intimate partner violence were perceived to potentially "dilute the human rights framework."[4] Over the last thirty-five years, however, through the operation of conventions, declarations, and resolutions, as well as the work of the special rapporteur on violence against women, nonbinding international norms (also known as "soft law") on violence against women and intimate partner violence have developed, creating "an increasingly robust climate of accountability for gendered violence."[5]

International Agreements

On the international level, the right to be free from intimate partner violence is derived from three sources: the right to life, protected in a number of declarations and conventions, including the Universal Declaration of Human Rights and the International Covenant on Economic, Social, and Cultural Rights; the right to be free from torture, as defined by the Convention against Torture and Other Cruel, Inhuman, or Degrading Treatment or Punishment and the International Covenant on Civil and Political Rights (ICCPR); and the right to be free from gender-based discrimination, most notably covered by the Convention on the Elimination of All Forms of Discrimination against Women (CEDAW). Of those three, the prohibition on gender-based discrimination is the most frequently cited source of the right to be free from violence. Gender-based violence, law professor Rhonda Copelon argues, is "inherently discriminatory in that it both reflects inequality and perpetuates it."[6] Gender-based violence generally, and intimate partner violence specifically, reflects women's subordination to individual men, as well as society's unwillingness to provide women with the tools to prevent and address violence, a manifestation of gender-based discrimination. Intimate partner violence prevents women from exercising a number of rights, thus reinforcing women's inequality.

In 1979, CEDAW established a firm human rights norm against gender-based discrimination. Called "an international bill of rights for women," CEDAW defines discrimination against women as a distinction made on the basis of sex that prevents women from exercising their political, civil, economic, social, and cultural rights and freedoms.[7] CEDAW requires that signatories condemn discrimination against women and work toward its eradication by adopting constitutional and legislative provisions, refraining from engaging in discrimination, and taking measures to protect women from discrimination by individuals and organizations. What CEDAW did not do, though, was to explicitly state that violence against women constituted discrimination against women.

In 1992, however, the CEDAW Committee, the body charged with monitoring compliance with CEDAW, issued General Recommendation 19, naming gender-based violence a form of discrimination. General recommendations are not considered binding law. But the CEDAW Committee has stated that gender-based violence constitutes a form of discrimination against women under Article 1 of CEDAW.

Relying on CEDAW as a source of the right to be free from intimate partner violence is nonetheless problematic. As noted above, CEDAW does not explicitly prohibit gender-based or intimate partner violence, and there is not universal agreement that General Recommendation 19 is binding pursuant to Article 1 of CEDAW. Without the legal authority of Article 1, General Recommendation 19 is considered soft law, imposing political rather than legal obligations on national governments. During her 2009–15 tenure as the special rapporteur on violence against women, Rashida Manjoo repeatedly called for the adoption of a treaty on violence against women and girls at the international level, arguing that soft law does not contain a mechanism for holding states accountable. "With a legally binding instrument," however, "a protective, preventive and educative framework would be established that reaffirms the commitment of the international community to its articulation that women's rights are human rights, and that violence against women is a pervasive and widespread human rights violation, in and of itself."[8] To address this gap, in 2012 human rights advocates collaborated to create a Draft Convention for the Elimination of Violence against Women and Girls. The Draft Convention has not yet been considered by the United Nations, and there is considerable disagreement as to whether such a document is necessary given General Recommendation 19.

Moreover, CEDAW's enforcement mechanism is weak. Nations cannot be compelled to comply with CEDAW. Signatories are required to submit compliance reports to the CEDAW Committee, but the committee has little recourse if countries submit reports that are inadequate, misleading, or inaccurate. Under an Optional Protocol adopted in 2000, which has been ratified by approximately two-thirds of CEDAW's signatories, women can bring complaints to the CEDAW Committee for investigation, but the committee's power to respond to those complaints is limited to providing recommendations to an offending nation. Compliance with CEDAW depends on the country's susceptibility to exposure and shaming as a result of violations. And the power to shame exists only if a nation is a signatory. The United States is one of only seven members of the United Nations—and the only Western democracy—that has not yet ratified CEDAW.

Another source of the right to be free from intimate partner violence is the Declaration on the Elimination of Violence against Women (DEVAW). Adopted in 1993, DEVAW asks countries to condemn violence against women and to implement policies that will prevent, punish, and provide redress for violence. These policies include the ratification of CEDAW. DEVAW defines violence against women as "any act of gender-based violence that results in, or is likely to result in, physical, sexual or psychological harm or suffering to women, including threats of such acts, coercion or arbitrary deprivation of liberty, whether occurring in public or in private life," including "[p]hysical, sexual and psychological violence occurring in the family." Because DEVAW is a resolution of the United Nations General Assembly, rather than a convention or treaty, it is not considered binding legal authority. Taken in conjunction with CEDAW's General Recommendation 19, however, it provides further support for the existence of a right to be free from intimate partner violence.

Other actions by the United Nations bolster the case for a right to be free from intimate partner violence. The United Nations has passed a number of resolutions on violence against women. In 2004, for example, the General Assembly adopted Resolution 59/167, reaffirming "that violence against women both violates and impairs or nullifies the enjoyment by women of their human rights and fundamental freedoms." Members were urged to take a "systematic, comprehensive, multisectoral, and sustained approach" to eliminate violence against women in 2007's General Assembly Resolution 61/143. In Resolution 69/147 in 2014, the General Assembly recognized gender-based violence as a form of discrimination and reiterated that violence against women and girls violated their human rights. Finally, the 2030 Agenda for Sustainable Development, adopted by the General Assembly in 2015, argues that sustainable development will be impossible if women are denied human rights, including the rights to be free from violence and discrimination. Goal 5.2 requires that nations "eliminate all forms of violence against all women and girls in the public and private spheres." Resolutions from the Commission on Human Rights and Human Rights Council contain similar language. All of these documents include intimate partner violence in their definition of violence against women.

Research from the United Nations touts the elimination of violence against women, including intimate partner violence, as a human rights norm. In 2006, United Nations Secretary General Kofi Annan released the *In-Depth Study on All Forms of Violence against Women.* The report characterized violence against women as a pervasive human rights violation, reiterated that violence against women constitutes discrimination under CEDAW, verified countries' responsibility to address intimate partner violence as a form of violence against women, and made recommendations at the national and international level for responding to violence against women.

In 1994, the United Nations signaled its commitment to monitoring human rights violations against women by appointing a "special rapporteur on violence against women, its causes and consequences." The special rapporteur works through the Human Rights Council, collecting information from member states about violence against women and recommending policies to end that violence. In the first decade of their work, special rapporteurs focused on naming forms of violence against women, including intimate partner violence, and articulating how countries should be responsible for eliminating that violence. The second phase of the work has been focused on implementation and evaluation of laws and policies designed to address violence against women. The special rapporteurs have had tremendous influence in shaping the human rights conversation about state responsibility for violence against women generally and intimate partner violence specifically.

Regional Agreements

Regional human rights agreements also provide redress for people subjected to intimate partner violence. Successful claims for human rights violations as a result of intimate partner violence have been brought under both the European Convention on Human Rights and the American Declaration on the Rights and Duties of Man. Moreover, conventions and protocols specifically targeting violence against women exist in the Americas, Africa, and Europe.

Adopted in 1994 and entered in effect in 1995, the Inter-American Convention on the Prevention, Punishment and Eradication of Violence against Women (better known as the Convention of Belém do Pará) was the first binding international instrument to declare violence against women a violation of human rights. The convention includes physical, sexual, or psychological violence in interpersonal relationships in its definition of violence against women and declares that women have the right to be free from violence in the public and private spheres. The convention recognizes that violence prevents women from exercising their civil, political, economic, social, and cultural rights. Signatories are required to prevent, investigate, and impose penalties for violations of the rights safeguarded by the convention, to adopt legal measures to safeguard those rights, and to provide remedies when those rights are violated. The convention charges signatories with devoting special attention to the needs of women who are vulnerable as a function of race, ethnicity, immigration status, age, and socioeconomic class. The agreement enables individual women to bring claims for violations of human rights under the convention to the Inter-American Commission on Human Rights. Thirty-two of the thirty-four countries in the Organization of American States are signatories. Only the United States and Canada have failed to ratify.

A second regional agreement, the Protocol to the African Charter on Human and Peoples' Rights on the Rights of Women in Africa, was adopted in 2003 and entered into force in 2005. Noting "the crucial role of women in the preservation of African values," the protocol's definition of violence against women includes physical, sexual, psychological, and emotional harm, as well as the imposition of restrictions on or deprivation of fundamental freedoms. Article 4 of the protocol requires signatories to identify the causes of, prevent, enact and enforce laws prohibiting, and provide reparations for violence against women in the private sphere.

Finally, in 2011 the Council of Europe adopted the Convention on Preventing and Combating Violence against Women and Domestic Violence, also known as the Istanbul Convention. The convention entered into force in 2014. Its express purpose is to protect women from violence and to prevent, prosecute, and eliminate all violence against women. The convention is noteworthy for its focus on intimate partner violence. Domestic violence is included in its title, and the convention includes obligations specific to intimate partner violence. It defines violence against women as both a violation of human rights and a form of discrimination and covers all gender-based violence (violence directed at a woman because she is a woman or violence that disproportionately affects women) that causes physical, sexual, psychological, and economic harm in public or private life. The convention details members' responsibility for prevention of violence, requiring signatories to combat gender stereotypes and prejudices, enact legislative and other measures, and engage society, especially men and boys, in preventing violence. Protection from violence must "be based on a gendered understanding of violence against women and domestic violence and shall focus on the human rights and safety of the victim." The convention also specifies that the victim of violence need not press charges or testify against an offender in order to receive services. It mandates that signatories enact civil remedies allowing for recovery against private actors for violations of the convention and provides people subjected to violence with a right to recover against state signatories if they fail "in their duty to take the necessary preventive or protective measures within the scope of their powers." Nations' compliance is monitored by a committee of experts (known as GREVIO), which reports to a Committee of the Parties to the Convention. Of the Council of Europe's forty-seven members, twenty-two have ratified the convention.

Enforcement is a challenge for each of these agreements. For example, the African Court on Human and People's Rights is charged with adjudicating "matters of interpretation" arising out of the protocol. The protocol lacked any enforcement mechanism for the first six years of its existence, until the African Court on Human and People's Rights became fully operational in 2009. Moreover, only individuals and nongovernmental organizations from countries that have opted in to the Court's jurisdiction can bring claims before the African Court. As of October 2016, just thirty of the more than fifty African countries had entered into the protocol establishing the African Court, and only seven of those thirty recognize the Court's authority to hear individual and nongovernmental organizations' claims. Not surprisingly, enforcement of the protocol through the African Court has been limited; the Court has not yet decided a case involving violence against women under the protocol. The Inter-American system has decided a number of cases involving violence against women under the Convention of Belem do Para, but that system has experienced resource shortages and significant delays in case processing. Although the European Court of Human Rights has referenced the Istanbul Convention in its decisions, enforcement of the convention itself is limited to monitoring through the process described above. And those agreements can be enforced only against those who have ratified them, narrowing their reach.

Nonetheless, both the international and regional agreements do essential work in addressing violence against women generally and intimate partner violence specifically. Documents like CEDAW, DEVAW, and the regional agreements name and define the problem of violence against women using the language of human rights. These documents are essential in articulating norms condemning intimate partner violence. That expressive function operates on a number of levels, telling people subjected to abuse, their partners, and the broader society that intimate partner violence is unacceptable. The existence of these documents enables antiviolence advocates to "exert moral pressure on recalcitrant"[9] signatory states and to shame them when they fail to comply with their requirements. As one U.S. congressman asked in connection with the case of Jessica Lenahan (discussed further below), "Do you know how embarrassing it would be for an international body to call the United States a violator of the rights of women and children?"[10] Ultimately, these norms can be used to persuade nations to recognize the gaps in their own laws and systems and induce countries to change law and policy. Ratification of these treaties enables signatories to take a leading role in monitoring and publicizing human rights violations in the world community.

Using the gender discrimination and violence against women frames to assert a right to be free from intimate partner violence has drawbacks, however. Because these documents are specifically focused on women, their scope is narrow. Most of the agreements do not reach intimate partner violence against men and boys. The exception is the Istanbul Convention, which recognizes that men can be victims of intimate partner violence, and extends protection to all victims, but directs signatories to "pay particular attention to women victims of gender-based violence in implementing the provisions of this Convention." Moreover, the patriarchal narrative found in documents like the Istanbul Convention, which asserts "that violence against women is a manifestation of historically unequal power relations between women and men, which have led to domination over, and discrimination against, women by men and to the prevention of the full advancement of women," fails to account for intimate partner violence in lesbian relationships. Although both men and women and hetero- and homosexual relationships are covered, the foundational narrative upon which the convention is based undermines the legitimacy of some claims.

THE LEGAL RIGHTS

Conventions and case law have established and fleshed out the substance of the right to be free from intimate partner violence. While documents such as the International Covenant on Civil and Political Rights clearly prevent a nation itself from engaging in violence against citizens, state responsibility for the harms arising from the acts of private citizens was not always part of human rights law. Over time, however, human rights law has imposed an affirmative duty on countries to protect citizens from violations of their human rights—even when the threat to those rights comes not from the government but from a private actor. A nation's responsibility to protect citizens from intimate partner violence depends on two intertwined concepts: the positive responsibility to protect citizens from human rights violations, including violence, and the requirement that a country exercise due diligence in preventing or responding to those violations.

Positive Responsibility to Protect Citizens

The Inter-American Court of Human Rights articulated the principle of positive responsibility in the first case that it decided—*Velásquez Rodriguez v. Honduras*. Armed men in civilian clothes kidnapped Angel Manfredo Velásquez Rodriguez and several others known to be enemies of the Honduran government, apparently at the government's request. The military and police denied that anyone had been detained. Investigations by the Honduran government into the circumstances surrounding the kidnappings were ineffective. The government denied responsibility for the kidnappings. Although the court determined that the Honduran government was responsible for the disappearances, it also held that even if state responsibility had not been proven, Honduras could nonetheless be held liable for human rights violations by private actors if the government failed to adequately prevent or respond to those violations. The court found that Honduras's failure to thoroughly investigate the kidnappings and the lack of response from the Honduran judicial system violated the American Declaration of the Rights and Duties of Man, explaining: "An illegal act which violates human rights and which is initially not directly imputable to the State (for example, because it is the act of a private person or because the person responsible has not been identified) can lead to international responsibility of the State, not because of the act itself but because of the lack of due diligence to prevent the violation or to respond to it as required."[11]

The European Court of Human Rights adopted a similar analysis in *Osman v. United Kingdom*, a case involving a teacher who harassed a student and ultimately shot and killed the student's father and husband. The student and her family repeatedly asked for government assistance in addressing the threat. The government responded that there was not sufficient evidence to charge the teacher prior to the fatal shootings. The *Osman* decision lays out a three-part test for determining when the positive obligation to protect attaches. First, the government is aware, or should be aware, that a danger exists. Second, the danger must be specific to an individual or group. Third, the government must have a reasonable possibility of preventing or avoiding the danger. If those conditions are met, a nation has a responsibility to intervene to protect a citizen from a private actor's violence. The European Court of Human Rights extended this analysis to human rights violations involving intimate partner violence in *Kontrová v. Slovakia,* a case in which a woman asked police for protection from her abusive husband, who later shot and killed their children and himself. The Inter-American Commission on Human Rights also used this reasoning in *Lenahan v. United States,* explaining that signatories to the American Declaration on Human Rights can be held responsible for failing to protect citizens from intimate partner violence.

The state's positive obligation to respond is linked to the right to be free from discrimination. When a country fails to address gender-based violence by a private actor, the government is not neutral. Instead, the government confers a gender-based benefit upon that private actor and therefore violates provisions of international law forbidding discrimination. The failure to respond appropriately to gender-based violence makes the government complicit in that violence. As the European Court of Human Rights noted in *Opuz v. Turkey,* that failure need not be intentional for it to constitute gender discrimination. Moreover, notwithstanding human rights protections for family privacy and family integrity, a country's concern about the sanctity of the family does not outweigh the positive responsibility to intervene. But the requirement that the government act is limited; the obligation to act cannot "impose an impossible or disproportionate burden on the state."[12]

Due Diligence

Velásquez Rodriguez and subsequent cases link the government's positive responsibility to protect citizens from human rights violations by private actors to the concept of due diligence. CEDAW's General Recommendation 19 and DEVAW both reference due diligence, as do the Convention of Belem do Para and the Istanbul Convention. Due diligence is the standard by which a nation's attempts to comply with its positive obligations to address violence against women generally, and intimate partner violence specifically, are measured under human rights law.

Due diligence operates on both the individual and systemic levels. Not only does a country owe an obligation to individuals and groups to address violence, the government must also "create, monitor and sustain a 'holistic model' of prevention, protection, punishment, and reparation," enabling human rights adjudicators to suggest remedies and reparation that benefit all women when violations occur.[13] Due diligence measures a country's efforts rather than results, but, former Special Rapporteur Rashida Manjoo noted in a 2013 report, those efforts must "have a real prospect of altering the outcome or mitigating the harm. . . . While due diligence does not require perfect deterrence in fact in each case, it requires the State to act in a way to reasonably deter violence."[14] Moreover, due diligence is more than simply passing legislation or criminalizing violence. If existing law fails to protect women from violence, nations are required to find more effective measures.

In the context of violence against women, due diligence obligates countries to prevent, protect against, prosecute, punish, and provide redress for violence against a private citizen that the state knew about or should have anticipated. Prevention requires that the nation identify and address the root causes of violence against women, including gender-based stereotyping and discrimination and structural economic and social inequality. Prevention "has the potential of involving the State in actively intervening in and transforming social and material structures that are at the root of [violence against women] . . . altering the intrinsic nature of the State to make it less patriarchal."[15]

To meet their responsibility to prevent violence against women, the special rapporteur has argued, nations should ratify all human rights instruments involving violence against women; develop national plans of action on violence against women; enact legislation targeting violence against women; engage in public awareness campaigns; provide education; mobilize communities; engage men; harness the power of the media and information technology; and promote public safety through training for professionals and intervention in cases involving violence against women. Some of these strategies are more controversial than others. There is little argument about the need for legislation addressing violence against women, and indeed, most nations have some form of legislation outlawing such violence. Working with men, however, has proven a bit more fraught. As the special rapporteur notes, "[I]f men constitute the vast majority of perpetrators of violence against women, then engaging them in discussions, educating them to resist and reject the nature and consequences of hypermasculinity and misogyny and to overcome patterns of violence is an obvious step towards the elimination of violence against women."[16] But, she notes, some forms of engaging men reaffirm patriarchal norms (for example, strategies that focus on women's roles as wives and mothers as justification for ending violence) and ignore the larger structural context within which violence against women occurs.

The various components of due diligence, and the strategies used to comply with its requirements, overlap. The due diligence prevention requirement intersects with the prosecution and punishment mandates. To prevent violence, simply having legislation is not sufficient; a country must prosecute and punish offenders. Moreover, the legislative response contributes not only to prevention, but also to protection, prosecution, and punishment.

While prevention is focused on the larger structural context, protection is more narrowly focused on meeting both the immediate and long-term needs of people subjected to abuse. Countries can provide protection through hotlines, health care services, counseling, short- and long-term shelter, and financial assistance. Nations can also protect through effective criminal and civil legal responses. Although nonprofit organizations have historically provided a number of these services, the obligation to protect rests with the state. The government cannot discharge that duty by relying solely upon the work of nongovernmental organizations, which are sometimes inaccessible, often underfunded, and unable to satisfy the demand for services. In the United States, for example, the National Network to End Domestic Violence's annual census attests to both the essential work that intimate partner violence service providers do daily and their inability to meet the overwhelming demand. Focusing on just one day each year, the census is a snapshot of the needs of and services provided to people subjected to intimate partner violence. The 2016 National Census of Domestic Violence Services, conducted on September 14, 2016, documented 11,991 requests for services, including emergency shelter, housing, transportation, childcare, and legal services, which providers were unable to meet. Protection requires that the government ensure that those needs are being met.

Most human rights complaints are based on a nation's failure to comply with the due diligence prosecution and punishment requirements. In case after case, countries are held responsible for human rights violations when police fail to adequately investigate, prosecutors fail to pursue charges, and courts fail to adjudicate claims against offenders who later cause grievous injury or death to their partners or others in the family. Sahide Goekce's husband shot her in 2002; Fatma Yildirim's husband stabbed her in 2003. Both women had gone to Austrian police repeatedly to make complaints before they were killed. In both cases, police failed to consistently report the violence. On those occasions when police did take reports, prosecutors declined to file charges against the men. Both women's families brought claims to the Committee on the Elimination of Discrimination against Women, the United Nations body charged with hearing claims pursuant to CEDAW. And in both cases, *Goekce v. Austria* and *Yildirim v. Austria,* the committee found that the women's human rights had been violated as a result of the failure to prosecute and punish the women's husbands.

In *Maria da Penha Maia Fernandes v. Brazil,* the Inter-American Commission on Human Rights found that Brazil violated Maria da Penha Fernandes's human rights by failing to prosecute and punish her husband for his repeated acts of violence against her. This violence culminated in his shooting her in 1983, leaving Ms. Fernandes a paraplegic. Authorities investigated the shooting in 1983, and charges were filed in 1984. The case did not come to trial for eight years. Fernandes's husband was eventually convicted, but the guilty verdict was vacated on appeal. Another five years passed before the second trial was held. Fernandes's husband was again found guilty and appealed the ruling. At the time that the Inter-American Commission announced its decision, four years after the second appeal was heard, no decision on the second appeal had been made. For the fifteen years that the case languished in Brazilian courts, Fernandes's husband was free. The commission found that "the domestic judicial decisions in this case reveal inefficiency, negligence, and failure to act on the part of the Brazilian judicial authorities and unjustified delay in the prosecution of the accused," in violation of the American Convention on Human Rights and the Convention of Belém do Pará. The Commission recommended that Brazil complete the criminal proceedings against Fernandes's husband, conduct an investigation into why the process had been handled so badly, adopt measures to enable Brazil to award Fernandes reparations, and continue its reforms to end state acceptance of intimate partner violence.[17]

As with prevention, enacting laws prohibiting intimate partner violence is not sufficient to satisfy the due diligence mandate. Governments must actually enforce those laws. Colorado, for example, had a law requiring that police make arrests for violations of protective orders. But on June 22, 1999, the night that Jessica (Gonzales) Lenahan's three daughters were kidnapped from her front yard by her estranged husband, Simon Gonzales, police refused to enforce her order, which restricted Mr. Gonzales's visitation rights with the children. Over the course of the night, police officers repeatedly rebuffed Ms. Lenahan's requests that they find her children and enforce her protective order. Almost ten hours after Jessica Lenahan's initial call to the Castle Rock, Colorado, police, Simon Gonzales appeared at the police station and opened fire. Police fired back. At the end of the incident, police discovered the bodies of the girls inside Simon Gonzales's truck. Denied a remedy by the United States Supreme Court in *Town of Castle Rock v. Gonzales,* Ms. Lenahan turned to the Inter-American Commission on Human Rights, arguing that the failure to enforce her protective order constituted a breach of her human rights. The Inter-American Commission agreed, finding that "it is not the formal existence of . . . remedies that demonstrates due diligence, but rather that they are available and effective."[18]

The due diligence duties to prosecute and punish clearly mandate that the government intervene to protect people from intimate partner violence. What is less clear is exactly when intervention is required. A nation has a positive obligation to protect when it knows or should know that a private actor poses a serious threat of harm to a citizen. In the context of intimate partner violence, though, there are times when the state does not intervene because the person subjected to abuse declines to pursue a legal remedy. Due diligence might require, however, that the state intervene despite the wishes of the person subjected to abuse in some circumstances. In *Opuz v. Turkey,* the European Court of Human Rights recognized that the state had failed to bring charges on several occasions because Nahide Opuz and her mother withdrew their complaints against Opuz's husband, who ultimately killed Nahide Opuz's mother. Nonetheless, the court found, given the history of violence in the case, due diligence required that the police and prosecutors act on their own initiative to prevent further violence. The court articulated a number of factors that prosecutors should have considered before declining to proceed, including the seriousness of the offense, the nature of the injury, whether a weapon was used, whether subsequent threats were made, the impact of the attack on children in the home, the likelihood of reoffending, whether a continued threat existed, the history of the parties' relationship, and the current status of the parties' relationship, inquiring specifically about the impact on that relationship of continuing with prosecution against a party's wishes. Following *Opuz,* commentators argued that European governments should "aggressively pursue criminal proceedings" and "consider amending domestic violence and criminal assault and battery laws to give prosecutors greater discretion to pursue independent claims."[19]

The due diligence requirement that the state hold offenders accountable for their actions through punishment is not satisfied by punishing an offender for the last (and often worst) in a series of violent events. In both *Goekce* and *Yildirim,* the Austrian government argued that it had complied with its duty to punish because both men had been sentenced to jail terms after killing their wives. The Committee on the Elimination of Discrimination against Women dismissed that argument, finding that notwithstanding prosecution for their wives' murders, Austria had failed to act with due diligence in punishing the men for the violations of their wives' human rights that occurred prior to their murders.

Finally, due diligence requires that states provide reparations for human rights violations involving intimate partner violence. Those reparations can take a number of forms, including the provision of legal and social rehabilitative and support services; repayment for out-of-pocket costs related to abuse; financial compensation for injuries (physical and psychological), lost work and educational opportunities, and harms to dignity and reputation; and the creation of processes designed to verify facts and disclose the truth surrounding an incident. Reparations must consist of more than simple restitution. Instead, reparations should "link individual reparation and structural transformation. This implies that reparations should aspire, to the extent possible, to subvert, instead of reinforce, pre-existing patterns of cross-cutting structural subordination, gender hierarchies, systemic marginalization and structural inequalities that may be at the root cause of the violence that women experience."[20]

In cases brought before various human rights bodies, countries have been admonished to beef up enforcement of laws governing intimate partner violence and provide better training for those involved with the criminal legal system (*Goekce v. Austria* and *Yildirim v. Austria*); investigate systemic failures in cases of violence against women (*Fernandes v. Brazil, Lenahan v. United States,* and *Gonzales et al. v. Mexico*); and enact new legislation in response to systemic failures (*Lenahan v. United States*). States have also been asked to provide financial reparations to address both symbolic and pecuniary harms (*Fernandes v. Brazil, Lenahan v. United States,* and *Gonzales et al. v. Mexico*). Human rights bodies have recommended the adoption of preventive measures designed to address stereotypes around violence against women (*Lenahan v. United States*). States have been ordered to hold public, nationally broadcast ceremonies acknowledging their responsibility for human rights violations and to erect public monuments to victims (*Gonzales et al. v. Mexico*).

The adoption of the due diligence standard by human rights conventions and bodies expands the understanding of and responses to intimate partner violence. Due diligence highlights the need for nations to engage in prevention rather than simply reacting to violence once it occurs. Due diligence requires that countries identify and work to remedy the root causes of violence, including gender stereotypes, economic inequality, and political and social disempowerment. While "the due diligence obligation is one of means and not results," the due diligence standard holds governments accountable for their failure to adequately address prevention and implement laws and policies that are likely to protect.[21]

There are dangers inherent in the due diligence standard, however. Due diligence is grounded in a state's obligation to prevent, protect, prosecute, punish, and provide redress for intimate partner violence. The assumption underlying this requirement is that government intervention is "useful and good."[22] But expanding the state's responsibility, and therefore its reach, may have negative implications for people subjected to abuse. In *Opuz,* the court noted the potential for tension between the requirement that the government respond to intimate partner violence and the right to respect for private and family life found in Article 8 of the European Convention on Human Rights. The court explained, however, that family privacy concerns could not outweigh the government's duty to act. What the *Opuz* court did not acknowledge is the right to autonomy of the person subjected to abuse. As law professor Bonita Meyersfield explains, "Privacy cannot be understood merely as the right to be left alone; rather, it is linked affirmatively to liberty, the right to autonomy and self-determination. . . . [I]n protecting the right to privacy, it is the state's duty to balance negative—non-intervention in the affairs of individuals—and positive steps—protection of individuals from intimate harm."[23] The *Opuz* court, like a number of human rights policy documents, embraces the use of mandatory interventions, like mandatory arrest and no-drop prosecution, policies that have harmed women subjected to abuse in the United States. Due diligence may require a nation to intervene against the wishes of the person subjected to abuse. If the requirements of due diligence are weighed against other human rights principles, including autonomy and dignity, and, on balance, intervention seems necessary to fulfill the state's responsibilities, a state must act.

Moreover, although human rights law has traditionally been viewed as limiting the coercive power of the criminal legal system, governments have largely used that system to comply with their due diligence obligations. That choice is problematic because it expands the reach of the carceral state, assumes that the criminal legal system is well suited to addressing intimate partner violence, and diverts resources that otherwise might be directed to community-based restorative efforts to confront intimate partner violence. "[W]e need to be careful that in the push for State accountability, we don't romanticize the role of the State or the ability of the criminal justice system to effectively address the problem of gender violence."[24] The due diligence principle should allow the state to delegate its responsibilities to community and nongovernmental organizations when doing so better meets the needs of people subjected to abuse.

Despite its failure to adopt or ratify CEDAW, DEVAW, or the Convention of Belem do Para, the United States has enacted some of the comprehensive laws and policies that the due diligence standard requires. Every state has the ability to prosecute intimate partner violence, either through assault and other general criminal laws or through laws specifically targeting intimate partner violence. Every state has legislation outlining the process for obtaining a civil restraining order. Some states have additional legislation protecting the economic rights of people subjected to abuse in the context of employment and housing, as well as rights to custody of and visitation with children. VAWA provides funding for activities associated with meeting the due diligence requirements. But as is clear from the ruling of the Inter-American Commission on Human Rights in *Lenahan v. United States,* significant gaps remain. The United States Supreme Court has twice undermined efforts to increase accountability for intimate partner violence. First, in *United States v. Morrison,* the Supreme Court struck down the civil rights remedy contained in the first iteration of VAWA. The civil rights remedy would have enabled people subjected to abuse to sue their abusers for damages in federal court. The Supreme Court found that Congress lacked the authority to pass such a law. Secondly, in *Town of Castle Rock v. Gonzales,* the Supreme Court held that the mandatory enforcement language in Jessica Lenahan's civil protective order failed to create a constitutional right to have the order enforced or to sue for damages when the government failed to enforce the law, essentially immunizing police departments from suits. In her 2011 report on her mission to the United States, the special rapporteur noted that these precedents left women subjected to abuse without a federal statutory or constitutional remedy. She concluded, "[T]he lack of substantive protective legislation at federal and state levels, and the inadequate implementation of current laws, policies and programs, has resulted in the continued prevalence of violence against women and the discriminatory treatment of victims, with particularly detrimental effects on poor, minority, and immigrant women."[25]

"HUMAN RIGHTS AT HOME": APPLYING INTERNATIONAL HUMAN RIGHTS NORMS IN THE UNITED STATES

Given that the United States has shown no interest in ratifying the international human rights conventions pertaining to violence against women and intimate partner violence, applying the human rights lens to intimate partner violence in the United States might seem futile. But the language of international human rights is already being used in domestic litigation, legislation, and investigations involving intimate partner violence. State courts have referenced or cited human rights documents and cases in a number of contexts, using human rights norms as guidance or persuasive authority. In the specific context of intimate partner violence, the United States District Court for the Southern District of New York referenced the Universal Declaration on Human Rights and the International Covenant on Civil and Political Rights as support in *Nicholson v. Williams,* a case challenging New York City's policy of removing children from nonabusive mothers who had been subjected to abuse. Advocates cited to both the ICCPR and DEVAW in amicus briefs in the case. Advocates also used the ICCPR in an amicus brief in *United States v. Morrison,* arguing that Congress's authority to enact VAWA's civil rights remedy derived in part from its obligation to adopt legislation implementing the responsibilities it assumed under the ICCPR. The Inter-American Commission on Human Rights' decision in *Lenahan v. United States* might similarly be used as persuasive authority to establish law enforcement's duty to intervene in situations involving intimate partner violence.

Cities and states are embracing human rights norms on intimate partner violence by enacting legislation mirroring international human rights provisions. Although the United States has failed to ratify CEDAW, a number of local jurisdictions, beginning with San Francisco in 1998, have enacted ordinances or resolutions based on CEDAW. As of 2016, five additional cities had passed CEDAW legislation and at least eighteen had adopted resolutions incorporating CEDAW's principles. Consistent with CEDAW's General Recommendation 19, some of these ordinances and resolutions define intimate partner violence as a form of discrimination and/or specifically require that the government address intimate partner violence.

In the wake of the Inter-American Commission's ruling in *Lenahan v. United States,* cities throughout the United States passed resolutions declaring freedom from domestic violence a fundamental human right. Since 2011, approximately thirty city, county, and municipal governments have enacted similar resolutions. In 2014, President Barack Obama issued a proclamation in honor of the twentieth anniversary of VAWA recognizing the basic human right to be free from intimate partner violence. The wording of the resolutions varies. Some simply declare that the right to be free from violence exists, while others obligate the government to secure that right or to incorporate the principle into government policy and practice. A few of the resolutions require the government to evaluate systemic responses to intimate partner violence given the existence of the right or to study gaps and barriers in service delivery. Some jurisdictions have adopted specific policies in response to the resolutions. In 2014, for example, Miami-Dade County, referencing the resolution passed in 2012, added people subjected to intimate partner violence to the classes of individuals protected from discrimination in employment, family leave, public accommodations, housing, and banking practices.

Human rights discourse and processes can also help to engage communities in efforts to address intimate partner violence. The idea that freedom from domestic violence is a fundamental human right could provide a basis for mobilizing communities to safeguard that right through grassroots efforts like court watch programs, community accountability forums, and community-based justice forums. While human rights tribunals are most often associated with genocide and other mass atrocities, such tribunals are being used domestically to draw attention to intimate partner violence and violence against women. In 2002, the Wellesley Centers for Women's Battered Mothers' Testimony Project (BMTP) organized a Human Rights Tribunal on Domestic Violence and Child Custody at the Massachusetts state house. The tribunal was followed by an extensive report that detailed human rights violations in the Massachusetts family court's handling of custody cases involving intimate partner violence. The BMTP documented violations of the Universal Declaration on Human Rights, CEDAW, and DEVAW and made specific policy recommendations to remedy these harms. Similarly, in 2016, Black Women's Blueprint held the first meeting of the U.S. Black Women's Truth and Reconciliation Commission, a tribunal designed to explore the experiences of black women with rape and sexual violence. Such tribunals perform a valuable function on both the individual and societal levels, allowing those affected by human rights violations to share their stories with and receive validation from the wider community while also providing data about and support for policy changes needed to address those violations.

INTERSECTIONALITY AND HUMAN RIGHTS

Intersectionality is an essential component of the human rights response. Human rights documents like the Convention to Eliminate Racial Discrimination's General Recommendation 25 acknowledge that women may be targeted for racial discrimination because of their gender and that gender bias affects the remedies available to women experiencing discrimination. Because they are disproportionately targeted by the criminal legal system and subjected to abuse by police when they call for assistance, for example, African American women may be reluctant to engage with the state in response to intimate partner violence. In her 2011 report on her mission to the United States, the special rapporteur noted that discrimination against certain groups of women has made them more vulnerable to violence and magnified the harmful consequences of that violence. Human rights bodies have recognized the ways in which violence against women is exacerbated and complicated by the intersecting identities of those affected. In *Gonzáles Pérez v. Mexico,* for example, the Inter-American Commission found that the pain and humiliation suffered by women who had been raped by military personnel was heightened by their status as members of an indigenous group. In *Lenahan,* the Inter-American Commission noted that the failure to enforce protective orders disproportionately affects women of color and low-income women. The commission recommended that the United States "promote the eradication of discriminatory socio-cultural patterns that impede women and children's full protection from domestic violence acts."[26] Applying both a human rights and an intersectional lens will better serve the most marginalized people experiencing intimate partner violence.

Assessing state efforts using the due diligence standard would also facilitate the development of comprehensive solutions. Law and policy on intimate partner violence in the United States, with its myopic focus on the criminal legal system, addresses only two of the five facets of due diligence—prosecution and punishment. Although human rights tribunals assessing state compliance with due diligence requirements frequently recommend criminal justice reform, the human rights response requires more. As Special Rapporteur Radhika Coomaraswamy wrote in 1996, "The due diligence standard is not limited to . . . criminalization."[27] The inquiry into the root causes of intimate partner violence required by the prevention prong of the due diligence standard also highlights the social, cultural, and economic dimensions of the issue, undermining the claim that intimate partner violence is solely, or even primarily, a criminal justice problem. The requirement that states provide reparations distinct from criminal punishment makes clear that justice demands more than retribution. Human-rights-driven policy solutions could focus on economic, social, civil, and political rights, challenging the government to consider the ways in which the operation of the criminal system violates human rights and encouraging state and community actors to think beyond that system.

Adopting a human rights framework could also create pressure to reform problematic aspects of the criminal legal response. The draft

Convention for the Elimination of Violence against Women and Girls, for example, forbids making the availability of services contingent upon a "victim's willingness to press charges or testify against any perpetrator." Such a prohibition is at odds with even soft no-drop prosecution policies, which use the provision of services as an incentive for people subjected to abuse to testify in cases of intimate partner violence.

In a 2006 report, the secretary general of the United Nations explained,

> "Understanding violence against women as a human rights concern does not preclude other approaches to preventing and eliminating violence, such as education, health, development and criminal justice efforts. Rather, addressing violence against women as a human rights issue encourages an indivisible, holistic and multisectoral response that adds a human rights dimension to work in all sectors."[28]

The human rights approach recognizes that intimate partner violence is, in fact, a complex problem that requires a balanced, multifaceted solution. What such a solution might look like is the subject of the final chapter.

6. A Balanced Policy Approach

A woman who has just been subjected to abuse stands at the intersection of two paths. On the first path, the woman (or a neighbor or passerby) calls the police. The police might arrest her partner; if the jurisdiction has a mandatory arrest policy, she will have no input into that decision. It's also possible that the police will arrest her instead of or in addition to her partner. Because her city has a nuisance property law, she risks losing her housing as a result of calling the police.

The case goes to the prosecutor. If the jurisdiction has a no-drop policy, prosecutors may decide whether to proceed without consulting the woman, and the case may go forward with or without the woman's consent or willing involvement. If both parties were arrested, the woman might be prosecuted for injuries she inflicted when she fought back against her partner. If the woman tells prosecutors that she's not interested in being part of the case against her partner, she might be arrested and held until she agrees to testify in the trial. The woman is interested in accessing services, but to get the services she wants, she must comply with the prosecutor's requests.

The woman's partner is convicted. The woman might feel vindicated by the conviction, or she might regret ever calling the police. Her partner is sentenced—to jail, where he witnesses and is subjected to more violence, or probation or time served. He loses his job as a result of his arrest, conviction, or failure both to work and to keep up with his appointments with his probation officer. It's possible that he was abused as a child or has PTSD after serving in the military, but no one links the trauma he experienced to his violence against his partner. He learns from this experience that the legal system will (or will not) intervene to protect his partner. The community may never know about the abuse; if the community is aware, it may not know how to help.

The other path starts long before the place where the woman stands. Behind her, there are programs designed to prevent child abuse and neglect and teach children and adults about intimate partner violence. There are policies regulating access to guns and alcohol. From where the woman stands, she has a number of options. She can participate in programs that put money into her hands in a variety of ways, eliminating economic dependency as a reason for staying with her partner. Safe and stable housing is available to her. She can enlist the support of her community to hold her partner accountable for his violence and help her find justice. This path has options for her partner as well: assistance in finding and keeping employment and effective counseling that understands his history of trauma but does not use it to excuse his actions. These options are housed in a centrally located, well-known site within her community and don't require the woman or her partner to engage with the state to access them. She can, if she chooses, turn to the criminal legal system for assistance, but without worrying that she will be forced to participate should she change her mind. On this path, the criminal system focuses its most intrusive interventions on serial offenders, connecting lower-level offenders to community-based resources designed to prevent further offending. And if people are incarcerated, they are held in places that don't feed their violence or expose them to trauma. It's a wider path, one that envisions not just prosecution and punishment of intimate partner violence, but also protection and providing reparations, as well as forming partnerships with other social justice movements to address structural racism, poverty, and other conditions that exacerbate the impact of intimate partner violence.

The first path—criminalization—has been the primary response to intimate partner violence in the United States for the last thirty years. The results have, frankly, been disappointing. The failure of the criminal legal system to seriously decrease the incidence and severity of intimate partner violence highlights the limits of a one-dimensional approach to a multidimensional problem. Intimate partner violence has overlapping economic, community, public health, and human rights facets. Viewing intimate partner violence through each of these frames opens up new avenues for addressing the problem.

Shifting the intimate partner violence policy frame reveals new ideas, enables us to recycle forgotten ones, and provides support for taking pilot projects to scale. Some policy choices become apparent through a variety of lenses: access to housing, for example, is an economic issue, a community issue, and a fundamental human right. Other policies could create a chain reaction. Ensuring that people who use violence are working would increase family income, which could improve the family's ability to secure housing, which could, in turn, help to stabilize the community, all of which could result in decreased rates of intimate partner violence. And for each policy proposal, we should ask what effect that proposal will have on the prevalence and severity of intimate partner violence, who will benefit, and what the consequences of implementation might be—a sort of intimate partner violence impact statement—before committing to a course of action.

This chapter surveys the laws and policies that could result from shifting to an economic, a public health, a community, or a human rights frame. Some proposals are more detailed, because theory and research have laid a solid foundation for implementation; what is needed now is either to pilot programs or scale up interventions that have been successfully tested. In other areas, existing research and insights should be used to develop creative solutions from scratch—and to cultivate support for moving away from criminal solutions.

ECONOMICS

Intimate partner violence will continue unabated if policymakers fail to focus on economic inequality and instability. The evidence is clear that intimate partner violence is more prevalent and more severe in the context of economic distress. Poor people, particularly poor women, are the most vulnerable to intimate partner violence, and few policy dollars are allocated to programs and policies that would directly ameliorate that risk. What women subjected to abuse most need, but least often receive, are tangible supports like housing, food, and financial assistance. Women who receive assistance in securing these kinds of material resources are significantly less likely to experience physical and psychological abuse after leaving shelter and report greater improvements in their quality of life. Economic policy may have more potential to seriously decrease intimate partner violence in the United States than any other policy intervention.

Provide Economic Resources

Intimate partner violence policy should put resources directly into the hands of people subjected to abuse. There are several ways to achieve this goal. Cash transfer programs direct grants of money to low-income people. Most programs target women, who are more likely to reinvest the funds they receive for the family's well-being. Cash transfer programs can decrease physical and emotional violence and controlling behaviors, though the evidence varies as to the magnitude of the impact. Cash transfers significantly decreased the risk of controlling behavior and physical and sexual violence in Ecuador.[1] The receipt of conditional cash transfers also decreased intimate partner violence in Peru.[2] These reductions in intimate partner violence were likely related to decreased economic stress within the home. In the United States, however, decades of stingy antipoverty policy, couched in the language of "welfare reform," have made it increasingly difficult to qualify for and continue to receive even the limited cash assistance provided by the federal and state governments. The United States should reconsider its cramped approach to welfare eligibility for all low-income people; doing so would tremendously benefit people subjected to abuse.

Another way to put resources into the hands of people subjected to abuse is through microfinance—providing loans and financial services to those who would otherwise be ineligible for such services as a result of their poverty. Microfinance makes money available for low-income women to start or expand existing businesses. Women who start businesses have higher household incomes and net worth; the benefits of microfinance are greatest for African-American women and Latinas.[3] Microfinance can provide a number of additional benefits to poor communities, including increased savings rates and improvements in children's nutrition, education, family health, housing, and general welfare.

Enrolling women in microfinance programs has been linked to lower rates of intimate partner violence. South Africa's IMAGE program, for example, coupled microfinance with training on gender and HIV. Two years after the initial training, women involved in the program had increased their assets and expenditures and were more likely to participate in informal savings groups. Among these same women, rates of intimate partner violence declined 55 percent. Women involved in IMAGE reported decreases in controlling behavior as well. Researchers posit that "these reductions in violence resulted from a range of responses that enabled women to challenge the acceptability of such violence, expect and receive better treatment from partners, leave violent relationships, give material and moral support to those experiencing abuse, mobilize new and existing community groups, and raise public awareness about the need to address . . . gender-based violence."[4]

The impact of microfinance programs on intimate partner violence in Bangladesh has been mixed. While some women have experienced less intimate partner violence after becoming involved with microfinance, others have found that violence increased. This disparity may be attributable to the point at which women are polled. Although women experience slight increases in intimate partner violence when they first become involved in microfinance, violence substantially decreases over time. Moreover, the increased risk of violence may be associated with the conservatism of the community and the number of women participating. In communities where women are more empowered, and in communities where a greater percentage of women are engaged in microfinance, the risk of violence diminishes significantly.

While microfinance provides people subjected to abuse with tangible economic resources, some have urged caution in expanding microfinance programs. The very small amount of income that microloans provide may be insufficient to spur the kind of empowerment needed to change gender norms within households. Moreover, microfinance does not address the structural inequalities built into economic systems. Microfinance has been criticized as promoting the neoliberal notions that the government has no responsibility for the poor and that economic inequality can be cured using markets. Microlending markets could also suffer from the same boom-and-bust cycles as the subprime mortgage markets, whose collapse drove the 2008 global recession. Like the subprime mortgage market, microfinance targets low-income borrowers, who may find themselves trapped in a cycle where they use the next loan to pay off the last, making them completely dependent upon the loans, a condition known as "credit bicycling."[5]

The impact of microfinance on intimate partner violence has not been tested in the United States in the way that it has in other parts of the world. It should be. Microfinance programs could serve both people subjected to abuse and their partners, given the links between intimate partner violence and offenders' economic stress and under- and unemployment. It may be impossible for microfinance to build the kind of lasting economic independence needed to eliminate intimate partner violence, but it could start people down that path. Given the evidence of its impact on rates of intimate partner violence in other parts of the world, microfinance is a promising policy intervention.

Work provides economic stability. Antiviolence policy should support programs that provide people subjected to abuse with the skills and training necessary to find meaningful work at a living wage. GreenHouse 17, a shelter in Lexington, Kentucky, is a particularly innovative program. GreenHouse 17 uses the principles of therapeutic horticulture to teach residents how to engage in farming and farm-related activities, including cooking, arranging flowers, and making crafts and beauty products from materials harvested on the farm. Shelter residents earn income while working on the farm, learn business skills, and have a reference to provide to potential employers when they leave the shelter. Similarly, FreeFrom, a nonprofit organization based in Oakland, California, trains and mentors women leaving abusive relationships in business creation and development, helping them to find customers, build credit, brand their businesses, and develop marketing plans. Christine, who started a business selling aromatherapy products with the assistance of FreeFrom, appreciates the "peace and safety and knowing that no one can take this away from us" that comes with owning her own business.[6] Work opportunities can arise in unexpected ways, and not always through formal programming. In Halifax, Nova Scotia, for example, a group of immigrant women, many of whom had been subjected to violence, banded together in an informal support group; from that group, they developed a catering business that employed all of the women. Antiviolence advocates should be prepared to recognize and nurture those kinds of opportunities.

Finding work for those who abuse should also be a priority. Under- and unemployed men are more likely to be violent toward their partners. Employing these men may do more to end intimate partner violence than punishing them criminally (which, ironically, makes it more difficult for them to find work). Increasing the minimum wage could also have an impact on rates of intimate partner violence. A 2016 report by the White House Council of Economic Advisers found that raising the minimum wage to twelve dollars an hour by the year 2020 could reduce criminal activity—including intimate partner violence assaults—by 3 to 5 percent. Funding currently supporting the criminal legal system could be better used to provide employment at a living wage for those who abuse. Full employment could be among the most effective strategies for preventing intimate partner violence. Moreover, job stability is more important than employment itself in preventing violence.[7] Antiviolence advocates should champion policies that preserve workers' job security and should explore partnerships with labor unions to that end. Unions are increasingly involved in social issues, and intimate partner violence is a key issue for some unions, like the American Federation of State, County, and Municipal Employees. Working together, labor unions and antiviolence advocates could highlight and organize around the connection between exploitative working conditions and gender-based violence.[8]

Change the Law

VAWA has consistently prioritized criminal legal solutions over economic ones. Although antiviolence advocates justified Congress's authority to enact VAWA's civil rights remedy (the provision found unconstitutional in *United States v. Morrison*) using data demonstrating the overwhelming economic impact of intimate partner violence, VAWA itself has done little to address individual or structural economic issues. But VAWA could, and should, include economic development measures. VAWA could make funding available to pilot microfinance or cash transfer programs, invest in small businesses, seed community revitalization efforts, even provide employment training and assistance to those who have used violence.

Changes to the substantive law could relieve economic stress for people subjected to abuse as well. In theory, federal tax law provides a defense for spouses subjected to abuse who sign fraudulent or otherwise problematic tax returns. But in practice, both the Internal Revenue Service and judges have been reluctant to grant relief, citing concerns that people are fabricating their claims of abuse. Although, as law professor Stephanie McMahon explains, "courts are increasingly sensitive to the issue of abuse in claims for innocent spouse relief . . . that sensitivity does not mean that courts often find abuse to be a mitigating factor sufficient to outweigh other factors weighing against relief."[9] New laws could provide clear guidance to courts and the Internal Revenue Service on the application of the innocent spouse relief factors. Similarly, amendments to the Fair Credit Reporting Act (FCRA) could provide relief for victims of coerced debt; current law restricts relief to victims of identity theft. The FCRA could be amended to extend protection to those who can show that they were subjected to a pattern of abuse or control and whose debt was accrued involuntarily, as a result of fraud or duress.[10]

Legislation that prevents adverse employment actions against people subjected to abuse and protects them in the workplace is also essential to economic stability. Title VII of the Civil Rights Act of 1964 covers some, but not all, instances of workplace discrimination against people subjected to abuse. Title VII governs adverse employment actions based on sex. An employer who fires an employee specifically because of stereotypes about "battered women" might be liable under Title VII; an employer who fires an employee because that employee has missed work because of court dates, medical appointments, or other issues associated with the violence would not. Moreover, federal law does not address using employee sick leave or vacation time to respond to needs associated with intimate partner violence. Federal law is also silent as to whether people subjected to abuse who are forced to leave their employment as a result of violence are eligible for unemployment insurance. The Security and Financial Empowerment Act, repeatedly introduced in Congress since 2005, would address many of these issues. It has yet to become law.

Some states, however, have enacted laws to address these issues. Domestic violence leave legislation in eleven states and the District of Columbia enables people subjected to abuse to take time off for court appearances, to find housing, or for treatment associated with violence. Nine states prohibit discrimination against a person based on their status as a victim of intimate partner violence. Recognizing that people subjected to abuse might need modifications to their work schedules or environments to ensure their safety, three states require that workplaces accommodate the needs of victims of intimate partner violence. A number of states have also made people subjected to abuse eligible for unemployment insurance if they are forced to leave their jobs as a result of violence. Every state and the federal government should have such laws.

Stable, Affordable Housing

In 2016, the National Network to End Domestic Violence's National Census of Domestic Violence Services found that 66 percent of the unmet requests for services were for shelter or transitional housing. While the census does not count requests for permanent housing, that number is likely as high, if not higher. NNEDV reports that it can take ten months or more for people subjected to abuse to find stable, permanent housing.[11]

Securing affordable housing is an obstacle for all low-income people. But it is particularly difficult for people who have been subjected to economic and other forms of abuse and whose credit may be damaged, who may have been evicted, or who have no savings as a result. Moreover, because court records are now widely available online, landlords have easy access to information about a person's history of abuse and may deny housing, move to evict a tenant, or refuse to renew a lease upon learning of violence in the home. In response, some states have enacted legislation making it unlawful for landlords to terminate tenancies, refuse to renew leases, or refuse to enter rental agreements as a result of intimate partner violence. States have also passed laws enabling people subjected to abuse to break their leases if necessary to protect their safety, preventing them from facing eviction proceedings and the difficulties in finding housing that such proceedings often create. All states should have such laws. Tenants must also be protected if they choose to call police to protect them from violence. Cities and counties should repeal their nuisance property laws.

Protecting tenants' rights will not be enough, however, to ensure housing for people subjected to abuse. States should also provide incentives for developers to house people subjected to abuse through tax benefits, housing trust funds, and subsidized housing. Moreover, states could require that any new development be subject to community benefits agreements, which allow community groups to negotiate with developers and states to ensure that such development benefits local and low-income residents. Antiviolence advocates could be involved in negotiating such agreements, ensuring that the needs of people subjected to abuse are considered when communities and developers meet. Finally, addressing the structural racism of housing policy could have a significant impact on intimate partner violence. Insurance regulations and mortgage and lending policies have contributed to race- and income-based residential segregation in the United States. Given the relationship between neighborhood affluence, race, and intimate partner violence, dismantling the policies that shore up racial and economic segregation is an essential antiviolence strategy.

Antiviolence agencies can also make housing their top priority. Participants in the Washington State Coalition against Domestic Violence's Domestic Violence Housing First Project, for example, made finding permanent housing for clients their primary goal. Once housing stability was achieved, any other issues that created an impediment to a person's safety and stability could be addressed. The Domestic Violence Housing First Project also provided flexible financial assistance to participants to cover transportation, childcare, education, and employment-related expenses. Participants entering the program identified a number of barriers to stability, including unemployment, lack of language skills, past evictions or criminal history, and struggles with substance abuse, in addition to intimate partner violence. But eighteen months after entering the program, 96 percent of the participants had maintained their housing, and 76 percent were receiving only minimal services at the final follow-up. Eighty-four percent of survivors said that the program had increased their safety.

Building an Anti-Poverty Movement

Antiviolence advocates' efforts to eradicate poverty should not be confined to people subjected to abuse. The antiviolence movement has long engaged in what has come to be known as "domestic violence exceptionalism"—the idea that policymakers should care more about people subjected to abuse than other victims of trauma or marginalized groups. But that exceptionalism has costs, both in denying assistance to those whose trauma is as painful and needs are as acute, and to people subjected to abuse, who are forced to identify themselves as having experienced intimate partner violence in order to receive assistance. Rather than continuing to embrace this notion that people subjected to abuse are somehow worthier of assistance than others, the antiviolence movement should become part of a broader antipoverty movement. Gains made for all low-income people will ultimately benefit the people subjected to abuse that the movement serves.

And working in coalition with antipoverty (and antiracism) organizations will create the potential for more robust alliances around antiviolence causes.

PUBLIC HEALTH

The criminal legal system's response to intimate partner violence is reactive; interventions occur after someone has used violence, after someone has been hurt. Preventing that violence from occurring in the first instance should be as important, if not more important, in crafting policy. Employing a public health framework ensures that prevention is the primary goal of intimate partner violence policy.

Although there are settings, like schools, in which public health–based programs and policies are being implemented, public health efforts to address intimate partner violence are underdeveloped, underfunded, and insufficiently evaluated. Prevention efforts need to build on existing successes and move into new settings, using multiple strategies to reach their target audiences. Primary prevention efforts must do more than raise awareness of a problem's existence; they should "provide pathways for individuals to move from being passive witnesses to active participants who reject and interrupt violence, and recognition that everyone has to be part of the solution."[12]

Increased funding for the creation and evaluation of community-based prevention efforts should be a central component of intimate partner violence policy. But the work of prevention is not just for nongovernmental organizations and researchers. Policymakers can engage in prevention as well by decreasing the use of alcohol and access to guns. Slowing alcohol consumption—by increasing alcohol taxes, limiting the days and hours of alcohol sales, minimizing the number of sale sites in a neighborhood, strictly enforcing laws on sales to minors, and providing treatment options for those who abuse alcohol—requires the active intervention of policymakers.

Gun policy could affect both tertiary and primary prevention. Surrender statutes should forbid not just the possession but also the purchase of firearms, preventing those who use violence from rearming with impunity. Law enforcement should be empowered to remove ammunition as well as guns, and the law should establish clear procedures for judges and police to follow in enforcing these laws. And where good laws exist, police, prosecutors, and judges all need to be engaged in efforts to remove firearms. In California, for example, although defendants were required to surrender their firearms within twenty-four hours of being served with a protective order (and immediately upon a law enforcement demand), enforcement of the law was spotty. Two California counties piloted a program that required law enforcement to screen all protective orders for evidence of gun ownership and attempt to recover those firearms. Researchers found that hundreds of guns were recovered from those subject to protective orders without significant problems.[13] Talking with law enforcement about the need to enforce these provisions is a key to their effectiveness; once police, judges, and attorneys understood why gun removal was so necessary to keep people subjected to abuse safe, they were much more likely to ensure that those provisions were included in court orders and enforced.[14]

To ensure that individuals who may pose a threat to their partners but whose behavior may not qualify as abusive under protective order statutes don't have access to firearms, states could also enact legislation authorizing courts to issue gun violence restraining orders. Currently available in three states, gun violence protective orders enable judges to temporarily prohibit individuals from purchasing or possessing firearms or ammunition and empower law enforcement to remove firearms or ammunition if the court finds that the individual poses a threat. Modeled after domestic violence restraining orders, gun violence restraining order laws require courts to consider factors including whether the individual has made a recent threat of violence, recently violated a protective order, or engaged in a pattern of violent acts or threats before the order was issued. Upon issuance of a gun violence restraining order, the individual must relinquish all firearms and ammunition immediately and is not permitted to purchase new firearms or ammunition during the life of the order.

Laws regulating gun ownership by those already convicted of intimate partner violence could serve as effective tertiary prevention. But the data from intimate partner violence fatality reviews shows that a significant number of homicide victims have no involvement with the legal system, criminal or civil, before they are killed; one study found that only half of the women killed by intimate partners had had contact with the criminal system in the year before they were killed. One way to reach those people might be to ask them for their opinion before their partner is allowed to purchase a gun, as is required by New Jersey law. The most effective prevention, though, would be to pass strong gun control laws that apply to the general population. Primary prevention requires restricting access to guns generally. Doing so will prevent intimate partner homicides.

Perhaps the greatest contribution to primary prevention would be to develop an understanding of why people use violence and what might make them stop. The criminal legal frame renders questions about why people act the way they do irrelevant; it only matters that they have acted, and acted with the state of mind required by the law.[15] The public health literature, however, explains that understanding causation is essential to finding a cure. Only by understanding what motivates violent behavior can policymakers make informed choices about how to try to curtail it.

The traditional feminist narrative explains intimate partner violence as a function of a person's desire to have power and control over their intimate partner. But it is possible that while securing power and control is an outcome of abusive behavior, the desire for power and control is not necessarily the motivation. The inquiry tends to stop at power and control, without asking why someone might want or need to feel empowered or in control. If the goal of policy interventions is to change problematic behaviors, answering that second question is essential.

Responding to adverse childhood experiences is certainly part of the equation, as is identifying and addressing trauma, both personal and historical. Childhood abuse, neglect, and trauma all undermine a person's sense of control. Many, if not most, of those who use violence, Dr. Gabor Maté explains, have been traumatized in some way, either directly or through the resonance of historical trauma visited on a parent or grandparent. New research suggests that trauma may be unwittingly passed down through generations. Intimate partner violence policy, then, must be able to simultaneously see those who use violence as victims and offenders. That duality requires us to confront intimate partner violence with compassion both for the person who uses violence and the person subjected to it.[16]

The Strength at Home Men's Program (SAH-M) takes just such an approach. SAH-M serves active duty members and veterans of the military who have experienced trauma and have subjected a partner to intimate partner violence within the last six to twelve months. SAH-M is a twelve-week group therapy intervention that works with service members to understand both intimate partner violence and reactions to trauma, recognize the impact of trauma on their own relationships, and develop coping skills and communications strategies. While "[t]he role of trauma is discussed throughout the group," the program emphasizes that "all group members are ultimately accountable and responsible for their own behavior." Both those who participated in the program and their partners report significant reductions in physical and psychological violence, particularly with respect to asserting control through isolation and monitoring.[17]

Understanding the ways in which respect, shame, and violence interact may also help to illuminate the causes of intimate partner violence. In his work with thousands of prisoners in Massachusetts and San Francisco, psychologist James Gilligan found that the desire for respect spurred many of the men to violence. He writes, "The purpose of violence is to force respect from other people. The less self-respect people feel, the more they are dependent on respect from others; for without a certain minimal amount of respect, from others or the self, the self begins to feel dead inside, numb and empty."[18] Gilligan argues that the preconditions for violence include the failure to develop the feelings that prevent violence, like guilt and remorse, empathy and love. Violence also flourishes when offenders have not developed a rational self-interest in avoiding punishment and are unable to see alternatives to violence for maintaining or establishing self-respect. Gilligan contends that shame erodes a person's self-respect, making them more likely to use violence: "Violence occurs when people see no means of undoing or preventing their own humiliation except by humiliating others; indeed, that is the underlying purpose of inflicting violence on others."[19] That shame could come from a number of sources: a reaction to the powerlessness of being abused as a child, the inability to find work, or the failure to live up to the hypermasculine ideal that rewards the use of violence.

Psychologist Tage Rai, by contrast, argues that when people use violence, they are motivated by morality: "By 'moral', I mean that people are violent because they feel they must be; because they feel their violence is obligatory." Rai explains that violence is used to order social relationships. The justifications people offer for their violence reveal their moral commitments and their perception of their community's moral standards. Rai uses former Baltimore Raven Ray Rice, who assaulted his then-fiancée in an Atlantic City casino elevator, as an example: "If the American football player Ray Rice claims that his fiancée hit and spat on him before he punched her in 2014, it's because he feels it mitigates his crime in the eyes of the people he cares about. If people actually do care whether his statement is true, then Rice is right. The excuses that perpetrators offer reveal the moral standards of those being appealed to." Rai is arguing not that people know that violence is wrong and use it nonetheless, but that people believe that violence is right, in that its use upholds the individual's or the community's moral standards. Punishing violence won't change the perception that the use of violence was moral; interventions must instead make it clear that the use of violence is immoral. As Rai writes, "Only when violence in *any* relationship is seen as a violation of *every* relationship will it diminish."[20] And the way to change perceptions of violence is through community, through an offender's primary social groups.

Rise?

Gilligan's and Rai's ideas move beyond the concept of power and control to examine the internal deficits or commitments that cause a person to use violence. Antiviolence advocates have been reluctant to engage in such explorations, fearing that they would provide those who abuse with excuses for their behavior. But understanding what motivates violence is essential if the goal is to change that behavior. If the lack of self-respect or the inability to develop empathy motivates violence, prevention efforts could work with those at risk of using violence to cultivate those feelings. If shaming is more likely to cause violence, interventions should avoid shaming techniques and focus on helping those who use violence to overcome their feelings of shame. Interventions could also help those who use violence to learn behaviors that will bring them respect and empowerment and control or alleviate their shame. If, as Rai argues, violence is an expression of morality, shifting individual and community conceptions of the morality of intimate partner violence will be essential.

These counternarratives about the causes of violence are a reminder that the current state of the knowledge on what causes intimate partner violence is imperfect. Gilligan's theories on respect, shame, and violence and Rai's on the moral motivations for violence may not fit all of those who use violence, but they are certainly worth exploring. The causes of violence are complex. Acknowledging that complexity will free researchers and policymakers to search for those causes and develop interventions that are responsive to them.

ENGAGE COMMUNITIES

Law enforcement officers aren't usually the first responders to intimate partner violence—family, friends, and others in the community are. Ensuring that policy responses bolster the efforts of these first responders, strengthen communities so that they can offer support, and provide mechanisms for finding justice in community should be priorities in a balanced approach.

Collective Efficacy and Community Accountability

Building collective efficacy is an essential component of the effort to reengage communities in preventing and responding to intimate partner violence. Recall that collective efficacy requires communities to believe in their capacity to end violence and take active steps toward that goal. Fostering relationships and trust within communities is the first step. To build those relationships, antiviolence programs could work with residents to plan community gatherings or block parties, with the goal of creating connections within the community rather than providing training or education. While concrete information on how to recognize and intervene when violence is happening will certainly be necessary, providing that information should be secondary to incubating the kinds of relationships within the community that will encourage people to use the information—relationships first, then active steps toward ending violence.

Where communities are ready to engage, providing a community accountability framework can facilitate that engagement. The toolkit developed by Creative Interventions provides one model for fostering community accountability; antiviolence advocates could develop others tailored to the needs and strengths of their own communities. Intervention strategies can and should vary based on the goals of the person subjected to abuse and that person's sense of what will have the greatest impact on the violence. For some people, simply having a space to share one's story might be sufficient. For others, direct intervention by family, friends, or other figures of authority within a community might be appropriate.

The community can also provide ongoing support to those who have used violence through Circles of Support and Accountability (CoSA). The CoSA model has been used with ex-offenders (known as core members) who are at high risk of reoffending. Circles engage community volunteers, professionals, and a coordinator who work together to prevent further offending—the core member by pledging not to reoffend and to avoid situations that could create the risk of reoffending, the community members by holding the core member accountable through regular meetings and check-ins. Professional supports are also available to the core member and the volunteers as they grapple with various issues. All parties involved sign a contract outlining expectations and responsibilities. Circles of Support and Accountability rely heavily on the moral authority the circle exercises, a moral authority derived from the strong relationships developed between the core member and the community members.

A pilot CoSA program in Vermont has been extremely successful in preventing recidivism. Over three years, only one of the twenty-one core members involved was charged with a new crime. Most of the core members believed that they would have returned to prison had they not been part of a CoSA. The relationships developed between CoSA core members and volunteers are essential to preventing further offending; the more deeply and interpersonally the team engages with the core member, the greater the success. The honest and trusting relationships developed between core members and volunteers enable volunteers to convey their expectations about the core member's behavior. CoSA success stories may seem small: stable relationships, housing, employment, friendships. But, as

ounder Yvonne Byrd notes, "[H]aving a job, paying your bills, other people—that's a success."[21]
e CoSA model currently focuses on reentry and ex-offenders, reason that the model could not be used to address intimate lence that has not yet come to the attention of the state. Community volunteers paired with service providers could develop the same kinds of relationships with individuals who have not been incarcerated but who pose a risk to another community member. The CoSA structure is simply a more formalized community accountability framework.

Restorative Justice

Community restorative justice opportunities should be available to those who are not interested in retributive justice and should be specifically designed to address intimate partner violence. Restorative justice in cases involving intimate partner violence should be driven by restorative principles rather than by an uncritical adherence to a particular process. Restorative processes must be victim driven and victim centered. If the person subjected to abuse is unwilling to engage in a restorative process, the process should not begin. Because people subjected to abuse may need time to feel fully prepared to engage in the process, restorative justice efforts should proceed on the person's schedule. Facilitators must take care to ensure that restorative processes do not become unintentionally coercive or put the person subjected to abuse in the position of making undesirable concessions to achieve consensus. And restorative approaches must accept people who have been harmed as they are. Victim advocate Mary Achilles asks, "Can we make room for victims in a restorative process when they are screaming out in pain or when they are vengeful, angry and full of rage? Can we make room for victims when they are not interested in what happens to the offender or, if they are interested in what happens, their interest does not fit with what some of us would refer to as a restorative response?"[22] The criminal legal system is often hostile to women's anger and pain. Anger is inconsistent with stereotypes of people subjected to abuse; judges and jurors use that anger to cast doubt on the credibility of women's accounts of violence. A restorative response should not make the same mistake.

The person who has done harm must be unequivocally willing to accept responsibility for that harm "*as described by the victim*. . . . If the perpetrator strongly wishes to argue that there are distortions of fact in the victim's account, this effectively should preclude the case" from being referred to a restorative process.[23] Participants should be screened carefully to ensure that they are genuinely taking responsibility rather than manipulating the system to evade criminal liability. Community members must also accept the victim's account of the violence and be willing to hold the person who has done harm accountable. Both support for the person subjected to abuse and enforcement of accountability agreements are central components of the community's role. Community should be broadly defined—around geographic place, common interests, cultural identities and life experiences, and circumstance. Looking at community expansively can help to abate concerns that the person subjected to abuse or her partner's community will not embrace antiviolence norms. Finally, restorative processes in these cases should not be neutral. Instead, they should adopt an explicit antiviolence perspective, preventing participants from minimizing or denying violence or blaming the victim for that violence. Such an orientation is consistent with John Braithwaite's argument that restorative justice is not morally neutral in the face of domination and injustice.[24]

Restorative processes in intimate partner violence cases may also look different because of the context within which they are taking place. Facilitators should have experience with intimate partner violence. The preprocess preparation is likely to be lengthier and more intensive than in other restorative interventions. Direct contact or conversations between the person subjected to abuse and the person who has used violence may not be appropriate. Shuttle negotiations or telephonic contact might be necessary to ensure the safety and comfort of the person subjected to abuse. Restorative justice processes in cases involving intimate partner violence should be linked to services and supports for both the victim and offender, and those services and supports should be available before, during, and after the process itself. Conference agreements and other resolutions should be monitored for compliance, with specific sanctions agreed to by all parties in the event of their failure. Developing such processes will be challenging. But "acknowledging the level of difficulty (and messiness) in a decision-making process that is indeed more open works against unrealistic hopes for restorative justice practices, and increases the likelihood that stakeholders will proceed with caution."[25]

A number of obstacles to testing and evaluating restorative processes in the context of intimate partner violence exist. First, some state statutes forbid the use of restorative processes in cases of intimate partner violence. In Vermont, for example, cases involving intimate partner violence cannot be referred to community justice centers funded by the state. In other states, the prohibition on using restorative justice in the context of intimate partner violence applies only to cases being diverted (either at pretrial or at sentencing) from the criminal system. The practical impact of these laws, however, is to make restorative practitioners wary about taking such cases, even when those cases do not come through the criminal system. That wariness prevents restorative practitioners from developing expertise in facilitating intimate partner violence cases. In other states, although no formal prohibition exists, the reluctance to use restorative justice in intimate partner violence cases is sufficient to stifle the practice. Rather than discouraging the practice, states should implement laws and policies that promote the use of restorative justice in intimate partner violence cases and enable restorative practitioners to develop expertise and expand their services.

VAWA has also been cited as an obstacle to developing restorative justice programs for people subjected to abuse. Since its inception VAWA has refused to provide funding for the use of mediation in response to intimate partner violence. Some have read that prohibition to include restorative justice as well. But in 2017, the Office on Violence against Women issued its first solicitation for a grant funding a pilot project on restorative responses to intimate partner and sexual violence on college and university campuses. The Office on Violence against Women is also funding a survey of programs (led by, among others, restorative justice pioneers Gale Burford and Joan Pennell) that use restorative justice to address intimate partner violence, with an eye toward the development of guidelines for such programs. These small steps are important—VAWA should no longer be seen as creating a barrier to experimenting with restorative practices. Ultimately, if these projects are successful, VAWA funding could and should be diverted from prosecution to restorative practices: circles, conferencing, and even new forms of restorative practice like community-based justice forums.

The goal of community-based justice is to provide space for people subjected to abuse to find justice without having to interact with state systems. Community-based justice forums are another way to meet that need. Community-based justice forums could be established in a variety of neighborhood spaces, including child-care centers, schools, churches, recreation centers, barbershops, and hair salons, to ensure that justice is visible on the ground. Members of the community justice forum could reach out to potential participants through general neighborhood information sources (newspapers, online forums, community organizations) and in a more targeted manner, through organizations and service providers working with people subjected to abuse.

Community-based justice forums would employ a victim-centered process. People subjected to abuse would have to choose community justice; this decision to participate should help to assuage concerns that the claims of women and other marginalized groups would be devalued and that people who have used violence will manipulate the process. Testimony could be given publicly or in camera, orally or in writing, anonymously or by name. The forums would not be bound by the rules of the adversarial system or restricted to information deemed relevant by a judge. Community justice forums would be able to consider a broad range of information without sacrificing the ability to ascertain truth. Eschewing the adversarial process creates a climate within which those subjected to abuse can feel freer and more comfortable in telling their stories.

People who have abused would also be permitted to provide testimony, but only after admitting and accepting responsibility for their abusive behavior and only with the permission of their partners. Providing public testimony helps to increase the accountability of offenders both to their partners and to the community. Playing an active role in the victim's healing process also increases offender accountability. Hearing from abusers may be central to meeting the justice goals of individual people subjected to abuse and is a crucial component in analyzing the ways in which the community may have enabled abuse to occur.

Community members would be engaged in a number of roles. Community-based justice forums could be staffed by local community organizations serving people subjected to abuse and abusers, those with the expertise to provide support and services to participants. After appropriate training on intimate partner violence, other community members would be engaged as witnesses, charged with hearing the stories of the participants. Transparency of process and ensuring that people sensitive to stories of abuse are well represented among those chosen would be essential in the selection of witnesses. But witnesses should come from all sectors of the community, given the goal of transforming community perceptions of intimate partner violence. Involving the community as listeners serves a number of additional goals. Listeners can convey the community's moral condemnation of violence and can set community standards for responding to intimate partner violence through their reactions to the stories of people subjected to abuse. Engaging the community can create a greater sense of safety and security for people subjected to abuse. Moreover, community members would be charged with unearthing and acknowledging the community's own complicity in perpetuating intimate partner violence, as well as with determining what changes the community might make in response to the stories it hears.

Community-based justice forums can enforce accountability on a number of levels. For those who use violence, having to publicly answer for one's actions can be a powerful form of accountability. Community-based justice forums can also hold institutions and systems accountable, providing people subjected to abuse with the opportunity to explore both individual and collective accountability. Participants would be encouraged to detail not just what their partners did, but how the community or the state reacted or failed to react in ways that exacerbated the person's suffering. The forums would explore the interconnections between the actions of individual offenders and the community or state, helping the community to identify sites for structural change as well as individual reparation. The community justice process should enable state and community actors to recognize their own roles in intimate partner violence, not in an attempt to shame or humiliate them but rather to help them work to end abuse and rebuild community.

The community justice forum's mandate would also include a specific charge to study how intimate partner violence affects people of color; lesbian, gay, bisexual, and transgender people; disabled people; low-income people; and others from marginalized communities. Having to engage the state keeps some people subjected to abuse, particularly gay men and transgender people, from seeking assistance. Failing to anticipate the needs of these groups or defining them out of alternative systems could prevent them from turning to these systems, depriving them of any opportunity to seek justice.

These forums would need to engage in ongoing evaluation to determine whether their efforts are successful. Success should be evaluated on both the individual and community levels. Success would hinge on whether people subjected to abuse believe that the process has given them the justice they sought, however they might define it. Success would also be reflected in changes in community norms around intimate partner violence.

The broadest goal of these community-based justice forums would be societal reconstruction. Transforming societal conceptions of intimate relationships, creating community norms that reject abuse, and conceptualizing the pursuit of justice as the right of the individual subjected to abuse rather than as society's right and responsibility could fundamentally change the responses to intimate partner violence. Ultimately, the power to create justice would be redistributed from the state to the community by charging the community with administration of these systems.

Exploring alternatives to the criminal legal system doesn't mean abandoning the idea of justice for people subjected to abuse. Instead, such exploration facilitates more expansive thinking about what justice means and gives people subjected to abuse the opportunity to seek justice in a wider variety of forums. Looking beyond the criminal system creates space to begin to answer the question posed by Farah Tanis, the executive director of Black Women's Blueprint: What would justice look like if the criminal system did not exist?

HUMAN RIGHTS

That freedom from intimate partner violence is a fundamental human right should be a fairly uncontroversial statement. But operationalizing the concept of intimate partner violence as a human rights problem requires that the United States adopt a more robust human rights framework.

Since the end of the Second World War, the United States has cast itself as the world's leading arbiter of international human rights norms and obligations. Moreover, through State Department programs like the International Visitor Leadership Program, which educates legal professionals and antiviolence advocates from around the world on issues including intimate partner violence, and through publications like the *Trafficking in Persons* report, the United States has repeatedly asserted its role in defining, providing training on, and policing global violence against women. But the United States' refusal to ratify international agreements like the Convention on the Elimination of All Forms of Discrimination against Women, the Declaration on the Elimination of Violence against Women, and the Convention of Belém do Pará undermines the credibility of these claims and sends the message that while the United States expects other nations to safeguard human rights abuses against women, it has no need to do so itself.

Adopting and ratifying CEDAW, DEVAW, and other human rights conventions would tangibly benefit women subjected to abuse in the United States, establishing the government's responsibility to prevent, protect individuals from, prosecute, punish, and provide reparation for gender-based violence and creating a remedy in cases where the government fails to act (a right at least partially foreclosed by the United States Supreme Court's decision in *Castle Rock v. Gonzales*). These instruments could encourage U.S. courts to rely upon and cite human rights law and principles in domestic decisions involving intimate partner violence and housing, family law, employment, and immigration. Adopting the due diligence analysis required by these documents would help the United States create a more balanced policy response to intimate partner violence, focused not just on the criminal system, but also on economic, cultural, and social rights.

If the United States continues to refuse to adopt and ratify these documents, states and localities should continue their efforts to make international human rights norms part of domestic law by enacting local versions of CEDAW and DEVAW and resolutions declaring freedom from violence a fundamental human right. Those laws and resolutions can then be used to leverage studies determining whether the state's response to intimate partner violence is compliant with human rights norms and to demand changes in policy and service provision consistent with those findings.

DECRIMINALIZING DOMESTIC VIOLENCE

One could make a credible, even strong, case for decriminalizing intimate partner violence. There is little to no evidence that criminalization deters intimate partner violence, and there is reason to believe that criminalization actually helps to create conditions that stimulate intimate partner violence. The costs of criminalization, particularly when prosecution leads to incarceration, are quite high. Criminalization undermines the economic and social structures of marginalized neighborhoods, depriving ex-offenders of employment opportunities and destroying relationships within communities. The traumatic effects of the inhumane conditions and exposure to violence within prisons feed a destructive cycle of violence when those who abuse are released into the community and resume their intimate relationships. The costs of incarceration particularly, and criminalization generally, far outweigh the limited benefits criminalization provides. And relying on criminalization is preventing the development of alternatives that could provide justice for people subjected to abuse without the harms associated with the carceral system.

But complete decriminalization of intimate partner violence is unlikely, and probably unwise. It is unrealistic to believe that there would be widespread support for repealing laws addressing intimate partner violence. Politicians and many antiviolence advocates are committed to the criminalization of intimate partner violence and unlikely to turn away from it completely. Arrest and prosecution play an important role in securing safety and justice for some people subjected to abuse. Whatever one thinks of the choice to criminalize as a means of making the private public or expressing society's interest in stemming intimate partner violence, the message sent by repealing such statutes at this point would be problematic at best. While the prosecution of each individual act of intimate partner violence, however small, may not appreciably benefit society, the need still exists to ensure that serious, repeat offenders (who are not deterred by current sanctions) are prevented from continuing to harm their partners. Even those who are most concerned about the detrimental aspects of

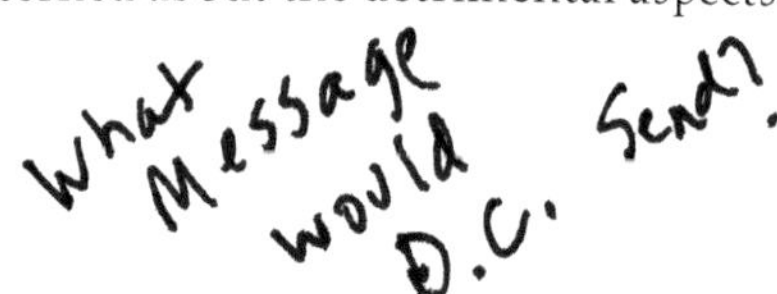

criminalization have experience with offenders who they believe should be isolated from society.

Instead of completely decriminalizing intimate partner violence, then, policymakers should rethink the current criminal legal regime. First, policymakers should repeal policies that are harming those they were originally intended to protect. Second, the punishment meted out for intimate partner violence should address the harm done without creating the potential for increased violence. Finally, rather than viewing punishment for intimate partner violence as a binary—an offender is either found guilty and incarcerated or not—criminalization and punishment should be viewed as a spectrum, with a range of possible responses.

Repeal Mandatory Policies

Mandatory policies have been controversial among antiviolence advocates since the first mandatory arrest policy was adopted in 1977. From their inception, some antiviolence advocates, particularly women of color, questioned both the effectiveness of mandatory interventions and the disproportionate impact these policies would have on communities of color. By 2003, law professor Holly Maguigan would conclude, "The claimed benefits [of mandatory policies] have not even been demonstrated; and in light of the burdens imposed, they do not support an argument for maintaining current levels of criminal justice intervention."[26]

Research over the past forty years has continually borne out these concerns. Mandatory arrest and prosecution policies are responsible for a significant portion of the harm done to women subjected to abuse when they become involved with the criminal legal system. Dual arrests and arrests of women increased as a result of mandatory arrest. People are forced to testify despite their own assessments of the utility of prosecution and are punished for their failure to testify or for giving testimony inconsistent with prior statements. Both mandatory arrest and no-drop prosecution policies deprive people subjected to abuse of the power to choose how the violence in their lives should be addressed. The desire to avoid mandatory reporting statutes may prevent some from seeking assistance. Although the two are often conflated, criminalizing domestic violence does not require the implementation of mandatory policies. Repealing mandatory policies could prevent a substantial amount of harm to people subjected to abuse.

Reconsidering Punishment

The relationship between punishment and shame helps to explain why the criminal legal system is so ineffective in deterring intimate partner violence. The criminal legal system holds people accountable for their bad acts by shaming them—labeling them criminals and imposing humiliating punishment on them. That punishment is not always incarceration. A judge in Guilford County, North Carolina, has sentenced several men convicted of domestic violence to stand outside the county courthouse for seven days holding a sign stating, This Is the Face of Domestic Abuse. One of the men, Joshua Hill, told a reporter, "This is belittling. I was born and raised here, everybody knows me. . . . [P]eople kind of shake their heads, look at me like I'm a bad person or ask me why I'm doing this." Hill says that he would have "preferred jail over the humiliation of holding the sign."[27] This kind of shaming, psychologist James Gilligan might argue, is exactly the kind of punishment that spurs further violent behavior. As Gilligan writes, "The criminal justice and penal systems have been operating on the basis of a huge mistake, namely, the belief that punishment will deter, prevent, or inhibit violence, when in fact it is the most powerful stimulus of violence that we have yet discovered."[28]

The United States has largely failed to explore alternatives to this shame-based system. Rather than starting from the premise that all cases require the punitive intervention of the criminal legal system, however, one might envision a system in which sanctions are graduated and where punishment is secondary to changing behavior and stimulating empathy.

Criminologist John Braithwaite outlines such a system in *Restorative Justice and Responsive Regulation*.[29] Braithwaite's initial response to harm would be restorative, giving the offender and victim of harm the opportunity to engage in the type of restorative dialogue described in chapter 5. If restorative approaches to addressing harm are unsuccessful, Braithwaite advocates moving through a number of levels of intervention before reaching the top of what he calls the regulatory pyramid—incarceration. While Braithwaite concedes that immediate criminal system intervention may be necessary at times, the goal is to "always start at the base of the pyramid, then escalate to somewhat punitive approaches only reluctantly and only when dialogue fails, and then to escalate to even more punitive approaches only when the more modest forms of punishment fail."[30]

Using "less costly, less coercive, more respectful" options before resorting to incarceration serves several functions. Restorative approaches engage offenders in thinking about the impact of their actions on their victims, helping to engender empathy; punishment-focused interventions, by contrast, make it difficult to think about anything but avoiding punishment. Starting with restorative approaches also underscores the importance of treating all citizens with dignity and respect. As Braithwaite writes, "[I]f we want a world with less violence and less dominating abuse of others, we need to take seriously rituals that encourage approval of caring behavior so that citizens will acquire pride in being caring and nondominating."[31] Making the criminal system the last, as opposed to the first, response prevents those who otherwise might not recidivate from being exposed to the collateral consequences of criminal intervention and the potentially criminogenic effect of spending time in prison.

In 1994, Braithwaite and criminologist Kathleen Daly developed a regulatory pyramid specific to the context of intimate partner violence. The bottom of the pyramid includes a number of restorative interventions: self-sanctioning, expressing social disapproval, and confrontation with family. If those interventions are unsuccessful, police are called, a warrant may be issued, and advocates become involved. Next is community conferencing, with escalated levels of intervention if conference agreements are not followed. Finally, the criminal legal system is invoked if all else fails, beginning with arrest and imposition of strict probation conditions and, at the pyramid's apex, incarceration. Braithwaite and Daly understand that

> [s]ome may recoil at the thought of one conference failing, more violence, another failed conference, more violence still, being repeated in a number of cycles before the ultimate sanction of incarceration is invoked. But there can be considerable intervention into a violent man's life when moving from one failed conference to another. For example, there could be escalation from weekly reporting by all family members of any violent incidents to the man's aunt or brother-in-law (conference 1), to a relative or other supporter of the woman moving into the household (conference 2), to the man moving to a friend's household (conference 3).[32]

Braithwaite and Daly's is just one vision of how sanctions could be graduated from restorative to retributive; others could be developed as well. But their model provides a starting point for conversations about expanding our conceptions of the appropriate societal response to intimate partner violence. Historically the criminal legal system was used strategically, as one option among many for dealing with conflict. Developing a range of options beyond the criminal legal system would allow for the consideration of goals other than punishment and avoid some of the harms of criminalization.

Advocating for graduated sanctions is grounded in the belief that those who use violence against their partners can and will desist from that violence. Although the research on desistance is limited, there is reason to believe that some offenders recognize the need to change their behavior and do, in fact, stop using violence. That process of change involves the interaction between an external structural factor (a negative consequence of using violence) and an internal negative emotional response to that consequence. While the trigger could be intervention by the criminal legal system, it could also be community intervention. Desistance does not require incarceration. It requires that an offender recognize, for whatever reason, that change is needed. Moreover, offenders are more likely to maintain the change when they have support and encouragement from family, friends, and partners, the kind of networks created through restorative practices and destroyed by incarceration.

Focus on Habitual Offenders

Criminal legal interventions should target habitual offenders. Focusing on habitual offenders directs resources to where they are most needed. Serial offenders were responsible for a substantial amount of intimate partner violence handled by the Quincy, Massachusetts, domestic violence courts.[33] Similarly, over a ten-year period, the thirty most frequent offenders in the Winnipeg Family Violence Courts were in court on 2,263 occasions, charged with 1,843 crimes, the subject of 551 cases, and convicted 319 times. Just as in the general criminal population, a small percentage of offenders are responsible for a disproportionate amount of offending. Moreover, "[d]omestic violence offenders tend to be serial offenders in two ways." Not only do they commit multiple acts of violence against their partners, they also have "robust criminal histories including a wide range of both domestic violence and non-domestic violence offenses."[34]

Interaction with the criminal legal system as currently configured is not deterring these repeat offenders. Criminologist Michael Salter notes that "[f]or this group of men whose violence appears to be, at least in part, an effort to shore up a fragile and unstable sense of masculine honour and entitlement, the threat of punishment appears as an additional affront to their authority and may trigger a compensatory escalation in violence."[35] What these men need are sanctions that bring them within the ambit of systems that provide strong but supportive boundaries that will inhibit their violence while at the same time addressing the needs that push them toward violence.

In High Point, North Carolina, the police department has concentrated its resources on habitual intimate partner violence offenders, using a strategy known as "focused deterrence." Focused deterrence is based on the belief that offenders perceive the risk of being prosecuted as low; reoffending rates will remain high until offenders have reason to think that they have underestimated those risks. Rather than relying on the remote possibility of punishment to act as a deterrent, focused deterrence identifies "levers," specific legal sanctions like probation or parole violations or new charges that can be imposed on chronic offenders who commit crimes of intimate partner violence. Offenders are informed that if they fail to desist, these levers will be pulled.

The first principle of focused deterrence interventions is do no harm; the National Network for Safe Communities, created by criminologist David Kennedy in 2009, explains, "Criminal justice is strong medicine: it can help, but applied too heavily or in the wrong way, it can hurt."[36] The goal of focused deterrence, then, is to deploy the lowest level of state involvement possible to stop violence. Officers in High Point separate incoming reports of intimate partner violence into classes. D-class offenders (those who are not arrested) are told that they are being put on a watch list. If an arrest is made, a C-class offender is visited by the police chief or his counterpart while in jail and told that if they offend again, the sanctions will be increased—higher bail, stricter conditions of probation, greater likelihood of prosecution. As Police Chief Jerry Thompson told one C-class offender during his meeting, "They got your name flagged. If you get charged again, it's going to be different than you've ever seen before. . . . You got to think about your kids. You have an eight-month-old? You want your child to be visiting you in prison? You got to think different. You are a grown man now."[37] Another assault moves an offender into B-class, leading to a meeting at city hall with the local domestic violence task force. At that meeting, the individual is offered services like job training and warned that if they reoffend, police and prosecutors will attempt to have them incarcerated for significant periods. The first B-class meeting, held in February of 2012, involved a number of community members who stressed both their disgust for intimate partner violence and their willingness to provide the offenders with assistance. Those who ignored the warnings or had a history of serious violence are categorized A-class; prosecutors vigorously pursue the cases of A-class offenders. Since the inception of the focused deterrence program, intimate partner homicides have decreased substantially, as have cases involving injuries to the victim.

Antiviolence advocates have been involved with the High Point Intimate Partner Violence Intervention since its inception. Recognizing that interventions with chronic offenders could put victims at risk of harm, advocates worked with people subjected to abuse to ensure that interventions would not jeopardize their safety and would serve their needs. In cases where people did not want the criminal system to intervene, advocates helped them identify interventions that might make them safer or stop the violence. No action was taken without that input. People subjected to abuse were offered specific services at each level of intervention: a letter describing available services at the D-level; an in-person offer of services at C-level; notice before and direct contact after the B-level meeting to get feedback on the impact of the meeting and to offer safety planning and third-party reporting opportunities (enabling family, neighbors, or friends to report directly to police if they believed the person was at risk and could not call police directly); and support and safety planning after the arrest of an A-level offender. People subjected to abuse report satisfaction with the approach; as one woman explained, "Until Lt. Carter reached out to me I felt like I was screaming and no one could hear me. I now know that I do have a voice."[38]

Reliable risk assessments could help to identify habitual and high-risk offenders. Risk assessment allows law enforcement, mental health professionals and others to "speculat[e] in an informed way"[39] about an individual's potential for future violence. Distinguishing offenders who are likely to pose a serious or recurring danger from others enables professionals to focus their efforts on and reserve their resources for those individuals most in need of interventions. Several tools to assess risk of future intimate partner violence have been developed and validated. These tools, which include the Ontario Domestic Assault Risk Assessment, the Brief Spousal Assault Form for the Evaluation of Risk, the Domestic Violence Risk Appraisal Guide, and the Danger Assessment, can reliably predict risk of future harm, measuring variables including a history of assault and antisocial behavior, stability of relationships and employment, mental health, childhood abuse, and attitudes toward women. Most of these tools are limited, measuring only the risk of future physical assault and ignoring other forms of abuse, including coercive control and psychological abuse. For the purposes of distinguishing which offenders should face criminal sanctions, however, the focus on physical assault, cramped though it is, is appropriate given the narrow parameters of what the criminal law punishes.

Use Probation and Community Monitoring Effectively

Probation and other forms of community monitoring are usually touted as the most promising alternatives to incarceration. Programs like Hawaii's HOPE project guarantee "less crime and less punishment"—decreased recidivism without the use of long periods of incarceration.[40] They achieve these results by marrying intensive monitoring with swift and certain penalties. In the HOPE project, for example, probation officers closely monitor probationers. Each time a probationer violates the terms of probation, the judge is immediately notified; the probationer is arrested on the spot and sentenced to a short term of incarceration. With every additional violation, the penalty escalates. By imposing short, immediate terms of imprisonment for violations of conditions of probation, HOPE is intended to show probationers that judges are serious about their compliance. In response, probationers are more likely to comply with the terms of probation.

Programs like HOPE beg the question of the purpose of community sanctions. Traditionally, community supervision was intended to ease an offender's postincarceration adjustment to the community. Today, however, probation is often used as a punishment and a stepping stone to incarceration. Treatment-based supervision strategies targeting a probationer's particular risk factors are more effective than sanctions in reducing recidivism, yet most probation officers spend their time in "control" related activities—taking urine samples, searching homes. Given the focus on catching probationers in bad behavior, it is not surprising that failure rates among probationers are high and that the impact of probation on recidivism is insignificant.

The numerous conditions probationers must meet undoubtedly contribute to high failure rates. Probationers are often required to pay the costs of monitoring, as well as fees for any other programs they are required to attend as a condition of probation. Some judges impose their own special conditions of probation—for example, a prohibition on changing residences without court permission. Conditions of probation sometimes conflict. Maintaining employment (a frequent condition of probation) can be difficult when probationers are also required to attend counseling, participate in other services, and regularly visit their probation officers. And these required services may not be responsive to the probationer's needs. As of 2005, only 19 percent of community corrections agencies had intimate partner violence intervention services, for example.[41] The consequences of minor violations of probation can be severe; incarceration for failure to pay fees and fines is common.

Probation and other community-based services are viable alternatives to incarceration only to the extent that they do not simply transfer state control from prisons to the community. Rather than using probation officers as "overseers," probation officers could be "compassionate navigators who walk their probationers through the system, offering support, connecting people to needed resources, encouraging them to change and maintain the change that will keep them from returning to the system."[42] Recognizing that "rewards are better shapers of behavior than punishments," experts recommend that probation officers recognize and reward progress through "earned compliance credits" (reducing the time that people spend on probation) and reductions in probation fees.[43] Probation should focus on creating opportunities for those who have been incarcerated to reintegrate into communities, rather than penalizing them for even the most minor infractions. Otherwise, we are simply creating "prisonlike substitutes for the prison."[44]

Reduce the Trauma of Incarceration

Some offenders are so dangerous that they must be incapacitated. But incarceration should not increase the likelihood that they will use violence after their release.

The conditions in many U.S. prisons are horrific. Overcrowding is the norm. Violence is rampant. Programming and treatment are scarce. And "these negative effects of hyper-incarceration increase the risks for domestic violence."[45]

But incarceration need not be inhumane. In Germany, for example, prisons are open and sunny, full of fresh air. Prisoners live in rooms and sleep in beds. They cook their own meals. "There is little to no violence—including in communal kitchens where there are knives and other potentially dangerous implements."[46] The correctional system is designed to restrict inmates' freedom as little as necessary. Norway's prisons are similarly open, because "[t]he punishment is that you lose your freedom. If we treat people like animals when they are in prison they are likely to behave like animals. Here we pay attention to you as human beings."[47] The Norwegian Correctional Service works to ensure housing, employment, and access to a support network for each prisoner before they are released. Norway's prisons operate from a restorative philosophy, with a focus on repairing the harms of crime. Although almost half of the prisoners in one Norwegian prison are incarcerated for violent offenses, violent incidents within the prison are rare.

The approach that correctional officers take to their work can make a tremendous difference as well. In Ada County, Iowa, corrections officials recognize the loss of humanity that comes with incarceration. They are trained to treat prisoners with empathy and respect. Correctional officers talk to inmates rather than giving them orders and explain the requests that they make. The Ada County jail uses steel mesh rather than bars and features open dorms. The guards' office windows allow guards to monitor the dorms and enable inmates to see what the guards are doing. Guards maintain an open-door policy, encouraging inmates to come and talk with them. As a result, use-of-force incidents are rare and the prison is less chaotic. Training correctional officers to honor the dignity of prisoners and creating physical spaces that reinforce that message could help to prevent the violence that traumatizes inmates, trauma that they take back to their communities.

If incarceration for intimate partner violence is used more judiciously and only for serious violence, fewer people should be jailed, but they are likely to be held for longer periods. During that time, they should be preparing to reenter society. Given the links between intimate partner violence, poverty, and employment, it is most essential to offer educational programs that prepare them for living wage work. For some, that might include higher education. The Violent Crime Control and Law Enforcement Act of 1994—the same omnibus bill that included VAWA—eliminated Pell Grant eligibility for inmates, preventing many from seeking college degrees. In 2015, however, the Obama administration made Pell Grants available to twelve thousand prisoners through a pilot program known as Second Chance Pell. Ending the ban on Pell Grants for inmates would likely have a positive impact on postrelease rates of intimate partner violence.

Incarcerated people should also have access to programs that help them identify, understand, and question their use of violence. In California's New Folsom Prison, inmates are invited to participate in a group called Inside Circle, which enables men to reflect upon their use of violence with the support of other men. Before joining Inside Circle, Eldra Jackson III explains, "I immersed myself in a world of toxic masculinity. I saw victimizing others as not merely a choice but a right." While "doing work" in the Circle, Jackson examined his own history, connecting his use of violence to the trauma and pain he experienced in his childhood. Jackson, like many of the men in the Circle, "learned early on to meet feelings of vulnerability with violence and force." Through the Circle, Jackson learned that "[h]arming others does not work. Harming oneself does not work. Manipulation does not work. Control and dominance do not work."[48]

Another way to reduce the trauma of incarceration is to allow offenders to maintain ties to the world outside of prison. Using social media to make contact with their families and extended communities makes reintegration easier and can help incarcerated people develop professional relationships and find employment postrelease. Of course, in the context of intimate partner violence, this poses obvious challenges. The posting of nonconsensual (or "revenge") pornography, online harassment, and monitoring of partners through phones and other technology are all potential risks when those who are incarcerated for intimate partner violence use social media.

People subjected to abuse should be permitted to block contact from those who used violence against them, and social media should never be used to abuse a former partner. Monitoring is clearly necessary. But rather than cutting off access for all inmates, including those who have used violence, prisons should encourage incarcerated people to stay connected.

In order to minimize the trauma of incarceration it is also essential to enforce measures intended to protect prisoners from violence. Although institutional rules, laws, and constitutional precedent to protect prisoners all exist, prison authorities routinely ignore these mandates. The Prison Rape Elimination Act (PREA), for example, is designed to protect prisoners from rape or sexual assault by guards or other inmates during their incarceration. National commissions have documented preventive measures prisons could take, consistent with PREA's mandate, to eliminate violence. Nonetheless, rates of sexual assault remain high in many prisons and jails. Holding individual prison authorities accountable for the failure to comply with PREA has been a challenge, despite the Supreme Court's finding that rape and sexual assault are not simply unfortunate consequences of being incarcerated and that states, therefore, are responsible for protecting prisoners from violence. Congress's unwillingness to sanction states for failing to enforce PREA in any meaningful way underscores the ambivalence about protecting prisoners from violence. But shielding prisoners from sexual violence is not only essential in and of itself, it is also a means of preventing intimate partner violence in the community. Decreasing offenders' exposure to all forms of violence should be a priority for prison systems.

When incarceration is used, it should be imposed with a clear understanding of its limitations. Incarceration has had a limited impact on the rate of serious crime. Keeping those who commit intimate partner violence in prison for long periods of time is unlikely to deter further violence. Longer sentences do not have a greater deterrent effect on offenders. Incarceration is unlikely to change the behavior of those who commit intimate partner violence. Even the staunchest advocates of criminalization do not argue that prison is successful in changing behavior, only that it punishes well.

The criminal legal system, on its own, cannot eliminate intimate partner violence. This is not a novel insight. From the very beginning of the antiviolence movement, women of color understood that criminalization was likely to be a problematic policy choice. Activist Angela Davis warned in 2000 that criminalization would not be any more effective in ending intimate partner violence than it had been in preventing crime generally. Law enforcement officers also recognized the limitations of criminalization. As prosecutor Kim Tate told Congress in 1994, "To ask that the criminal justice system alone solve the problem of domestic violence is to ask that a system designed to be punitive should accomplish remediation, that a system designed for reaction should effect proactive purposes, that a system designed to focus on the accused should be made to serve the victim, and that a prosecution with the highest burden of proof in the world shall be capable of infinite flexibility."[49] Nonetheless, by pouring funding, time, and effort into the criminal legal system, at the expense of other responses to intimate partner violence, we have asked the system to do all of the things Tate describes—and it has failed. Rates of intimate partner violence have decreased less than the rates of other crimes, and intimate partner violence remains one of the most underreported crimes. And the reliance on the criminal legal system must be juxtaposed against the larger context of mass incarceration, as the United States continues to grapple with the consequences of incarcerating 2.3 million of its citizens.

Deemphasizing the criminal response to intimate partner violence could be a first step toward reversing the damage that has been done by mass incarceration. To decrease the unacceptably high number of individuals currently incarcerated in the United States, policymakers must rethink responses to violent crimes. Decriminalization of domestic violence could provide valuable data as to whether alternative approaches can, in fact, be effective in preventing the harms criminalization seeks to control. If such approaches can work in the realm of intimate partner violence, they might also be effective in addressing other forms of violent crime. Reconsidering the criminal response could also help to distinguish offenders who require immediate punishment from those who might be amenable to change, who are willing and able to be accountable for their behavior, and whose violence might be preventable.

In 2015, 806,050 incidents of intimate partner violence were reported in the United States. Arresting, trying, convicting, and incarcerating each offender would substantially increase the already overwhelming number of inmates in U.S. prisons and jails. The United States is not going to arrest and prosecute its way out of its problem with intimate partner violence. As Anne Sparks asked in 1997, "How many prisons are we willing to build for batterers?"[50]

Intimate partner violence is a complex problem, one that cannot be solved by the criminal system alone. To build an alternative path requires fundamental changes in both philosophy and policy. The United States must reject governing through crime, abandon its practice of shunting people into the criminal system while ignoring the issues that lead to their incarceration, and bring the research, resources, policies, and practices of a number of different fields to bear on the issue of intimate partner violence. We must elect politicians and appoint policymakers who understand the value of a multifaceted approach. Policymakers should fund, enact, and evaluate initiatives to prevent intimate partner violence. We should shift funding away from courts, police, and prosecutors and put money and programmatic control into communities, nongovernmental organizations, and the hands of people subjected to abuse. National policymakers should adopt human rights treaties like CEDAW and DEVAW; states and localities should enact their own versions of these laws and operationalize their protections through local government initiatives on behalf of people subjected to abuse. Criminal legal system actors should partner with communities to identify and implement the kinds of graduated penalties that would allow the criminal system to focus penal resources on repeat, dangerous offenders. Communities should hold state officials accountable for ensuring humane prison conditions and treatment of offenders through monitoring and, ultimately, through voting.

Antiviolence advocates must abandon our dependency on the criminal system. Doing so will require us to name and confront our fears about moving away from criminalization and be open to experimentation. State domestic violence and sexual assault coalitions across the country, led by Washington, Idaho, Vermont, and others, are exploring alternatives to criminalization—we should learn from their experiences. We should publicize efforts like Survived and Punished, a coalition of freedom projects and organizations assembled to demand the immediate release of women who have been doubly victimized—first by their partners, then by the criminal legal system. We should replicate the innovative work being done by organizations like the Center for Survivor Agency and Justice and the District Alliance for Safe Housing, which focus on meeting the economic needs of people subjected to abuse, and Black Women's Blueprint, which is interrogating what justice would mean for people subjected to abuse if the criminal system did not exist. We should help communities build their capacity to identify and address intimate partner violence and support people subjected to abuse and their partners. We should return to feminist first principles and convene groups around the country to listen to what people subjected to abuse most need; we should use that information to draft and lobby for a decarceral VAWA.[51] We should acknowledge that some of these efforts will fail, but that failure should not drive us back to the criminal legal system, which has been failing for years.

We should play an active role in social justice coalitions working to end racism, poverty, discrimination, violence against LGBTQI individuals, and other forms of marginalization that exacerbate the damage done by intimate partner violence. We should join in local prisoner's rights efforts as well as the prison reform work done by organizations like the Vera Institute. Some might argue that engaging in these other struggles will divert time, attention, and energy from our core work on intimate partner violence. But (to borrow from Australian Aboriginal activist Lilla Watson), the liberation of people subjected to abuse and their partners is bound up with these other struggles. We must all walk together if we hope to eradicate intimate partner violence.

Notes

INTRODUCTION

1. Historically, violence by one partner against another has been known by a number of names, including spouse abuse, family violence, and domestic violence. I have chosen to use the term "intimate partner violence," which is the term most frequently used by contemporary researchers and scholars and which captures the specific phenomenon of violence (physical, emotional, psychological, sexual, reproductive, religious, and other) perpetrated within the context of an intimate relationship (as opposed to those related by blood or adoption or others included in state law definitions of family or domestic violence).

2. I generally use the phrase "people subjected to abuse" to describe the individuals others refer to as victims or survivors. *Victim* and *survivor* are limiting terms that define people only by reference to the things that have been done to them. Using the term "people subjected to abuse" also highlights the active role of someone who is otherwise obscured in these labels: the person's partner in the violent relationship. Margaret E. Johnson, "Redefining Harm, Reimagining Remedies, and Reclaiming Domestic Violence Law," *University of California Davis Law Review* 42, no. 4 (2009): 1107–64. Although women are more likely to be subjected to intimate partner violence, and are substantially more likely to experience serious, coercive violence, the antiviolence movement has become more inclusive in its language and its policy stances since its inception. In this book I will refer to "people subjected to abuse" whenever possible in order to capture the violence done to both women and men in intimate relationships. In those sources where comments or research describe women, however, women will be specifically referenced.

3. Susan Schechter, *Women and Male Violence: The Visions and Struggles of the Battered Women's Movement* (Boston: South End Press, 1982): 13.

4. Ibid., 15.

5. William L. Hart, "Attorney General's Task Force on Family Violence: Final Report," Washington, D.C.: United States Department of Justice, 1984. http://files.eric.ed.gov/fulltext/ED251762.pdf.

6. Donna Coker, "Crime Control and Feminist Law Reform in Domestic Violence Law: A Critical Review," *Buffalo Criminal Law Review* 4, no. 2 (2001): 801, 803–4.

7. Jill Theresa Messing et al., "The State of Intimate Partner Violence Intervention: Progress and Continuing Challenges," *Social Work* 60, no. 4 (2015): 305–13.

8. Beth E. Richie, "Keynote: Reimagining the Movement to End Gender Violence: Anti-Racism, Prison Abolition, Women of Color Feminisms, and Other Radical Visions of Justice," *University of Miami Race and Social Justice Law Review* 5, no. 2 (2015): 268.

9. Ibid.

10. Marc Mauer and David Cole, "How to Lock up Fewer People," *New York Times*, May 23, 2015, https://www.nytimes.com/2015/05/24/opinion/sunday/how-to-lock-up-fewer-people.html?mtrref=www.google.com&gwh=59DE1A213CFC482C6F8BABA5423F9797&gwt=pay&assetType=opinion.

11. Alexandra Natapoff, "Underenforcement," *Fordham Law Review* 75, no. 3 (2006): 1719.

12. Michele C. Black et al., *The National Intimate Partner and Sexual Violence Survey: 2010 Summary Report*, Atlanta: Centers for Disease Control and Prevention (2011).

13. Kersti Yllö, "Through a Feminist Lens: Gender Diversity, and Violence: Extending the Feminist Framework," in *Current Controversies on Family Violence*, ed. Donileen R. Loseke, Richard J. Gelles, and Mary M. Cavanaugh (Thousand Oaks, CA: Sage Publications, 2005), 22.

14. Adele M. Morrison, "Queering Domestic Violence to 'Straighten Out' Criminal Law: What Might Happen When Queer Theory and Practice Meet Criminal Law's Conventional Response to Domestic Violence," *Southern California Review of Law and Women's Studies* 13, no. 1 (2003): 92.

15. Angela P. Harris, "Heteropatriarchy Kills: Challenging Gender Violence in a Prison Nation," *Washington University Journal of Law and Policy* 37, no. 13 (2011): 38.

1. A CRIMINAL JUSTICE PROBLEM?

1. Claire Houston, "How Feminist Theory Became (Criminal) Law: Tracing the Path to Mandatory Criminal Intervention in Domestic Violence Cases," *Michigan Journal of Gender and the Law* 21, no. 2 (2014): 259.

2. Lawrence W. Sherman et al., "Crime, Punishment, and Stake in Conformity: Legal and Informal Control of Domestic Violence," *American Sociological Review* 57, no. 5 (1992): 680.

3. Congress later amended this provision, requiring states applying for VAWA funds to implement either mandatory or preferred (an arrest should, rather than must, be made whenever probable cause exists to do so) policies.

4. George W. Bush, "Remarks on Domestic Violence Prevention, October 8, 2003," *The American Presidency Project*, http://www.presidency.ucsb.edu/ws/?pid=222.

5. I use the term *offender* to describe people who use violence in their intimate relationships. *Offender* is an imperfect term because, like victim or survivor, it defines someone solely through their experiences. Moreover, the term fails to acknowledge that often those who use violence are victims of violence as well. I have used the term solely as a matter of expediency, to avoid the tortured syntax that would otherwise be required.

6. William R. Kelly, *Criminal Justice at the Crossroads: Transforming Crime and Punishment* (New York: Columbia University Press, 2015), 1.

7. Marie Gottschalk, *Caught: The Prison State and the Lockdown of American Politics* (Princeton: Princeton University Press, 2015), 1–2.

8. Erik Luna, "Overextending the Criminal Law," in *Go Directly to Jail: The Criminalization of Almost Everything*, ed. Gene Healy (Washington, DC: Cato Institute, 2004), 1, 7.

9. Angela Davis, "Masked Racism: Reflections on the Prison Industrial Complex," *ColorLines*, September 10, 1998, http://www.colorlines.com/articles/masked-racism-reflections-prison-industrial-complex.

10. Angela Davis, "Keynote." (The Color of Violence: Violence against Women of Color, Santa Cruz, CA, April 28, 2000).

11. Mimi E. Kim, "Dancing the Carceral Creep: The Anti-Domestic Violence Movement and the Paradoxical Pursuit of Criminalization, 1973–1986," in ISSI Graduate Fellows Working Paper Series no. 2013–2014.70, October 14, 2015, https://escholarship.org/uc/item/804227k6.

12. Ibid.

13. Jonathan Simon, *Governing through Crime: How the War on Crime Transformed American Democracy and Created a Culture of Fear* (New York: Oxford University Press, 2007), 180.

14. Gottschalk, *Caught: The Prison State*, 244.

15. Alesha Durfee, "Situational Ambiguity and Gendered Patterns of Arrest for Intimate Partner Violence," *Violence against Women* 18, no. 1 (2012): 75.

16. Connie Burk, "ABA Summit Keynote" (American Bar Association LGBT Domestic Violence Legal Issues Summit, April 11, 2008.

17. Aya Gruber, "A 'Neo-Feminist' Assessment of Rape and Domestic Violence Law Reform," *Journal of Gender, Race and Justice* 15, no. 3 (2012): 583–84.

18. Laureen Snider, "Criminalising Violence Against Women: Solution or Dead End?" *Criminal Justice Matters* 74, no. 1 (2008): 38.

19. "Complaint and Jury Demand," Singleton v. Cannizzaro, Case No. 2:17-cv-10721 (E.D. La. 2017).

20. Matthew Desmond et al., "Police Violence and Citizen Crime Reporting in the Black Community," *American Sociological Review* 81, no. 5 (2016): 865.

21. Mary Haviland, Victoria Frye, Valli Raja, Juhu Thukral, and Mary Trinity, *The Family Protection and Domestic Violence Intervention Act of 1995: Examining the Effects of Mandatory Arrest in New York City*, New York: Urban Justice Center, 2001, http://www.connectnyc.org/docs/Mandatory_Arrest_Report.pdf.

22. Andrea J. Ritchie, *Invisible No More: Police Violence against Black Women and Women of Color* (Boston: Beacon Press, 2017), 187.

23. Nils Christie, "Conflicts as Property," *British Journal of Criminology* 17, no. 1 (1977): 7 (emphasis in original).

24. Paul H. Robinson and John M. Darley, "Does Criminal Law Deter? A Behavioural Science Investigation," *Oxford Journal of Legal Studies* 24, no. 2 (2004): 174.

25. N. Zoe Hilton, Grant T. Harris, and Marnie E. Rice, "The Effect of Arrest on Wife Assault Recidivism: Controlling for Pre-Arrest Risk," *Criminal Justice and Behavior* 34, no. 10 (2007): 1340.

26. Eve Buzawa, Gerald T. Hotaling, Andrew Klein, and James Byrne, *Response to Domestic Violence in a Pro-Active Court Setting*, 1999, https://www.ncjrs.gov/pdffiles1/nij/grants/181427.pdf: 146.

27. Ibid. at 164–65. The authors note, however, that the system could have deterred potential offenders, leading to an overrepresentation of "hard-core recidivists" in their sample. Ibid. at 166.

28. Ellen Pence, "Some Thoughts on Philosophy," in *Coordinating Community Responses to Domestic Violence: Lessons from Duluth and Beyond*, ed. Melanie F. Shepard and Ellen L. Pence (Thousand Oaks, CA: Sage Publications, 1999), 25, 29.

29. Simon, *Governing through Crime*, 152.

30. Gottschalk, *Caught: The Prison State*, 91

31. National Research Council, *The Growth of Incarceration in the United States: Exploring Causes and Consequences* (Washington, D.C.: National Academies Press, 2014), 234, 267.

32. Annie E. Casey Foundation, *A Shared Sentence: The Devastating Toll of Parental Incarceration on Kids, Families and Communities* (Baltimore: The Annie E. Casey Foundation, 2016), http://aecf.org/m/resourcedoc/aecf-asharedsentence-2016.pdf: 3.

33. National Research Council, *The Growth of Incarceration*, 268.

34. Annie E. Casey Foundation, *A Shared Sentence*, 2.

35. Iniamai M. Chettier, "The Many Causes of America's Decline in Crime," *The Atlantic*, February 11, 2015, https://www.theatlantic.com/politics/archive/2015/02/the-many-causes-of-americas-decline-in-crime/385364/.

36. Gottschalk, *Caught: The Prison State*, 244.

37. Elliott Currie, "Violence and Social Policy," in *Routledge Handbook of Critical Criminology*, ed. Walter S. DeKeseredy and Molly Dragiewicz (New York: Routledge, 2012), 472.

38. Maya Schenwar, *Locked Down, Locked Out: Why Prison Doesn't Work and How We Can Do Better* (San Francisco: Berrett-Koehler Publishers, 2014), 48.

39. Michael L. Benson and Greer L. Fox, *Concentrated Disadvantage, Economic Distress, and Violence against Women in Intimate Relationships*, 2004: II-3-5 to II-3-6.

40. Ibid.

41. Donna Coker and Ahjané Macquoid, "Why Opposing Hyper-Incarceration Should Be Central to the Work of the Domestic Violence Movement," *University of Miami Race and Social Justice Law Review* 5, no. 2 (2015): 612.

42. Harris, "Heteropatriarchy Kills," 64.

43. SpearIt, "Gender Violence in Prison and Hyper-Masculinities in the 'Hood: Cycles of Destructive Masculinity," *Washington University Journal of Law and Policy* 37, no. 13 (2011): 89.

44. Tony N. Brown and Evelyn Patterson, "Criminal Injustice: Wounds from Incarceration That Never Heal," *The Conversation*, June 28, 2016, http://theconversation.com/criminal-injustice-wounds-from-incarceration-that-never-heal-60843.

45. Sherry Hamby et al., "Intervention Following Family Violence: Best Practices and Helpseeking Obstacles in a Nationally Representative Sample of Families with Children," *Psychology of Violence* 5, no. 3 (2015): 325.

46. Danielle Keats Citron, "Law's Expressive Value in Combating Cyber Gender Harassment," *Michigan Law Review* 108, no. 3 (2009): 407.

2. AN ECONOMIC PROBLEM

1. Lisa D. Brush, *Poverty, Battered Women, and Work in U.S. Pubic Policy* (New York: Oxford University Press, 2011), 68.

2. Emily F. Rothman and Phaedra S. Corso, "Propensity for Intimate Partner Abuse and Workplace Productivity: Why Employers Should Care," *Violence against Women* 14, no. 9 (2008): 1054.

3. Richard M. Tolman and Daniel Rosen, "Domestic Violence in the Lives of Women Receiving Welfare: Mental Health, Substance Dependence, and Economic Well-Being," *Violence against Women* 7, no. 2 (2001): 147–48.

4. Angela M. Moe and Myrtle P. Bell, "Abject Economics: The Effects of Battering and Violence on Women's Work and Employability," *Violence against Women* 10, no. 1 (2004): 30.

5. Melanie M. Hughes and Lisa D. Brush, "The Price of Protection: A Trajectory Analysis of Civil Remedies for Abuse and Women's Earnings," *American Sociological Review* 80, no. 1 (2015): 158.

6. Brush, *Poverty, Battered Women, and Work*, 71.

7. Moe and Bell, "Abject Economics," 34.

8. Rothman and Corso, "Propensity for Intimate Partner Abuse," 1055.

9. Amy Salomon et al., *Secondary Data Analysis on the Etiology, Course, and Consequences of Intimate Partner Violence against Extremely Poor Women* (Washington, D.C.: National Institute of Justice, 2004), II-9-3.

10. Donna Coker et al., *Responses from the Field: Sexual Assault, Domestic Violence, and Policing* (New York: American Civil Liberties Union, 2015), 7.

11. Cynthia K. Sanders, "Economic Abuse in the Lives of Women Abused by an Intimate Partner: A Qualitative Study," *Violence against Women* 21, no. 1 (2015): 4

12. Coker et al., *Responses from the Field*, 7.

13. Micahael A. Benson and Greer Litton Fox, *Economic Distress, Community Context, and Intimate Violence: An Application and Extension of Social Disorganization Theory* (Washington, D.C.: National Institute of Justice, 2002), 53.

14. Lisa A. Goodman et al., "When Crises Collide: How Intimate Partner Violence and Poverty Intersect to Shape Women's Mental Health and Coping," *Trauma, Violence, and Abuse* 10, no. 4 (2009): 3.

15. Tolman and Rosen, "Domestic Violence in the Lives of Women Receiving Welfare," 142.

16. Sara Shoener, *The Price of Safety: Hidden Costs and Unintended Consequences for Women in the Domestic Violence Service System* (Nashville: Vanderbilt University Press, 2016), 44

17. Adrienne E. Adams et al., "The Impact of Intimate Partner Violence on Low-Income Women's Economic Well-Being : The Mediating Role of Job Stability," *Violence against Women* 18, no. 12 (2013): 1349.

18. Brush, *Poverty, Battered Women, and Work*, 56–57.

19. Ibid.

20. Donna Coker, "Shifting Power for Battered Women: Law, Material Resources, and Poor Women of Color," *University of California Davis Law Review* 33, no. 4 (2000): 5.

21. Benson and Fox, *Economic Distress, Community Context and Intimate Violence*, 100; Carol B. Cunradi et al., "Neighborhood Poverty as a Predictor of Intimate Partner Violence among White, Black, and Hispanic Couples in the United States: A Multilevel Analysis," *Annals of Epidemiology* 10, no. 5 (2000): 298, 301.

22. Benson and Fox, *Economic Distress, Community Context and Intimate Violence*, 114.

23. Adrienne E. Adams et al., "Development of the Scale of Economic Abuse," *Violence against Women* 14, no. 5 (2008): 564.

24. Moe and Bell, "Abject Economics," 39.

25. Adrienne E. Adams et al., "Evidence of the Construct Validity of the Scale of Economic Abuse," *Violence and Victims* 30, no. 3 (2015): 368.

26. Judy L. Postmus et al., "Measuring Economic Abuse in the Lives of Survivors: Revising the Scale of Economic Abuse," *Violence against Women* 22, no. 6 (2016): 701.

27. Ibid., 701; Judy L. Postmus et al., "Understanding Economic Abuse in the Lives of Survivors " *Journal of Interpersonal Violence* 27, no. 3 (2012).

28. Cynthia K. Sanders, "Economic Abuse in the Lives of Women Abused by an Intimate Partner," *against*12.

29. Cynthia K. Sanders, *Domestic Violence, Economic Abuse, and Implications of a Program for Building Economic Resources for Low-Income Women*, (St. Louis: Center for Social Development, 2007), 39.

30. Susan Lloyd and Nina Taluc, "The Effects of Male Violence on Female Employment," *Violence against Women* 5, no. 4 (1999): 374.

31. Angela Littwin, "Escaping Battered Credit: A Proposal for Repairing Credit Reports Damaged by Domestic Violence," *Pennsylvania Law Review* 161, no. 2 (2013): 372; Angela Littwin, "Coerced Debt: The Role of Consumer Credit in Domestic Violence," *California Law Review* 100, no. 4 (2012): 957–59.

32. Richard M. Tolman and Hui-Chen Want, "Domestic Violence and Women's Employment: Fixed Effects Models of Three Waves of Women's Employment Study Data," *American Journal of Community Psychology* 36, no. 1–2 (2005): 155.

33. Claire M. Renzetti, *Economic Stress and Domestic Violence*, VAWnet.org, September 2009, https://uknowledge.uky.edu/cgi/viewcontent.cgi?article=1000&context=crvaw_reports.

34. Adams et al., "The Impact of Intimate Partner Violence on Low-Income Women's Economic Well-Being," 1360–61.

35. Postmus et al., "Understanding Economic Abuse in the Lives of Survivors," 3.

36. Linda DeRiviere, *The Healing Journey: Intimate Partner Abuse and Its Implications in the Labour Market* (Winnipeg: Fernwood Publishing, 2014), 116.

37. Noel Bridget Busch and Terry A. Wolfer, "Battered Women Speak Out: Welfare Reform and Their Decisions to Disclose," *Violence against Women* 8, no. 5 (2002): 578.

38. Brush, *Poverty, Battered Women, and Work*, 5.

39. Moe and Bell, "Abject Economics," 46.

40. Littwin, "Coerced Debt," 7.

41. Sanders, "Economic Abuse in the Lives of Women Abused by an Intimate Partner," 15.

42. *Saving Money and Reducing Tragedies through Prevention (SMART Prevention)*, U.S. Code 42 (2013) § 14043(c)(10).

43. Equal Rights Center, *No Vacancy: Housing Discrimination against Survivors of Domestic Violence in the District of Columbia* (2008), 2.

44. Gretchen W. Arnold, "From Victim to Offender: How Nuisance Property Laws Affect Battered Women," *Journal of Interpersonal Violence* (2016): 2–3, http://journals.sagepub.com/doi/pdf/10.1177/0886260516647512.

45. Matthew Desmond and Nicol Valdez, "Unpolicing the Urban Poor: Consequences of Third-Party Policing for Inner-City Women," *American Sociological Review* 78, no. 1 (2012): 134.

46. Arnold, "From Victim to Offender," 9–13.

47. Desmond and Valez, "Unpolicing the Urban Poor," 134.

48. Ibid., 137 (emphasis in original).

49. Arnold, "From Victim to Offender," 9

50. Ibid., 10.

51. Dickinson v. Zanesville Metropolitan Housing Authority, 975 F. Supp. 2d. 863 (2013).

52. Deborah M. Weissman, "Countering Neoliberalism and Aligning Solidarities: Rethinking Domestic Violence Advocacy," *Southwestern Law Review* 45, no. 4 (2016): 18–19.

53. Eric Dunn and Marina Grabchuk, "Background Checks and Social Effects: Contemporary Residential Tenant-Screening Problems in Washington State," *Seattle Journal of Social Justice* 9, no. 1 (2010): 337.

54. Sanders, "Domestic Violence, Economic Abuse, and Implications," 23.

55. Judy L. Postmus, "Economic Empowerment of Domestic Violence Survivors," VAWnet.org, October 2010, http://vawnet.org/sites/default/files/materials/files/2016-09/AR_EcoEmpowerment.pdf.

56. Sanders, "Domestic Violence, Economic Abuse, and Implications," 81.

57. Jennifer Cole, *First Look at Economic Empowerment Program Outcome Evaluation* (Lexington: University of Kentucky, Center on Drug and Alcohol Research, 2015).

58. Postmus, "Economic Empowerment of Domestic Violence Survivors."

59. Weissman, "Countering Neoliberalism and Aligning Solidarities," 36.

60. Deborah M. Weissman, "The Personal Is Political—and Economic: Rethinking Domestic Violence," *Brigham Young University Law Review* 2007, no. 2 (2007): 418–20.

61. Weissman, "The Personal Is Political—and Economic,"411.

62. Ibid., 431.

63. James Gilligan, *Preventing Violence* (New York: Thames and Hudson, 2001), 75–76.

64. National Institute of Justice, *When Violence Hits Home: How Economics and Neighborhood Play a Role,* (Washington, D.C.: United States Department of Justice, 2004), 2.

65. Jacquelyn C. Campbell et al., "Risk Factors for Femicide in Abusive Relationships: Results from a Multisite Case Control Study," *American Journal of Public Health* 93, no. 7 (2003): 1092.

66. National Institute of Justice, *When Violence Hits Home*, 4.

67. Coker, "Shifting Power for Battered Women," 1037.

68. Sanders, "Domestic Violence, Economic Abuse, and Implications," 35–36.

69. Ibid., 35.

70. Deborah M. Weissman, "Law, Social Movements, and the Political Economy of Domestic Violence," *Duke Journal of Gender Law and Policy* 20, no. 2 (2013): 222.

71. Ariane Hegewish and Emma Williams-Baron, *The Gender Wage Gap: 2017* (Washington, D.C. : Institute for Women's Policy Research, 2018).

72. Department of Economic and Social Affairs, *Women's Control Over Economic Resources and Access to Financial Resources, Including Microfinance* (New York: United Nations, 2009): 29.

73. Ken Jacobs et al., "Producing Poverty: The Public Cost of Low-Wage Production Jobs in Manufacturing," *UC Berkley Labor Center,* May 10, 2016, http://laborcenter.berkeley.edu/producing-poverty-the-public-cost-of-low-wage-production-jobs-in-manufacturing/.

74. Brush, *Poverty, Battered Women, and Work*, 40.

75. Weissman, "The Personal Is Political—and Economic," 415.

76. Yakin Ertürk, *Report of the Special Rapporteur on Violence against Women, Its Causes and Consequences: Political Economy and Violence against Women* (New York: United Nations Human Rights Office of the High Commissioner, June 2009): 6, http://www.ohchr.org/EN/Issues/Women/SRWomen/Pages/SRWomenIndex.aspx.

77. Jacqui True, *The Political Economy of Violence against Women* (New York: Oxford University Press, 2012), 105.

78. Ibid., 106.

79. Ibid., 95.

3. A PUBLIC HEALTH PROBLEM

1. "Domestic Violence as a Public Health Issue," Human Resource and Intergovernmental Relations Committee, Committee on Government Operations, House of Representatives (October 5, 1994): 2.

2. Emiko Petrosky et al., "Racial and Ethnic Differences in Homicides of Adult Women and the Role of Intimate Partner Violence—United States, 2003–2014," *Morbidity and Mortality Weekly Report* 66, no. 28 (2017), https://www.cdc.gov/mmwr/volumes/66/wr/mm6628a1.htm?s_cid=mm6628a1_w#suggestedcitation.

3. National Center for Injury Prevention and Control, *Costs of Intimate Partner Violence against Women in the United States* (Atlanta: Centers for Disease Control and Prevention, 2003), 15.

4. "Domestic Violence as a Public Health Issue,", 69.

5. World Health Organization/London School of Hygiene and Tropical Medicine, *Preventing Intimate Partner and Sexual Violence against Women: Taking Action and Generating Evidence* (Geneva: World Health Organization, 2010), 3.

6. Etienne G. Krug et al., eds., *World Report on Violence and Health* (Geneva: World Health Organization, 2002): 3, http://who.int/violence_injury_prevention/violence/world_report/en/introduction.pdf.

7. Ibid., 34.

8. Michele R. Decker, Elizabeth Miller, and Nancy Glass, "Gender-Based Violence Assessment in the Health Sector and Beyond," in *Preventing Intimate Partner Violence*, ed. Claire M. Renzetti, Diane R. Follingstad, and Anne L. Coker (Bristol: Policy Press, 2017).

9. Michael Marmot, "Social Determinants of Health Inequalities," *The Lancet* 365, no. 9464 (2005): 1099.

10. Richard Wilkinson and Michael Marmot, *Social Determinants of Health: The Solid Facts*, Copenhagen: World Health Organization Europe, 2003, 10, http://www.euro.who.int/__data/assets/pdf_file/0005/98438/e81384.pdf.

11. Marmot, "Social Determinants of Health Inequalities," 1103.

12. Lori L. Heise, "What Works to Prevent Partner Violence? An Evidence Overview" *STRIVE Research Consortium* (2011): 6–7, http://researchonline.lshtm.ac.uk/21062/1/Heise_Partner_Violence_evidence_overview.pdf.

13. Ibid.

14. Shannan Catalano, *Intimate Partner Violence: Attributes of Victimization, 1993–2011* (Washington, D.C.: Bureau of Justice Statistics, 2013), 12, https://www.bjs.gov/content/pub/pdf/ipvav9311.pdf.

15. Gary J. Gates, *How Many People Are Lesbian, Gay, Bisexual, and Transgender?* (Los Angeles: The Williams Institute, 2011), 6, https://williams institute.law.ucla.edu/wp-content/uploads/Gates-How-Many-People-LGBT -Apr-2011.pdf.

16. Michael Flood, "Preventing Male Violence," in *Oxford Textbook of Violence Prevention*, ed. Peter D. Donnelly and Catherine L. Ward (Oxford: Oxford University Press, 2015), 201.

17. Michael Kaufman, "The White Ribbon Campaign: Involving Men and Boys in Ending Global Violence against Women," in *A Man's World? Changing Men's Practices in a Globalized World*, ed. Bob Pease and Keith Pringle (London: Zed Books, 2001), 41.

18. Philippe Bourgois, "In Search of Masculinity: Violence, Respect and Sexuality among Puerto Rican Crack Dealers in East Harlem," *British Journal of Criminology* 36, no. 3 (1996): 416.

19. Rachel Jewkes et al., "From Work with Men and Boys to Changes of Social Norms and Reduction of Inequities in Gender Relations: A Conceptual Shift in Prevention of Violence against Women and Girls," *The* Lancet 385, no. 9977 (2014): 1583, http://dx.doi.org/10.1016/S0140-6736(14)61683-4.

20. G. Barker et al., "Questioning Gender Norms with Men to Improve Health Outcomes: Evidence of Impact," *Global Public Health* 5, no. 5 (2010): 540.

21. Richard M. Tolman, Tova Walsh, and Jeffrey Edleson, "Engaging Men in Violence Prevention," in *Sourcebook on Violence gainst Women*, 3rd ed., ed. Claire M. Renzetti, Jeffrey L. Edleson, and Raquel Kennedy Bergen (Sage Publications, 2017), 341.

22. E.M. Broido, "The Development of Social Justice Allies during College: A Phenomenological Investigation," *Journal of College Student Development* 41, no. 1 (2000): 3.

23. Kaufman, "The White Ribbon Campaign," 50.

24. Juliana Carlson et al., "Strategies to Engage Men and Boys in Violence Prevention: A Global Organizational Perspective," *Violence against Women* 21, no. 11 (2016): 1420.

25. Kaufman, "The White Ribbon Campaign," 45.

26. Ibid., 45–46.

27. Michael A. Messner, Max A. Greenberg, and Tal Peretz, *Some Men: Feminist Allies and the Movement to End Violence against Women* (New York: Oxford University Press, 2015), 121–22.

28. Ibid., 136.

29. Ibid., 15.

30. Ibid., 175.

31. Michael Salter, "Managing Recidivism amongst High Risk Violent Men," *Australian Domestic Violence and Family Violence Clearinghouse* 23 (2012): 4.

32. Charles L. Whitfield et al., "Violent Childhood Experiences and the Risk of Intimate Partner Violence in Adults," *Journal of Interpersonal Violence* 18, no. 2 (2003): 178, 181.

33. Heise, "What Works to Prevent Partner Violence?," 32.

34. Sherry Hamby and John Grych, *The Web of Violence: Exploring Connections among Different Forms of Interpersonal Violence and Abuse* (Dordrecht: Springer, 2013), 17.

35. "Nurse-Family Partnership: About Us," https://www.nursefamilypartnership.org/about/.

36. Claire Crooks, "The Science of Prevention/Interrupting the Cycle of Violence," in *Preventing Violence against Women and Children: Workshop Summary* (Washington, D.C.: National Academies Press, 2011), 93.

37. "Nurse-Family Partnership," *StoryCorps*, June 29, 2017, https://archive.storycorps.org/interviews/i-can-stand-up-set-those-boundaries-and-make-the-decisions-that-are-best-for-not-just-me-but-for-my-daughter/.

38. Megan H. Bair-Merritt et al., "Reducing Maternal Intimate Partner Violence after the Birth of a Child: A Randomized Controlled Trial of the Hawaii Healthy Start Home Visitation Program," *Archives of Pediatrics and Adolescent Medicine* 164, no. 1 (2010); Ann Duggan et al., "Randomized Trial of a Statewide Home Visiting Program to Prevent Child Abuse: Impact in Reducing Parental Risk Factors," *Child Abuse and Neglect* 28, no. 6 (2004).

39. Angela J. Taft et al., "Mothers' AdvocateS in the Community (MOSAIC)—Non-professional Mentor Support to Reduce Intimate Partner Violence and Depression in Mothers: A Cluster Randomized Trial in Primary Care," *BMC Public Health* 11, no. 178 (2011), https://bmcpublichealth.biomedcentral.com/track/pdf/10.1186/1471-2458-11-178.

40. John Eckenrode et al., "Preventing Child Abuse and Neglect with a Program of Nurse Home Visitation: The Limiting Effects of Domestic Violence," *Journal of the American Medical Association* 284, no. 11 (2000): 1385.

41. Flood, "Preventing Male Violence," 202.

42. Carla Smith Stover, "Fathers for Change: A New Approach to Working with Fathers Who Perpetrate Intimate Partner Violence," *Journal of the American Academy of Psychiatry and Law* 41, no. 1 (2013): 65.

43. Elizabeth Miller et al., "'Coaching Boys into Men': A Cluster-Randomized Controlled Trial of a Dating Violence Prevention Program," *Journal of Adolescent Health* 51, no. 5 (2012): 432.

44. Ibid., 436.

45. Ravi K. Thiara and Jane Ellis, "Concluding Remarks," in *Preventing Violence against Women and Girls: Educational Work with Children and Young People*, ed. Jane Ellis and Ravi K. Thiara (Bristol: Policy Press, 2014), 249.

46. Vangie A. Foshee et al., "Assessing the Long-Term Effects of the Safe Dates Program and a Booster in Preventing and Reducing Adolescent Dating Violence Victimization and Perpetration," *American Journal of Public Health* 94, no. 4 (2004): 623.

47. Deborah A. Levesque et al., "Teen Dating Violence Prevention: Cluster-Randomized Trial of *Teen Choices,* an Online, Stage-Based Program for Healthy, Nonviolent Relationships," *Psychology of Violence* 6, no. 3 (2016).

48. David A. Wolfe et al., "Dating Violence Prevention with At-Risk Youth: A Controlled Outcome Evaluation," *Journal of Consulting and Clinical Psychology* 71, no. 2 (2003); David A. Wolfe et al., "A School-Based Program to Prevent Adolescent Dating Violence: A Cluster Randomized Trial," *Archives of Pediatrics and Adolescent Medicine* 163, no. 8 (2009).

49. A. Singhal et al., "Entertainment-Education Strategy in Development Communication," in *Development and Communication in Africa,* ed. C. Okigobo and F. Eribo (Lanham: Rowman and Littlefield Publishers, 2004), 141–53.

50. S. Usdin et al., "Achieving Social Change on Gender-Based Violence: A Report on the Impact Evaluation of Soul City's Fourth Series," *Social Science and Medicine* 61, no. 11 (2005): 2439.

51. Jewkes et al., "From Work with Men and Boys," 1584.

52. L. Kevin Hamberger, "Typologies and Characteristics of Batterers," *Intimate Partner Violence: A Health-Based Perspective,* ed. Connie Mitchell and Deirdre Anglin (New York: Oxford University Press, 2009), 123.

53. William Fals-Stewart, "The Occurrence of Partner Physical Aggression on Days of Alcohol Consumption: A Longitudinal Diary Study," *Journal of Consulting and Clinical Psychology* 71, no. 1 (2003).

54. Martie P. Thompson and J.B. Kingree," The Roles of Victim and Perpetrator Alcohol Use in Intimate Partner Violence Outcomes," *Journal of Interpersonal Violence* 21, no. 2 (2006): 172.

55. Sara Markowitz, "The Price of Alcohol, Wife Abuse, and Husband Abuse," *Southern Economic Journal* 67, no. 2 (2000): 299.

56. Michael Grossman and Sara Markowitz, *Alcohol Regulation and Violence on College Campuses* (Cambridge: National Bureau of Economic Research, 1999), http://nber.org/papers/w7129.pdf.

57. Megan C. Kearns, Dennis E. Reidy, and Linda Anne Valle, "The Role of Alcohol Policies in Preventing Intimate Partner Violence: A Review of the Literature," *Journal of Studies on Alcohol and Drugs* 76, no. 1 (2015), https://www.ncbi.nlm.nih.gov/pmc/articles/PMC4770459/.

58. Carol B. Cunradi et al., "Alcohol Outlets, Neighborhood Characteristics, and Intimate Partner Violence: Ecological Analysis of a California City," *Journal of Urban Health: Bulletin of the New York Academy of Medicine* 88, no. 2 (2011): 191.

59. National Institute of Justice, *Program Profile: South Dakota's 24/7 Sobriety Project* (Washington, D.C.: United States Department of Justice, 2015), https://www.crimesolutions.gov/ProgramDetails.aspx?ID=404.

60. Susan B. Sorensen and Rebecca A. Schut, "Nonfatal Gun Use in Intimate Partner Violence: A Systematic Review of the Literature," *Trauma, Violence, and Abuse* (2016): 1–12.

61. April Zeoli, Rebecca Malinski, and Brandon Turchan, "Risks and Targeted Interventions: Firearms in Intimate Partner Violence," *Epidemiology Review* 38, no. 1 (2016): 125.

62. Jacquelyn C. Campbell et al., "Risk Factors for Femicide in Abusive Relationships: Results From a Multistate Case Control Study," *American Journal of Public Health* 93, no. 7 (2003): 1092.

63. Linda E. Saltzman et al., "Weapon Involvement and Injury Outcomes in Family and Intimate Assaults," *Journal of the American Medical Association* 267, no. 22 (1992): 3043.

64. Emily F. Rothman, Renee M. Johnson, and David Hemenway, "Gun Possession among Massachusetts Batterer Intervention Program Enrollees," *Evaluation Review* 30, no. 3 (2006): 283.

65. Ibid., 291.

66. Sorensen and Schut, "Nonfatal Gun Use in Intimate Partner Violence," 1.

67. Kerri M. Raissian, "Hold Your Fire: Did the 1996 Federal Gun Control Act Expansion Reduce Domestic Homicides?," *Journal of Policy Analysis and Management* 35, no. 1 (2016): 67–93.

68. Carolina Díez et al., "State Intimate Partner Violence-Related Firearm Laws and Intimate Partner Homicide Rates in the United States, 1991–2015," *Annals of Internal Medicine* 167, no. 8 (2017), http://annals.org/aim/fullarticle/2654047/state-intimate-partner-violence-related-firearm-laws-intimate-partner-homicide.

69. Elizabeth Richardson Vigdor and James A. Mercy, "Do Laws Restricting Access to Firearms by Domestic Violence Offenders Prevent Intimate Partner Homicide?," *Evaluation Review* 30, no. 3 (2006): 337.

70. Katherine A. Vittes et al., "Removing Guns from Batterers: Findings from a Pilot Survey of Domestic Violence Restraining Order Recipients in California," *Violence against Women* 19, no. 5 (2013): 611–12; Laura Choi, Rachel Elkin, and Monica Harasim, *Taking Aim at Family Violence: A Report on the Dallas County Gun Surrender Program* (Dallas: SMU Dedman School of Law, 2017), 44.

71. Daniel W. Webster et al., "Women with Protective Orders Report Failure to Remove Firearms from Their Abusive Partners: Results from an Exploratory Study," *Journal of Women's Health* 19, no. 1 (2010): 96.

72. "Results of Survey USA Mkt Research Study #23648," http://surveyusa.com/client/PollReportUC.aspx?g=a111d1a3-6bd7-445a-b873-f05742882310.

73. Daniel J. Whitaker et al., "Effectiveness of Primary Prevention Efforts for Intimate Partner Violence," *Partner Abuse* 4, no. 2 (2013): 176.

74. Thiara and Ellis, "Concluding Remarks," 248.

75. Messner, Greenberg, and Peretz, *Some Men*, 106–07.

76. Linda Hamilton Krieger, "De-biasing the Courtroom" (Safe Ireland Summit, Dublin, Ireland, November 2016).

77. "Domestic Violence as a Public Health Issue," 72.

4. A COMMUNITY PROBLEM

1. Alliance for Safety and Justice, *Crime Survivors Speak: The First-Ever National Survey of Victims' Views on Safety and Justice* (2016).

2. Jazmine Ulloa, "What Is a 'Violent Crime'? For California's New Parole Law, the Definition Is Murky—and It Matters," *Los Angeles Times*, January 27, 2017, www.latimes.com/politics/la-pol-sac-proposition-57-violent-crime-list-20170127-story.html.

3. Brian A. Reaves, *Police Response to Domestic Violence, 2006–2015* (Washington, D.C.: United States Department of Justice, 2017), 1.

4. Radhika Coomaraswamy, *Report of the Special Rapporteur on Violence against Women, Its Causes and Consequences* (New York: United Nations Commission on Human Rights, February 1997): 5, www.refworld.org/docid/3b00f4104.html.

5. Natalie Moore, *One Block, Zero Shootings: How One Mom Is Building Community in Englewood*, WBEZ News, August 22, 2016, www.wbez.org/shows/wbez-news/one-block-zero-shootings-how-one-mom-is-building-community-in-englewood/ad478912-c74c-439d-a1cf-52f0c58989b6.

6. Natalya Verbitsky-Savitz et al., *Preventing and Mitigating the Effects of ACEs by Building Community Capacity and Resilience: APPI Cross-Site Evaluation Findings* (Washington, D.C.: Mathematica Policy Research, 2016): 96–97.

7. David Bornstein, "Tapping a Troubled Neighborhood's Inner Strength," *New York Times*, August 10, 2016, https://www.nytimes.com/2016/08/10/opinion/tapping-a-troubled-neighborhoods-inner-strength.html?_r=0.

8. Emily M. Wright and Michael L. Benson, "Immigration and Intimate Partner Violence: Exploring the Immigrant Paradox," *Social Problems* 57, no. 3 (2010).

9. Adam J. Zolotor and Desmond K. Runyan, "Social Capital, Family Violence, and Neglect," *Pediatrics* 117, no. 6 (2006): 1127–28.

10. Christopher R. Browning, "The Span of Collective Efficacy: Extending Social Disorganization Theory to Partner Violence," *Journal of Marriage and Family* 64, no. 4 (2002): 833–50.

11. Emily M. Wright and Michael L. Benson, "Clarifying the Effects of Neighborhood Context on Violence 'Behind Closed Doors,'" *Justice Quarterly* 28, no. 5 (2011): 791.

12. Sonia Jain et al., "Neighborhood Predictors of Dating Violence Victimization and Perpetration in Young Adulthood: A Multilevel Study," *American Journal of Public Health* 100, no. 9 (2010): 1737–44.

13. Paul Kivel, "Social Service or Social Change?," www.paulkivel.com, 2006, http://coavp.org/sites/default/files/social percent20service percent20vs percent20change.pdf.

14. Madelaine Adelman et al., "Mobilizing Culture as an Asset: A Transdisciplinary Effort to Rethink Gender Violence," *Violence against Women* 18, no. 6 (2012): 696.

15. Ibid., 697.

16. Mieko Yoshihama et al., "Intimate Partner Violence Prevention Program in an Asian Immigrant Community: Integrating Theories, Data, and Community, Violence Against Women," *Violence against Women* 18, no. 7 (2012): 775.

17. Schechter, *Women and Male Violence*, 4.

18. Personal communication with Hannah Brancato, March 10, 2017.

19. Kathleen Daly, "Reconceptualizing Sexual Victimization and Justice," in *Justice for Victims: Perspectives on Rights, Transition, and Reconciliation,* ed. Inge Vanfraechem et al. (New York: Routledge, 2014), 378–95.

20. "Transformative Justice: A Liberatory Approach to Child Sexual Abuse and Other Forms of Intimate and Community Violence," *Generation Five,* 2007, http://www.generationfive.org/wp-content/uploads/2013/07/G5_Toward_Transformative_Justice-Document.pdf

21. Ibid.

22. Mimi Kim, "Alternative Interventions to Intimate Violence: Defining Political and Pragmatic Challenges," in *Restorative Justice and Violence against Women,* ed. James Ptacek (New York: Oxford University Press, 2010), 207.

23. "Pillars," *Support New York,* 2014, https://supportnewyork.files.wordpress.com/2014/02/supportnypillars.pdf.

24. Andrea Smith, *Conquest: Sexual Violence and American Indian Genocide* (Durham: Duke University Press, 2005), 140.

25. John Braithwaite, "The Fundamentals of Restorative Justice," in *A Kind of Mending: Restorative Justice in the Pacific Islands,* ed. Sinclair Dinnen (Canberra: ANU Press, 2011), 35.

26. Ibid.

27. Kay Pranis, "Restorative Values and Confronting Family Violence," in *Restorative Justice and Family Violence,* ed. Heather Strang and John Braithwaite (Cambridge: Cambridge University Press, 2002), 23–41.

28. Sered, *Accounting for Violence,* 17.

29. Jeremiah Bourgeois, "How Restorative Justice Ended My Cycle of Madness," *The Crime Report,* September 12, 2016, http://thecrimereport.org/2016/09/12/making-amends-for-real/.

30. Leah Sottile, "Abuser and Survivor, Face to Face," *The Atlantic,* October 5, 2015, www.theatlantic.com/health/archive/2015/10/domestic-violence-restorative-justice/408820/.

31. Sered, *Accounting for Violence,* 18.

32. John Braithwaite and Kathleen Daly, "Violence and Communitarian Control," in *Just Boys Doing Business,* ed. Tim Newburn and Betsy Stanko (London: Routledge, 1994), 235.

33. Karp et al., *A Report on Promoting Restorative Initiatives,* 3.

34. Lawrence W. Sherman and Heather Strang, *Restorative Justice: The Evidence* (London: The Smith Institute, 2007); Heather Strang et al., *Restorative Justice Conferencing (RJC) Using Face-to-Face Meetings of Offenders and Victims: Effects on Offender Recidivism and Victim Satisfaction: A Systematic Review* (Oslo: The Campbell Collaboration, 2013); Heather Strang and Lawrence W. Sherman, "Repairing the Harm: Victims and Restorative Justice," *Utah Law Review* 2003 no. 15 (2003).

35. Strang and Sherman, "Repairing the Harm," 40.

36. Jennifer Llewellyn, Jacob Macisaac, and Melissa Mackay, *Report from the Restorative Justice Process* (Halifax: Dalhousie University, 2015): 9.

37. Ibid., 10.

38. Ibid., 3.
39. Ibid., 10.
40. Ibid., 11.
41. Ruth Busch, "Domestic Violence and Restorative Justice Initiatives: Who Pays If We Get It Wrong?," in *Restorative Justice and Family Violence*, ed. Heather Strang and John Braithwaite (Cambridge: Cambridge University Press 2002), 242.
42. Julie Stubbs, "Domestic Violence and Women's Safety: Feminist Challenges to Restorative Justice," in *Restorative Justice and Family Violence*, ed. Heather Strang and John Braithwaite (Cambridge: Cambridge University Press 2002), 42–61.
43. Julie Stubbs, "Gendered Violence and Restorative Justice," in *A Restorative Approach to Family Violence: Changing Tack*, ed. Anne Hayden et al. (Surrey: Ashgate Press, 2014), 38.
44. C. Quince Hopkins, "Tempering Idealism with Realism: Using Restorative Justice Processes to Promote Acceptance of Responsibility in Cases of Intimate Partner Violence," *Harvard Journal of Law and Gender* 35, no. 2 (2012): 321.
45. Jill Davies et al., *Safety Planning with Battered Women: Complex Lives/Difficult Choices* (Thousand Oaks, CA: Sage Publications, 1998), 77.
46. Judith Lewis Herman, "Justice from the Victim's Perspective," *Violence against Women* 11, no. 5 (2005): 585.
47. Donna Coker, "Transformative Justice: Anti-Subordination Processes in Cases of Domestic Violence," in *Restorative Justice and Family Violence*, ed. Strang and Braithwaite,128–52.
48. House of Commons (United Kingdom) Justice Committee, *Restorative Justice: Fourth Report of Session 2016–17*, 2017, 15.
49. Braithwaite and Daly, "Violence and Communitarian Control," 208.
50. Ibid., 227.
51. Sarah Curtis-Fawley and Kathleen Daly, "Gendered Violence and Restorative Justice: The Views of Victim Advocates," *Violence against Women* 11, no. 5 (2005): 614.
52. Joan Pennell, "Safety for Mothers and Their Children," in *Widening the Circle: The Practice and Evaluation of Family Group Conferencing with Children, Youths, and Their Families*, ed. Joan Pennell and Gary Anderson (Washington, D.C.: NASW Press, 2005); Joan Pennell and Gale Burford, "Family Group Decision Making: Protecting Women and Children," *Child Welfare* 79 no. 2 (2000): 131.
53. Venezia Kingi, "The Use of Restorative Justice in Family Violence: The New Zealand Experience," in *A Restorative Approach to Family Violence: Changing Tack*, ed. Anne Hayden et al. (Surrey: Ashgate Press, 2014), 149–53.
54. Robyn Holder and Kathleen Daly, "Sequencing Justice: A Longitudinal Study of Justice Goals of Domestic Violence Victims," *British Journal of Criminology*, September 2017, https://academic.oup.com/bjc/advance-article-abstract/doi/10.1093/bjc/azx046/4259717.

55. House of Commons (United Kingdom) Justice Committee, *Restorative Justice*,15.

56. John Braithwaite, *Restorative Justice and Responsive Regulation* (New York: Oxford University Press, 2002), 35–36.

57. Lois Presser and Emily Gaarder, "Can Restorative Justice Reduce Battering? Some Preliminary Considerations," *Social Justice* 27, no. 1 (2000): 188.

5. A HUMAN RIGHTS PROBLEM

1. The University of Miami Human Rights Clinic, Columbia Law School Human Rights Initiative, and ACLU Women's Rights Project, *Domestic Violence and Sexual Assault in the United States: A Human Rights Based Approach and Practice Guide* (2014): 2, http://www.law.columbia.edu/sites/default/files/microsites/human-rights-institute/files/dv_sa_hr_guide_reduce.pdf.

2. The vast majority of the human rights literature focuses on violence against women; even the definition of gender-based violence in many international human rights documents references women specifically. Moreover, in human rights law, the right to be free from intimate partner violence has been situated, in significant part, in a woman's right to be free from discrimination. For this reason, this chapter is significantly less gender neutral than previous chapters of this book have been. Nonetheless, the human rights norms against intimate partner violence should be broadly applied to violence in all intimate relationships, and I have attempted to make that point whenever possible.

3. Rashida Manjoo, *Report of the Special Rapporteur on Violence against Women, Its Causes and Consequences*, (New York: United Nations Human Rights Office of the High Commissioner, September 2014): 5.

4. Rhonda Copelon, "International Human Rights Dimension of Intimate Violence: Another Strand in the Dialectic of Feminist Lawmaking," *Journal of Gender, Social Policy and the Law* 11, no. 2 (2003): 867.

5. Monica McWilliams and Fionnuala Ní Aoláin, "Moving Slowly to Regulate and Recognize: Human Rights Meets Intimate Partner Sexual Violence," in *Marital Rape: Consent, Marriage, and Social Change in Global Context*, ed. Kersti Yllö and M. Gabriela Torres (New York: Oxford University Press, 2016), 190.

6. Copelon, "International Human Rights Dimension of Intimate Violence," 869.

7. Sally Engle Merry, "Constructing a Global Law—Violence against Women and the Human Rights System," *Journal of Law and Social Inquiry* 28, no. 4 (2003): 950.

8. Rashida Manjoo, *Statement by Ms. Rashida Manjoo, Special Rapporteur on Violence against women, its causes and consequences*, (New York: United Nations Commission on the Status of Women, March 2015): 3, http://www.ohchr.org/Documents/Issues/Women/CSW2015.pdf.

9. Merry, "Constructing a Global Law," 968.

10. Caroline Bettinger-López, "Jessica Gonzales v. United States: An Emerging Model for Domestic Violence and Human Rights Advocacy in the United States," *Harvard Human Rights Journal* 21, no. 2 (2008): 193.

11. Velásquez Rodriguez v. Honduras (Inter-American Court of Human Rights 1988).

12. Opuz v. Turkey (European Court of Human Rights 2009).

13. Julie Goldscheid and Debra Liebowitz, "Due Diligence and Gender Violence: Parsing Its Power and Its Perils," *Cornell International Law Journal* 48, no. 2 (2015): 307.

14. Rashida Manjoo, *Report of the Special Rapporteur on Violence against Women, Its Causes and Consequences,* (New York: United Nations Human Rights Office of the High Commissioner, May 2013): 20.

15. Yakin Ertürk, *Fifteen Years of the United Nations Special Rapporteur on Violence against Women, Its Causes and Consequences (1994–2009)—A Critical Review,* (New York: United Nations Human Rights Office of the High Commissioner, May 2009): 33, www.unwomen.org/en/docs/2009/1/15-years-of-the-un-special-rapporteur-on-violence-against-women.

16. Manjoo, *Report of the Special Rapporteur,* September 2014, 19.

17. Maria da Penha Maia Fernandes v. Brazil (Inter-American Commission on Human Rights, 2001).

18. Jessica Lenahan v. United States (Inter-American Commission on Human Rights, 2011).

19. Tarik Abdel-Monem, "Opuz v. Turkey: Europe's Landmark Judgment on Violence against Women," *Human Rights Brief* 17, no. 1 (2009): 29.

20. Rashida Manjoo, *Report of the Special Rapporteur on Violence against Women, Its Causes and Consequences,* (New York: United Nations Human Rights Office of the High Commissioner, August 2011): 21.

21. Goldscheid and Liebowitz, "Due Diligence and Gender Violence," 310.

22. Ibid., 312.

23. Bonita Meyersfield, *Domestic Violence and International Law* (Oxford: Hart Publishing, 2010), 246.

24. Goldscheid and Liebowitz, "Due Diligence and Gender Violence," 345.

25. Rashida Manjoo, *Report of the Special Rapporteur on Violence against Women, Its Causes and Consequences,* (New York: United Nations Human Rights Office of the High Commissioner, June 2011): 27.

26. Lenahan v. United States.

27. Radhika Coomaraswamy, *Report of the Special Rapporteur on Violence against Women, Its Causes and Consequences,* (New York: United Nations Human Rights Office of the High Commissioner, February 1996): 38.

28. United Nations General Assembly, *In-Depth Study on All Forms of Violence against Women: Report of the Secretary-General,* A/61/122, (New York: United Nations, 2006): ¶ 42, https://documents-dds-ny.un.org/doc/UNDOC/GEN/N06/419/74/PDF/N0641974.pdf?OpenElement.

6. A BALANCED POLICY APPROACH

1. Melissa Hidrobo, Amber Peterman, and Lori Heise, "The Effect of Cash, Vouchers and Food Transfers on Intimate Partner Violence: Evidence from a Randomized Experiment in Northern Ecuador, *American Economic Journal: Applied Economics* 8, no. 3 (2016).

2. Elizaveta Perova, *Three Essays on Intended and Not Intended Impacts of Conditional Cash Transfers* (2010), https://escholarship.org/uc/item/2767982k.

3. Karuna Jaggar and Elizabeth de Renzy, *Closing the Wealth Gap Through Self-employment: Women of Color Achieving the American Dream* (San Francisco: Women's Initiative, 2008), 2.

4. Julia C. Kim et al., "Understanding the Impact of a Microfinance-Based Intervention on Women's Empowerment and the Reduction of Intimate Partner Violence in South Africa," *American Journal of Public Health* 97, no. 10 (2007): 1798.

5. Caroline Schuster, "Microfinance Could Wind up Being the New Subprime," *The Conversation*, May 23, 2016, http://theconversation.com/microfinance-could-wind-up-being-the-new-subprime-59001.

6. Olivia Solon, "Women-Led Startup Turns Domestic Abuse Survivors into Entrepreneurs," *The Guardian*, November 23, 2017, www.theguardian.com/society/2017/nov/23/domestic-abuse-survivors-free-from-entrepreneur-startups.

7. Benson and Fox, *Economic Distress, Community Context and Intimate Violence*, 127.

8. Weissman, "The Personal Is Political," 447.

9. Stephanie McMahon, "An Empirical Study of Innocent Spouse Relief: Do Courts Implement Congress' Legislative Intent," *Florida Tax Review* 12, no. 8 (2012): 705.

10. Littwin, "Escaping Battered Credit," 364–65, 400–01.

11. National Network to End Domestic Violence, *Eleventh Annual Domestic Violence Counts Report* (2016).

12. Lori Michau et al., "Prevention of Violence against Women and Girls: Lessons from Practice," *The Lancet* 385, no. 9978 (2015): 1680.

13. Garen J. Wintemute et al., "Identifying Armed Respondents to Domestic Violence Restraining Orders and Recovering Their Firearms: Process Evaluation of an Initiative in California," *American Journal of Public Health* 104, no. 2 (2014): 115.

14. Shannon Frattaroli, "Systems Change: Police/Criminal Justice" (Symposium on Violence Prevention, Bloomberg American Health Initiative, Baltimore, MD, December 8, 2017).

15. Krieger, "De-Biasing the Courtroom."

16. Gabor Maté, "The Biology of Loss" (SafeIreland Summit, Dublin, Ireland, November 15, 2016).

17. Casey T. Taft et al., "A Randomized Controlled Clinical Trial of the Strength at Home Men's Program for Partner Violence in Military Veterans," *Journal of Clinical Psychiatry* 77, no. 9 (2016): 1174.

18. Gilligan, *Preventing Violence*, 35.

19. Ibid., 53.

20. Tage Rai, "How Could They?," *Aeon*, June 18, 2015, https://aeon.co/essays/people-resort-to-violence-because-their-moral-codes-demand-it.

21. Steven Yoder, "Getting beyond Prison: A Vermont Case Study," *The American Prospect*, May 4, 2016, http://prospect.org/article/getting-beyond-prison-vermont-case-study.

22. Mary Achilles, "Can Restorative Justice Live up to Its Promise to Victims?," in *Critical Issues in Restorative Justice*, ed. Howard Zehr and Barb Toews (Monsey: Criminal Justice Press, 2004).

23. Ken McMaster, "Restoring the Balance: Restorative Justice and Intimate Partner Violence," in *A Restorative Approach to Family Violence: Changing Tack*, ed. Anne Hayden et al. (Surrey: Ashgate Press, 2014), 100.

24. Braithwaite, "The Fundamentals of Restorative Justice," 38.

25. Gordon Bazemore and Twila Hugley Earle, "Balance in the Response to Family Violence: Challenging Restorative Principles," in *Restorative Justice and Family Violence* (Cambridge: Cambridge University Press, 2002), 159.

26. Holly Maguigan, "Wading into Professor Schneider's 'Murky Middle Ground' between Acceptance and Rejection of Criminal Justice Responses to Domestic Violence," *American University Journal of Gender, Social Policy, and Law* 11, no. 2 (2003): 435.

27. Chris Coffi, "He Became the Poster Boy of Domestic Abuse. Now He Wishes He Chose Jail Instead," *Miami Herald*, March 29, 2017, www.miamiherald.com/news/nation-world/national/article141422664.html.

28. Gilligan, *Preventing Violence*, 116.

29. John Braithwaite, *Restorative Justice and Responsive Regulation*, 30.

30. Ibid.

31. Ibid., 80.

32. Ibid., 200. Of course, one could also ask why we don't recoil at the thought that arrest and incarceration fail to deter further violence, leading to further cycles of violence. My thanks to Aya Gruber for this observation.

33. Eve Buzawa et al., *Response to Domestic Violence in a Pro-Active Court Setting* (1999), www.ncjrs.gov/pdffiles1/nij/grants/181427.pdf [https://perma.cc/MHJ2-3Z8J].

34. David M. Kennedy, "Rethinking Law Enforcement Strategies to Prevent Domestic Violence," *Networks: Magazine of the National Center for Victims of Crime* 19, no. 2–3 (2004): 11.

35. Salter, "Managing Recidivism," 17.

36. National Network for Safe Communities, *Intimate Partner Violence Intervention: Overview* (New York: National Network for Safe Communities at John Jay College): 10.

37. John Buntin, "How High Point, N.C., Solved Its Domestic Violence Problem," *Governing*, March 2016, www.governing.com/topics/public-justice-safety/gov-domestic-violence-focused-deterrence.html.

38. National Network for Safe Communities, *Intimate Partner Violence Intervention: Overview*, 9.

39. Alma Au et al., "A Preliminary Validation of the Brief Spousal Assault Form for the Evaluation of Risk (B-SAFER) in Hong Kong," *Journal of Family Violence* 23 (2008): 727.

40. Todd R. Clear and Natasha A. Frost, *The Punishment Imperative: The Rise and Failure of Mass Incarceration in America* (New York: New York University Press, 2014), 174.

41. Kelly, *Criminal Justice at the Crossroads*, 214.

42. Jeff Deeney, "Making Overseers into Advocates," *The Marshall Project*, February 28, 2015, www.themarshallproject.org/2015/02/18/making-overseers-into-advocates#.NtXgiWy91.

43. Adam Gelb and Barbara Broderick, "It's Time to Refocus the Punishment Paradigm," *The Hill*, July 10, 2017, http://thehill.com/blogs/pundits-blog/crime/341274-its-time-to-refocus-the-punishment-paradigm.

44. Naomi Murakawa, *The First Civil Right: How Liberals Built Prison America* (New York: Oxford University Press, 2014), 155; Mark A. R. Kleiman, *When Brute Force Fails: How to Have Less Crime and Less Punishment* (Princeton: Princeton University Press, 2010), 99 (arguing that although intensive probation could "amount to a prison without walls," such measures are preferable to incarceration).

45. Coker and Macquoid, "Why Opposing Hyper-Incarceration Should Be Central," 587.

46. Ibid.

47. Christina Sterbenz, "Why Norway's Prison System Is So Successful," *Business Insider*, Dec. 11, 2014, http://www.businessinsider.com/why-norways-prison-system-is-so-successful-2014-12 (quoting Arne Wilson, the prison governor of Bastoy Prison).

48. Eldra Jackson III, "How Men at New Folsom Prison Reckon with Toxic Masculinity," *Los Angeles Times*, November 30, 2017, www.latimes.com/opinion/op-ed/la-oe-jackson-men-group-therapy-folsom-prison-the-work-toxic-masculinity-20171130-story.html.

49. "Domestic Violence as a Public Health Issue," 88.

50. Anne Sparks, "Feminists Negotiate the Executive Branch: The Policing of Male Violence," in *Feminists Negotiate the State: The Politics of Domestic Violence*, ed. Cynthia R. Daniels (Lanham: University Press of America, 1997), 52.

51. The idea for a decarceral VAWA came from Alisa Bierria at the Politicization of Safety conference held at the University of California, Irvine, on April 7, 2017.

Bibliography

Abdel-Monem, Tarik. "Opuz v. Turkey: Europe's Landmark Judgment on Violence against Women." *Human Rights Brief* 17, no. 1 (2009): 29–33.

Achilles, Mary. "Can Restorative Justice Live up to Its Promise to Victims?." In *Critical Issues in Restorative Justice*. Edited by Howard Zehr and Barb Toews. Monsey: Criminal Justice Press, 2004.

Adams, Adrienne E., Marisa L. Beeble, and Katie A. Gregory. "Evidence of the Construct Validity of the Scale of Economic Abuse." *Violence and Victims* 30, no. 3 (2015): 363–76.

Adams, Adrienne E., Cris M. Sullivan, Deborah Bybee, and Megan R. Greeson. "Development of the Scale of Economic Abuse." *Violence against Women* 14, no. 5 (2008): 563–88.

Adams, Adrienne E., Richard M. Tolman, Deborah Bybee, Cris M. Sullivan, and Angie C. Kennedy. "The Impact of Intimate Partner Violence on Low-Income Women's Economic Well-Being: The Mediating Role of Job Stability." *Violence against Women* 18, no. 12 (2013): 1345–67.

Adelman, Madelaine, Hillary Haldane, and Jennifer R. Wies. "Mobilizing Culture as an Asset: A Transdisciplinary Effort to Rethink Gender Violence." *Violence against Women* 18, no. 6 (2012): 691–700.

Alliance for Safety and Justice. *Crime Survivors Speak: The First-Ever National Survey of Victims' Views on Safety and Justice* (2016).

Annie E. Casey Foundation. *A Shared Sentence: The Devastating Toll of Parental Incarceration on Kids, Families and Communities*. Baltimore: The Annie E. Casey Foundation, 2016.

Arnold, Gretchen W. "From Victim to Offender: How Nuisance Property Laws Affect Battered Women." *Journal of Interpersonal Violence*, (2016): 1–24. http://journals.sagepub.com/doi/pdf/10.1177/0886260516647512

Au, Alma, George Cheung, Randall Kropp, Chan Yuk-chung, Gladys L.T. Lam, Pauline Sung. "A Preliminary Validation of the Brief Spousal Assault Form for the Evaluation of Risk (B-SAFER) in Hong Kong." *Journal of Family Violence* 23 (2008): 727–35.

Bair-Merritt, Megan H., Jacky M. Jennings, Rusan Chen, Lori Burrell, Elizabeth McFarlane, Loretta Fuddy, and Anne K. Duggan. "Reducing Maternal Intimate Partner Violence after the Birth of a Child: A Randomized Controlled Trial of the Hawaii Healthy Start Home Visitation Program." *Archives of Pediatrics and Adolescent Medicine* 164, no. 1 (2010): 16–23.

Barker, G., C. Ricardo, M. Nascimento, A. Olukoya, and C. Santos. "Questioning Gender Norms with Men to Improve Health Outcomes: Evidence of Impact." *Global Public Health* 5, no. 5 (2010): 539–53.

Bazemore, Gordon, and Twila Hugley Earle. "Balance in the Response to Family Violence: Challenging Restorative Principles." In *Restorative Justice and Family Violence.* Cambridge: Cambridge University Press, 2002.

Benson, Michael L., and Greer L. Fox. *Concentrated Disadvantage, Economic Distress, and Violence against Women in Intimate Relationships.* 2004. https://www.ncjrs.gov/pdffiles1/nij/199709.pdf

Benson, Michael L. and Greer Litton Fox. *Economic Distress, Community Context and Intimate Violence: An Application and Extension of Social Disorganization Theory.* Washington, D.C.: National Institute of Justice, 2002.

Bettinger-López, Caroline. "Jessica Gonzales v. United States: An Emerging Model for Domestic Violence and Human Rights Advocacy in the United States." *Harvard Human Rights Journal* 21, no. 2 (2008): 183–95.

Black, Michele C., Kathleen C. Basile, Matthew J. Breiding, Sharon G. Smith, Mike L. Walters, Melissa T. Merrick, Jieru Chen, and Mark R. Stevens. *The National Intimate Partner and Sexual Violence Survey: 2010 Summary Report.* Atlanta: Centers for Disease Control and Prevention, 2011.

Bornstein, David. "Tapping a Troubled Neighborhood's Inner Strength." *New York Times,* August 10, 2016. https://nytimes.com/2016/08/10/opinion/tapping-a-troubled-neighborhoods-inner-strength.html?_r=0.

Bourgeois, Jeremiah. "How Restorative Justice Ended My Cycle of Madness." *The Crime Report,* September 12, 2016. www.thecrimereport.org/2016/09/12/making-amends-for-real/.

Bourgois, Philippe. "In Search of Masculinity: Violence, Respect and Sexuality among Puerto Rican Crack Dealers in East Harlem." *British Journal of Criminology* 36, no. 3 (1996): 412–27.

Braithwaite, John. "The Fundamentals of Restorative Justice." In *A Kind of Mending: Restorative Justice in the Pacific Islands.* Edited by Sinclair Dinnen. Canberra: ANU Press, 2011.

Braithwaite, John. *Restorative Justice and Responsive Regulation.* New York: Oxford University Press, 2002.

Braithwaite, John, and Kathleen Daly. "Violence and Communitarian Control." In *Just Boys Doing Business.* Edited by Tim Newburn and Betsy Stanko. London: Routledge, 1994.

Broido, E.M. "The Development of Social Justice Allies During College: A Phenomenological Investigation." *Journal of College Student Development* 41, no. 1 (2000): 3–18.

Brown, Tony N., and Evelyn Patterson. "Criminal Injustice: Wounds from Incarceration That Never Heal." *The Conversation*, June 28, 2016. http://theconversation.com/criminal-injustice-wounds-from-incarceration-that-never-heal-60843.

Browning, Christopher R. "The Span of Collective Efficacy: Extending Social Disorganization Theory to Partner Violence." *Journal of Marriage and Family* 64, no. 4 (2002): 833–50.

Brush, Lisa D. *Poverty, Battered Women, and Work in U.S. Public Policy*. New York: Oxford University Press, 2011.

Buntin, John. "How High Point, N.C., Solved Its Domestic Violence Problem." *Governing*, March 2016. www.governing.com/topics/public-justice-safety/gov-domestic-violence-focused-deterrence.html.

Burk, Connie. "ABA Summit Keynote." Presentation at the American Bar Association LGBT Domestic Violence Legal Issues Summit, San Francisco, CA, April 11, 2008.

Busch, Noel Bridget, and Terry A. Wolfer. "Battered Women Speak Out: Welfare Reform and Their Decisions to Disclose." *Violence against Women* 8, no. 5 (2002): 566–84.

Busch, Ruth. "Domestic Violence and Restorative Justice Initiatives: Who Pays If We Get It Wrong?" In *Restorative Justice and Family Violence*. Edited by Heather Strang and John Braithwaite. Cambridge: Cambridge University Press, 2002.

Bush, George W. "Remarks on Domestic Violence Prevention." *The American Presidency Project*, October 8, 2003. www.presidency.ucsb.edu/ws/?pid=222.

Buzawa, Eve, Gerald T. Hotaling, Andrew Klein, and James Byrne. *Response to Domestic Violence in a Pro-Active Court Setting*. 1999. www.ncjrs.gov/pdffiles1/nij/grants/181427.pdf [https://perma.cc/MHJ2-3Z8J].

Campbell, Jacquelyn C., Daniel Webster, Jane Koziol-McLain, Carolyn Block, Doris Campbell, Mary Ann Curry, Faye Gray, Nancy Glass, Judith McFarlane, Carolyn Sachs, Phyllis Sharps, Yvonna Ulrich, Susan A. Wilt, Jennifer Manganello, Xiao Xu, Janet Schollenberger, Victoria Frye, and Kathryn Laughton. "Risk Factors for Femicide in Abusive Relationships: Results from a Multisite Case Control Study." *American Journal of Public Health* 93, no. 7 (2003): 1089–97.

Carlson, Juliana, Erin Casey, Jeffrey L. Edelson, Richard M. Tolman, Tova B. Walsh, Ericka Kimball. "Strategies to Engage Men and Boys in Violence Prevention: A Global Organizational Perspective." *Violence against Women* 21, no. 11 (2016): 1406–25.

Catalano, Shannan. *Intimate Partner Violence: Attributes of Victimization, 1993–2011*. Washington, D.C.: Bureau of Justice Statistics, 2013. https://www.bjs.gov/content/pub/pdf/ipvav9311.pdf.

Chettier, Iniamai M. "The Many Causes of America's Decline in Crime." *The Atlantic*, February 11, 2015. https://www.theatlantic.com/politics/archive/2015/02/the-many-causes-of-americas-decline-in-crime/385364/.

Choi, Laura, Rachel Elkin, and Monica Harasim. *Taking Aim at Family Violence: A Report on the Dallas County Gun Surrender Program.* Dallas: SMU Dedman School of Law, 2017.

Christie, Nils. "Conflicts as Property." *British Journal of Criminology* 17, no. 1 (1977): 1–15.

Citron, Danielle Keats. "Law's Expressive Value in Combating Cyber Gender Harassment." *Michigan Law Review* 108, no. 3 (2009): 373–416.

Clear, Todd R., and Natasha A. Frost. *The Punishment Imperative: The Rise and Failure of Mass Incarceration in America.* New York: New York University Press, 2014.

Coffi, Chris. "He Became the Poster Boy of Domestic Abuse. Now He Wishes He Chose Jail Instead." *Miami Herald,* March 29, 2017. www.miamiherald.com/news/nation-world/national/article141422664.html.

Coker, Donna. "Crime Control and Feminist Law Reform in Domestic Violence Law: A Critical Review." *Buffalo Criminal Law Review* 4, no. 2 (2001): 801–60.

Coker, Donna. "Shifting Power for Battered Women: Law, Material Resources, and Poor Women of Color." *University of California Davis Law Review* 33, no. 4 (2000): 1009–55.

Coker, Donna. "Transformative Justice: Anti-Subordination Processes in Cases of Domestic Violence." In *Restorative Justice and Family Violence.* Edited by Heather Strang and John Braithwaite. Cambridge: Cambridge University Press, 2002.

Coker, Donna, and Ahjané Macquoid. "Why Opposing Hyper-Incarceration Should Be Central to the Work of the Domestic Violence Movement." *University of Miami Race and Social Justice Law Review* 5, no. 2 (2015): 585–618.

Coker, Donna, Sandra Park, Julie Goldscheid, Tara Neal, and Valerie Halstead. *Responses from the Field: Sexual Assault, Domestic Violence, and Policing.* New York: American Civil Liberties Union, 2015.

Cole, Jennifer. *First Look at Economic Empowerment Program Outcome Evaluation.* Lexington: University of Kentucky, Center on Drug and Alcohol Research, 2015.

Coomaraswamy, Radhika. !!*Report of the Special Rapporteur on Violence against Women, Its Causes and Consequences.* New York: United Nations Commission on Human Rights, February 1997. www.refworld.org/docid/3b00f4104.html.

Coomaraswamy, Radhika. *Report of the Special Rapporteur on Violence against Women, Its Causes and Consequences.* New York: United Nations Commission on Human Rights, February 1996.

Copelon, Rhonda. "International Human Rights Dimension of Intimate Violence: Another Strand in the Dialectic of Feminist Lawmaking." *Journal of Gender, Social Policy and the Law* 11, no. 2 (2003): 865–76.

Crooks, Claire. "The Science of Prevention/Interrupting the Cycle of Violence." In *Preventing Violence against Women and Children: Workshop Summary.* Washington, D.C.: National Academies Press, 2011.

Cunradi, Carol B., Christina Mair, William Ponicki, and Lillian Remer. "Alcohol Outlets, Neighborhood Characteristics, and Intimate Partner Violence: Ecological Analysis of a California City." *Journal of Urban Health: Bulletin of the New York Academy of Medicine* 88, no. 2 (2011): 191–200.

Cunradi, Carol B., Raul Caetano, Catherine Clark, and John Schafer. "Neighborhood Poverty as a Predictor of Intimate Partner Violence Among White, Black, and Hispanic Couples in the United States: A Multilevel Analysis." *Annals of Epidemiology* 10, no. 5 (2000): 297–308.

Currie, Elliott. "Violence and Social Policy." In *Routledge Handbook of Critical Criminology*. Edited by Walter S. DeKeseredy and Molly Dragiewicz. New York: Routledge, 2012.

Curtis-Fawley, Sarah, and Kathleen Daly. "Gendered Violence and Restorative Justice: The Views of Victim Advocates." *Violence against Women* 11, no. 5 (2005): 603–38.

Daly, Kathleen. "Reconceptualizing Sexual Victimization and Justice." In *Justice for Victims: Perspectives on Rights, Transition, and Reconciliation*. Edited by Inge Vanfraechem, Antony Pemberton, and Felix Mukiwza Ndahinda. New York: Routledge, 2014.

Davies, Jill, Eleanor Lyon, and Diane Monti-Catania. *Safety Planning with Battered Women: Complex Lives/Difficult Choices*. Thousand Oaks, CA: Sage Publications, 1998.

Davis, Angela. "Keynote." The Color of Violence: Violence against Women of Color, University of California, Santa Cruz, Santa Cruz, CA, April 28, 2000.

Davis, Angela. "Masked Racism: Reflections on the Prison Industrial Complex." *ColorLines*, September 10, 1998. www.colorlines.com/articles/masked-racism-reflections-prison-industrial-complex.

Decker, Michele R., Elizabeth Miller, and Nancy Glass. "Gender-Based Violence Assessment in the Health Sector and Beyond." In *Preventing Intimate Partner Violence*. Edited by Claire M. Renzetti, Diane R. Follingstad, and Anne L. Coker. Bristol: Policy Press, 2017.

Deeney, Jeff. "Making Overseers into Advocates." *The Marshall Project*, February 28, 2015. www.themarshallproject.org/2015/02/18/making-overseers-into-advocates#.NtXgiWy91.

Department of Economic and Social Affairs. *Women's Control Over Economic Resources and Access to Financial Resources, Including Microfinance*. New York: United Nations, 2009.

DeRiviere, Linda. *The Healing Journey: Intimate Partner Abuse and Its Implications in the Labour Market* (Winnipeg: Fernwood Publishing, 2014).

Desmond, Matthew, and Nicol Valdez. "Unpolicing the Urban Poor: Consequences of Third-Party Policing for Inner-City Women." *American Sociological Review* 78, no. 1 (2012) 117–41.

Desmond, Matthew, Andrew V. Papachristos, and David S. Kirk. "Police Violence and Citizen Crime Reporting in the Black Community." *American Sociological Review* 81, no. 5 (2016): 857–76.

Dickinson v. Zanesville Metropolitan Housing Authority, 975 F. Supp. 2d 863 (2013).

Díez, Carolina, Rachel P. Kurland, Emily F. Rothman, Megan Bair-Merritt, Eric Fleegler, Ziming Xuan, Sandro Galea, Craig S. Ross, Bindu Kalesan, Kristin A. Goss, and Michael Siegel. "State Intimate Partner Violence-Related Firearm Laws and Intimate Partner Homicide Rates in the United States, 1991 to 2015." *Annals of Internal Medicine* 167, no. 8 (2017): 536–43. http://annals.org/aim/fullarticle/2654047/state-intimate-partner-violence-related-firearm-laws-intimate-partner-homicide.

"Domestic Violence as a Public Health Issue." Human Resource and Intergovernmental Relations Committee, Committee on Government Operations, House of Representatives. October 5, 1994.

Duggan, Anne, Loretta Fuddy, Lori Burrell, Susan M. Higman, Elizabeth McFarlane, Amy

Windham, and Calvin Sia. "Randomized Trial of a Statewide Home Visiting Program to Prevent Child Abuse: Impact in reducing Parental Risk Factors." *Child Abuse and Neglect* 28, no. 6 (2004): 623–43.

Dunn, Eric, and Marina Grabchuk. "Background Checks and Social Effects: Contemporary Residential Tenant-Screening Problems in Washington State." *Seattle Journal of Social Justice* 9, no. 1 (2010): 319–99.

Durfee, Alesha. "Situational Ambiguity and Gendered Patterns of Arrest for Intimate Partner Violence." *Violence against Women* 18, no. 1 (2012): 64–84.

Eckenrode, John, Barbara Ganzel, Charles L. Henderson, Elliott Smith, David L. Olds, Jane Powers, Robert Cole, Harriett Kitzman, and Kimberly Sidora. "Preventing Child Abuse and Neglect with a Program of Nurse Home Visitation: The Limiting Effects of Domestic Violence." *Journal of the American Medical Association* 284, no. 11 (2000): 1385–91.

Equal Rights Center. *No Vacancy: Housing Discrimination against Survivors of Domestic Violence in the District of Columbia* (2008).

Ertürk, Yakin. *Fifteen Years of the United Nations Special Rapporteur on Violence against Women, Its Causes and Consequences (1994–2009)—A Critical Review.* New York: United Nations Human Rights Office of the High Commissioner, May 2009. www.unwomen.org/en/docs/2009/1/15-years-of-the-un-special-rapporteur-on-violence-against-women.

Ertürk, Yakin. *Report of the Special Rapporteur on Violence against Women, Its Causes and Consequences: Political Economy and Violence against Women.* New York: United Nations Human Rights Office of the High Commissioner, June 2009. www.ohchr.org/EN/Issues/Women/SRWomen/Pages/SRWomenIndex.aspx.

Fals-Stewart, William. "The Occurrence of Partner Physical Aggression on Days of Alcohol Consumption: A Longitudinal Diary Study." *Journal of Consulting and Clinical Psychology* 71, no. 1 (2003): 41–52.

Flood, Michael. "Preventing Male Violence." In *Oxford Textbook of Violence Prevention.* Edited by Peter D. Donnelly and Catherine L. Ward. Oxford: Oxford University Press, 2015.

Foshee, Vangie A., Karl E. Bauman, Susan T. Ennett, G. Fletcher Linder, Thad Benefield, and Chirayath Suchindran. "Assessing the Long-Term Effects of the Safe Dates Program and a Booster in Preventing and Reducing Adolescent Dating Violence Victimization and Perpetration." *American Journal of Public Health* 94, no. 4 (2004): 619–24.

Frattaroli, Shannon. "Systems Change: Police/Criminal Justice." Presentation at the Symposium on Violence Prevention, Baltimore, MD, December 2017.

Gates, Gary J. *How Many People Are Lesbian, Gay, Bisexual, and Transgender?* Los Angeles: The Williams Institute, 2011. https://williamsinstitute.law.ucla.edu/wp-content/uploads/Gates-How-Many-People-LGBT-Apr-2011.pdf.

Gelb, Adam, and Barbara Broderick. "It's Time to Refocus the Punishment Paradigm." *The Hill*, July 10, 2017. www.thehill.com/blogs/pundits-blog/crime/341274-its-time-to-refocus-the-punishment-paradigm.

Gilligan, James. *Preventing Violence.* New York: Thames and Hudson, 2001.

Goldscheid, Julie, and Debra Liebowitz, "Due Diligence and Gender Violence: Parsing Its Power and Its Perils." *Cornell International Law Journal* 48, no. 2 (2015): 301–46.

Goodman, Lisa A., Katya Fels Smyth, Angela M. Borges, and Rachel Singer. "When Crises Collide: How Intimate Partner Violence and Poverty Intersect to Shape Women's Mental Health and Coping." *Trauma, Violence, and Abuse* 10, no. 4 (2009): 306–29.

Gottschalk, Marie. *Caught: The Prison State and the Lockdown of American Politics.* Princeton: Princeton University Press, 2015.

Grossman, Michael, and Sara Markowitz. *Alcohol Regulation and Violence on College Campuses.* Cambridge: National Bureau of Economic Research, 1999. http://nber.org/papers/w7129.pdf.

Gruber, Aya. "A 'Neo-Feminist' Assessment of Rape and Domestic Violence Law Reform." *Journal of Gender, Race and Justice* 15, no. 3 (2012): 583–616.

Hamberger, L. Kevin, "Typologies and Characteristics of Batterers." In *Intimate Partner Violence: A Health-Based Perspective.* Edited by Connie Mitchell and Deirdre Anglin. New York: Oxford University Press, 2009.

Hamby, Sherry, David Finkelhor, and Heather Turner. "Intervention Following Family Violence: Best Practices and Helpseeking Obstacles in a Nationally Representative Sample of Families with Children." *Psychology of Violence* 5, no. 3 (2015): 325.

Hamby, Sherry, and John Grych. *The Web of Violence: Exploring Connections among Different Forms of Interpersonal Violence and Abuse.* Dordrecht: Springer, 2013.

Harris, Angela P. "Heteropatriarchy Kills: Challenging Gender Violence in a Prison Nation." *Washington University Journal of Law and Policy* 37, no. 13 (2011): 13–65.

Hart, William L. *Attorney General's Task Force on Family Violence: Final Report*. Washington, D.C.: United States Department of Justice, 1984. www.files.eric.ed.gov/fulltext/ED251762.pdf.

Haviland, Mary, Victoria Frye, Valli Raja, Juhu Thukral, and Mary Trinity. *The Family Protection and Domestic Violence Intervention Act of 1995:*

Examining the Effects of Mandatory Arrest in New York City. New York: Urban Justice Center 2001. http://connectnyc.org/docs/Mandatory_Arrest_Report.pdf.

Hegenwish, Ariane, and Emma Williams-Baron. *The Gender Wage Gap: 2017.* Washington, D.C.: Institute for Women's Policy Research, 2018.

Heise, Lori L. "What Works to Prevent Partner Violence? An Evidence Overview." *STRIVE Research Consortium.* 2011. http://researchonline.lshtm.ac.uk/21062/1/Heise_Partner_Violence_evidence_overview.pdf.

Herman, Judith Lewis. "Justice from the Victim's Perspective." *Violence against Women* 11, no. 5 (2005): 571–602.

Hidrobo, Melissa, Amber Peterman, and Lori Heise. "The Effect of Cash, Vouchers and Food Transfers on Intimate Partner Violence: Evidence from a Randomized Experiment in Northern Ecuador." *American Economic Journal: Applied Economics* 8, no. 3 (2016): 284–303.

Hilton, N. Zoe, Grant T. Harris, and Marnie E. Rice. "The Effect of Arrest on Wife Assault Recidivism: Controlling for Pre-Arrest Risk." *Criminal Justice and Behavior* 34, no. 10 (2007): 1334–44.

Holder, Robyn and Kathleen Daly. "Sequencing Justice: A Longitudinal Study of Justice Goals of Domestic Violence Victims." *The British Journal of Criminology,* September 2017. https://academic.oup.com/bjc/advance-article-abstract/doi/10.1093/bjc/azx046/4259717.

Hopkins, C. Quince. "Tempering Idealism with Realism: Using Restorative Justice Processes to Promote Acceptance of Responsibility in Cases of Intimate Partner Violence." *Harvard Journal of Law and Gender* 35, no. 2 (2012): 311–56.

House of Commons (United Kingdom) Justice Committee. *Restorative Justice: Fourth Report of Session 2016–17* (2017).

Houston, Claire. "How Feminist Theory Became (Criminal) Law: Tracing the Path to Mandatory Criminal Intervention in Domestic Violence Cases." *Michigan Journal of Gender and the Law* 21, no. 2 (2014): 217–72.

Hughes, Melanie M., and Lisa D. Brush. "The Price of Protection: A Trajectory Analysis of Civil Remedies for Abuse and Women's Earnings." *American Sociological Review* 80, no. 1 (2015): 140–65.

Human Resource and Intergovernmental Relations Committee, Committee on Government Operations. House of Representatives. *Domestic Violence as a Public Health Issue,* October 5, 1994.

Jackson III, Eldra. "How Men at New Folsom Prison Reckon with Toxic Masculinity." *Los Angeles Times,* November 30, 2017. www.latimes.com/opinion/op-ed/la-oe-jackson-men-group-therapy-folsom-prison-the-work-toxic-masculinity-20171130-story.html.

Jacobs, Ken, Zohar Perla, Ian Perry, and Dave Graham-Squire. "Producing Poverty: The Public Cost of Low-Wage Production Jobs in Manufacturing." *UC Berkley Labor Center,* May 10, 2016. htpp://laborcenter.berkeley.edu/producing-poverty-the-public-cost-of-low-wage-production-jobs-in-manufacturing/.

Jaggar, Karuna, and Elizabeth De Renzy. *Closing the Wealth Gap through Self-Employment: Women of Color Achieving the American Dream.* San Francisco: Women's Initiative, 2008.

Jain, Sonia, Stephen L. Buka, S.V. Subramanian, and Beth E. Molnar. "Neighborhood Predictors of Dating Violence Victimization and Perpetration in Young Adulthood: A Multilevel Study." *American Journal of Public Health* 100, no. 9 (2010): 1737–44.

Jewkes, Rachel, Michael Flood, and James Lang. "From Work with Men and Boys to Changes of Social Norms and Reduction of Inequities in Gender Relations: A Conceptual Shift in Prevention of Violence against Women and Girls." *The Lancet* 385, no. 9977 (2014): 1580–89. http://dx.doi.org/10.1016/S0140-6736(14)61683-4.

Johnson, Margaret E. "Redefining Harm, Reimagining Remedies, and Reclaiming Domestic Violence Law." *University of California Davis Law Review* 42, no. 4 (2009): 1107–64.

Karp, David R., Julie Shackford-Bradley, Robin J. Wilson, Kaaren M. Williamsen. *A Report on Promoting Restorative Initiatives for Sexual Misconduct on College Campuses.* Saratoga Springs: Skidmore College Project on Restorative Justice, 2016. www.skidmore.edu/campusrj/documents/Campus_PRISM__Report_2016.pdf.

Kaufman, Michael. "The White Ribbon Campaign: Involving Men and Boys in Ending Global Violence against Women." In *A Man's World? Changing Men's Practices in a Globalized World.* Edited by Bob Pease and Keith Pringle. London: Zed Books, 2001.

Kearns, Megan C., Dennis E. Reidy, and Linda Anne Valle. "The Role of Alcohol Policies in Preventing Intimate Partner Violence: A Review of the Literature." *Journal of Studies on Alcohol and Drugs* 76, no. 1 (2015): 21–30.

Kelly, William R. *Criminal Justice at the Crossroads: Transforming Crime and Punishment.* New York: Columbia University Press, 2015.

Kennedy, David M. "Rethinking Law Enforcement Strategies to Prevent Domestic Violence." *Networks: Magazine of the National Center for Victims of Crime* 19, no. 2–3 (2004): 8–15.

Kim, Julia C., Charlotte H. Watts, James R. Hargreaves, Luceth X. Ndhlovu, Godfrey Phetla, Linda A. Morison, Joanna Busza, John D.H. Porter, Paul Pronyk. "Understanding the Impact of a Microfinance-Based Intervention on Women's Empowerment and the Reduction of Intimate Partner Violence in South Africa." *American Journal of Public Health* 97, no. 10 (2007): 1794–1802.

Kim, Mimi E. "Dancing the Carceral Creep: The Anti-Domestic Violence Movement and the Paradoxical Pursuit of Criminalization, 1973–1986." In *ISSI Graduate Fellows Working Paper* Series no. 2013-2014.70, October 14, 2015. https://escholarship.org/uc/item/804227k6.

Kim, Mimi. "Alternative Interventions to Intimate Violence: Defining Political and Pragmatic Challenges." In *Restorative Justice and Violence against Women.* Edited by James Ptacek. New York: Oxford University Press, 2010.

Kingi, Venezia. "The Use of Restorative Justice in Family Violence: The New Zealand Experience." In *A Restorative Approach to Family Violence: Changing Tack*. Edited by Anne Hayden, Loraine Gelsthorpe, Venezia Kingi, and Allison Morris. Surrey: Ashgate Press, 2014.

Kivel, Paul. "Social Service or Social Change?" www.paulkivel.com, 2006. http://coavp.org/sites/default/files/social%20service%20vs%20change.pdf.

Kleiman, Mark A.R. *When Brute Force Fails: How to Have Less Crime and Less Punishment*. Princeton: Princeton University Press, 2010.

Krieger, Linda Hamilton. "De-biasing the Courtroom." Safe Ireland Summit, Dublin, Ireland, November 2016.

Krug, Etienne G., Linda L. Dahlberg, James A. Mercy, Anthony B. Zwi, and Rafael Lozano, eds. *World Report on Violence and Health*. Geneva: World Health Organization, 2002. www.who.int/violence_injury_prevention/violence/world_report/en/introduction.pdf.

Lenahan v. United States (Inter-American Commission on Human Rights 2011).

Levesque, Deborah A., Janet L. Johnson, Carol A. Welch, Janice M. Prochaska, and Andrea L. Paira. "Teen Dating Violence Prevention: Cluster-Randomized Trial of *Teen Choices*, an Online, Stage-Based Program for Healthy, Nonviolent Relationships." *Psychology of Violence* 6, no. 3 (2016): 421–32.

Littwin, Angela. "Coerced Debt: The Role of Consumer Credit in Domestic Violence." *California Law Review* 100, no. 4 (2012): 951–1026.

Littwin, Angela. "Escaping Battered Credit: A Proposal for Repairing Credit Reports Damaged by Domestic Violence." *University of Pennsylvania Law Review* 161, no. 2 (2013): 363–430.

Llewellyn, Jennifer, Jacob Macisaac, and Melissa Mackay. *Report from the Restorative Justice Process*. Halifax: Dalhousie University, 2015. https://cdn.dal.ca/content/dam/dalhousie/pdf/cultureofrespect/RJ2015-Report.pdf.

Lloyd, Susan and Nina Taluc. "The Effects of Male Violence on Female Employment." *Violence against Women* 5, no. 4 (1999): 370–92.

Luna, Erik. "Overextending the Criminal Law." In *Go Directly to Jail: The Criminalization of Almost Everything*. Edited by Gene Healy. Washington, D.C.: Cato Institute, 2004.

Maguigan, Holly. "Wading into Professor Schneider's 'Murky Middle Ground' between Acceptance and Rejection of Criminal Justice Responses to Domestic Violence." *American University Journal of Gender, Social Policy, and Law* 11 no. 2 (2003): 427–46.

Manjoo, Rashida. *Report of the Special Rapporteur on Violence against Women, its Causes and Consequences: Addendum: Mission to the United States of America*. New York: United Nations Human Rights Office of the High Commissioner, June 2011.

Manjoo, Rashida. *Report of the Special Rapporteur on Violence against Women, Its Causes and Consequences.* New York: United Nations Human Rights Office of the High Commissioner, August 2011.

Manjoo, Rashida. *Report of the Special Rapporteur on Violence against Women, Its Causes and Consequences.* New York: United Nations Human Rights Office of the High Commissioner, May 2013.

Manjoo, Rashida. *Report of the Special Rapporteur on Violence against Women, Its Causes and Consequences.* New York: United Nations Human Rights Office of the High Commissioner, September 2014.

Manjoo, Rashida. *Statement by Ms. Rashida Manjoo, Special Rapporteur on Violence against Women, Its Causes and Consequences.* New York: United Nations Commission on the Status of Women, March 2015. http://www.ohchr.org/Documents/Issues/Women/CSW2015.pdf.

Maria de Penha Maia Fernandes v. Brazil (Inter-American Commission on Human Rights, 2001).

Markowitz, Sara. "The Price of Alcohol, Wife Abuse, and Husband Abuse." *Southern Economic Journal* 67, no. 2 (2000): 279–303.

Marmot, Michael. "Social Determinants of Health Inequalities." *The Lancet* 365, no. 9464 (2005): 1099–1104.

Maté, Gabor. "The Biology of Loss." Safe Ireland Summit: Dublin, Ireland, November 2016.

Mauer, Marc, and David Cole. "How to Lock up Fewer People." *New York Times*, May 23, 2015. https://nytimes.com/2015/05/24/opinion/sunday/how-to-lock-up-fewer-people.html?mtrref=www.google.com&gwh=59DE1A213CFC482C6F8BABA5423F9797&gwt=pay&assetType=opinion.

McMahon, Stephanie. "An Empirical Study of Innocent Spouse Relief: Do Courts Implement Congress' Legislative Intent." *Florida Tax Review* 12, no. 8 (2012): 629–708.

McMaster, Ken. "Restoring the Balance: Restorative Justice and Intimate Partner Violence." In *A Restorative Approach to Family Violence: Changing Tack*. Edited by Anne Hayden, Loraine Gelsthorpe, Venezia Kingi, and Allison Morris. Surrey: Ashgate Press, 2014.

McWilliams, Monica, and Fionnuala Ní Aoláin. "Moving Slowly to Regulate and Recognize: Human Rights Meets Intimate Partner Sexual Violence." In *Marital Rape: Consent, Marriage, and Social Change in Global Context*. Edited by Kersti Yllö and M. Gabriela Torres. New York: Oxford University Press, 2016.

Merry, Sally Engle. "Constructing a Global Law—Violence against Women and the Human Rights System." *Journal of Law and Social Inquiry* 28, no. 4 (2003): 941–78.

Messing, Jill Theresa, Allison Ward-Lasher, Jonel Thaller, and Meredith E. Bagwell-Gray. "The State of Intimate Partner Violence Intervention: Progress and Continuing Challenges." *Social Work* 60, no. 4 (2015): 305–13.

Messner, Michael A., Max A. Greenberg, and Tal Peretz. *Some Men: Feminist Allies and the Movement to End Violence against Women.* New York: Oxford University Press, 2015.

Meyersfield, Bonita. *Domestic Violence and International Law.* Oxford: Hart Publishing, 2010.

Michau, Lori, Jessica Horn, Amy Bank, Mallika Dutt, and Cathy Zimmerman. "Prevention of Violence against Women and Girls: Lessons from Practice." *The Lancet* 385, no. 9978 (2015): 1672–84.

Miller, Elizabeth, D.J. Tancredi, H.L. McCauley, M.R. Secker, M.C. Virata, H.A. Anderson, N. Stetkevich, E.W. Brown, F. Moideen, and J.G. Silverman. "'Coaching Boys into Men': A Cluster-Randomized Controlled Trial of a Dating Violence Prevention Program." *Journal of Adolescent Health* 51, no. 5 (2012): 431–38.

Moe, Angela M., and Myrtle P. Bell. "Abject Economics: The Effects of Battering and Violence on Women's Work and Employability." *Violence against Women* 10, no. 1 (2004): 29–55.

Moore, Natalie. "One Block, Zero Shootings: How One Mom Is Building Community in Englewood." WBEZ News, August 22, 2016. www.wbez.org/shows/wbez-news/one-block-zero-shootings-how-one-mom-is-building-community-in-englewood/ad478912-c74c-439d-a1cf-52f0c58989b6.

Morrison, Adele M. "Queering Domestic Violence to 'Straighten Out' Criminal Law: What Might Happen When Queer Theory and Practice Meet Criminal Law's Conventional Response to Domestic Violence." *Southern California Review of Law and Women's Studies* 13, no. 1 (2003): 81–162

Murakawa, Naomi. *The First Civil Right: How Liberals Built Prison America*. New York: Oxford University Press, 2014.

Natapoff, Alexandra. "Underenforcement." *Fordham Law Review* 75, no. 3 (2006): 1715–76.

National Center for Injury Prevention and Control, *Costs of Intimate Partner Violence Against Women in the United States*. Atlanta: Centers for Disease Control and Prevention, 2003.

National Institute of Justice. *Program Profile: South Dakota's 24/7 Sobriety Project*. Washington, D.C.: United States Department of Justice, 2015. https://www.crimesolutions.gov/ProgramDetails.aspx?ID=404.

National Institute of Justice. *When Violence Hits Home: How Economics and Neighborhood Play a Role*. Washington, D.C.: United States Department of Justice, 2004.

National Network for Safe Communities, *Intimate Partner Violence Intervention: Overview*. New York: National Network for Safe Communities at John Jay College. https://nnscommunities.org/uploads/IPVI_Paper.pdf

National Network to End Domestic Violence. *Eleventh Annual Domestic Violence Counts Report*, 2016. https://nnedv.org/mdocs-posts/census_2016_handout_report/.

National Research Council. *The Growth of Incarceration in the United States: Exploring Causes and Consequences*. Washington, D.C.: National Academies Press, 2014.

Nils, Christie. "Conflicts as Property." *British Journal of Criminology* 17, no. 1 (1977): 1–15.

"Nurse-Family Partnership: About Us." https://nursefamilypartnership.org/about/.

"Nurse-Family Partnership." *StoryCorps*. June 29, 2017. https://archive.storycorps.org/interviews/i-can-stand-up-set-those-boundaries-and-make-the-decisions-that-are-best-for-not-just-me-but-for-my-daughter/.

Opuz v. Turkey (European Court of Human Rights 2009).

Pence, Ellen. "Some Thoughts on Philosophy." In *Coordinating Community Responses to Domestic Violence: Lessons from Duluth and Beyond*. Edited by Melanie F. Shepard and Ellen L. Pence. Thousand Oaks, CA: Sage Publications, 1999.

Pennell, Joan. "Safety for Mothers and Their Children." In *Widening the Circle: The Practice and Evaluation of Family Group Conferencing with Children, Youths, and Their Families*. Edited by Joan Pennell and Gary Anderson. Washington, D.C.: NASW Press, 2005.

Pennell, Joan, and Gale Burford. "Family Group Decision Making: Protecting Women and Children." *Child Welfare* 79, no. 2 (2000): 131–58.

Petrosky, Emiko, Janet M. Blair, Carter J. Betz, Katherine A. Fowler, Shane P. D. Jack, and Bridget H. Lyons. "Racial and Ethnic Differences in Homicides of Adult Women and the Role of Intimate Partner Violence—United States, 2003–2014." *Morbidity and Mortality Weekly Report* 66, no. 28 (2017): 741–46. https://.cdc.gov/mmwr/volumes/66/wr/mm6628a1.htm?s_cid=mm6628a1_w#suggestedcitation.

Perova, Elizaveta. *Three Essays on Intended and Not Intended Impacts of Conditional Cash Transfers* (2010). https://escholarship.org/uc/item/2767982k.

"Pillars." *Support New York*, 2014. https://supportnewyork.files.wordpress.com/2014/02/supportnypillars.pdf.

Postmus, Judy L. "Economic Empowerment of Domestic Violence Survivors." VAWnet.org. October 2010. vawnet.org/sites/default/files/materials/files/2016-09/AR_EcoEmpowerment.pdf.

Postmus, Judy L., Sara-Beth Plummer, Sarah McMahon, N. Shaanta Murshid, and Mi Sung Kim. "Understanding Economic Abuse in the Lives of Survivors." *Journal of Interpersonal Violence* 27, no. 3 (2012): 411–30.

Postmus, Judy L., Sara-Beth Plummer, and Amanda M. Stylianou. "Measuring Economic Abuse in the Lives of Survivors: Revising the Scale of Economic Abuse." *Violence against Women* 22, no. 6 (2016): 692–703.

Pranis, Kay. "Restorative Values and Confronting Family Violence." In *Restorative Justice and Family Violence*. Edited by Heather Strang and John Braithwaite. Cambridge: Cambridge University Press, 2002.

Presser, Lois, and Emily Gaarder. "Can Restorative Justice Reduce Battering? Some Preliminary Considerations." *Social Justice* 27, no. 1 (2000): 175–95.

Rai, Tage. "How Could They?" *Aeon*. June 18, 2015. https://aeon.co/essays/people-resort-to-violence-because-their-moral-codes-demand-it.

Raissian, Kerri M. "Hold Your Fire: Did the 1996 Federal Gun Control Act Expansion Reduce Domestic Homicides?" *Journal of Policy Analysis and Management* 35, no. 1 (2016): 67–93.

Reaves, Brian A. *Police Response to Domestic Violence, 2006–2015*. Washington, D.C.: United States Department of Justice, 2017.

Renzetti, Claire M., *Economic Stress and Domestic Violence*, VAWnet.org, September 2009. https://uknowledge.uky.edu/cgi/viewcontent.cgi?article=1000&context=crvaw_reports.

"Results of Survey USA Mkt Research Study #23648." http://surveyusa.com/client/PollReportUC.aspx?g=a111d1a3-6bd7-445a-b873-f05742882310.

Richie, Beth E. "Keynote: Reimagining the Movement to End Gender Violence: Anti-Racism, Prison Abolition, Women of Color Feminisms, and Other Radical Visions of Justice." *University of Miami Race and Social Justice Law Review* 5, no. 2 (2015): 257–73.

Ritchie, Andrea J. *Invisible No More: Police Violence against Black Women and Women of Color*. Boston: Beacon Press, 2017.

Robinson, Paul H., and John M. Darley. "Does Criminal Law Deter? A Behavioural Science Investigation." *Oxford Journal of Legal Studies* 24, no. 2 (2004): 173–205.

Rothman, Emily F., and Phaedra S. Corso. "Propensity for Intimate Partner Abuse and Workplace Productivity: Why Employers Should Care." *Violence against Women* 14, no. 9 (2008): 1054–64.

Rothman, Emily F., Renee M. Johnson, and David Hemenway. "Gun Possession among Massachusetts Batterer Intervention Enrollees." *Evaluation Review* 30, no. 3 (2006): 283–95.

Salomon, Amy, Ellen Bassuk, Angela Browne, Shari S. Bassuk, Ree Dawson, and Nick Huntington, *Secondary Data Analysis on the Etiology, Course, and Consequences of Intimate Partner Violence against Extremely Poor Women*. Washington, D.C.: National Institute of Justice, 2004.

Salter, Michael. "Managing Recidivism amongst High Risk Violent Men." *Australian Domestic Violence and Family Violence Clearinghouse* 23 (2012): 1–25.

Saltzman, Linda A., James A. Mercy, Patrick W. O'Carroll, Mark L. Rosenberg and Philip H. Rhodes. "Weapon Involvement and Injury Outcomes in Family and Intimate Assaults." *Journal of the American Medical Association* 267, no. 22 (1992): 3043–47.

Sanders, Cynthia K. "Economic Abuse in the Lives of Women Abused by an Intimate Partner: A Qualitative Study." *Violence against Women* 21, no. 1 (2015): 3–29.

Sanders, Cynthia K. *Domestic Violence, Economic Abuse, and Implications of a Program for Building Economic Resources for Low-Income Women*. Saint Louis: Center for Social Development, 2007.

Saving Money and Reducing Tragedies through Prevention (SMART Prevention). U.S. Code 42 (2013) § 14043(c)(10).

Schechter, Susan. *Women and Male Violence: The Visions and Struggles of the Battered Women's Movement*. Boston: South End Press, 1982.

Schenwar, Maya. *Locked Down, Locked Out: Why Prison Doesn't Work and How We Can Do Better*. San Francisco, CA: Berrett-Koehler Publishers, 2014.

Schuster, Caroline. "Microfinance Could Wind up Being the New Subprime." *The Conversation*, May 23, 2016. http://theconversation.com/microfinance-could-wind-up-being-the-new-subprime-59001.

Sered, Danielle. *Accounting for Violence: How to Increase Safety and Break Our Failed Reliance on Mass Incarceration.* New York: Vera Institute of Justice, 2017.

Sherman, Lawrence W., Douglas A. Smith, Janell D. Schmidt, and Dennis P. Rogan. "Crime, Punishment, and Stake in Conformity: Legal and Informal Control of Domestic Violence." *American Sociological Review* 57, no. 5 (1992): 680–90.

Sherman, Lawrence W., and Heather Strang. *Restorative Justice: The Evidence.* London: The Smith Institute, 2007.

Shoener, Sara. *The Price of Safety: Hidden Costs and Unintended Consequences for Women in the Domestic Violence Service System.* Nashville: Vanderbilt University Press, 2016.

Simon, Jonathan. *Governing through Crime: How the War on Crime Transformed American Democracy and Created a Culture of Fear.* New York: Oxford University Press, 2007.

Singhal, A., S. Usdin, E. Scheepers, S. Goldstein, and G. Japhet. "Entertainment-Education Strategy in Development Communication." In *Development and Communication in Africa.* Edited by C. Okigobo and F. Eribo. Lanham: Rowman and Littlefield Publishers, 2004.

Singleton v. Cannizzaro, Case No. 2:17-cv-10721 (E.D. La. 2017).

Smith, Andrea. *Conquest: Sexual Violence and American Indian Genocide.* Durham: Duke University Press, 2005.

Smith Stover, Carla. "Fathers for Change: A New Approach to Working with Fathers Who Perpetrate Intimate Partner Violence." *Journal of the American Academy of Psychiatry and Law* 41, no. 1 (2013): 65–71.

Snider, Laureen. "Criminalising Violence against Women: Solution or Dead End?" *Criminal Justice Matters* 74, no. 1 (2008): 38–39.

Solon, Olivia. "Women-Led Startup Turns Domestic Abuse Survivors into Entrepreneurs." *The Guardian*, November 23, 2017. www.theguardian.com/society/2017/nov/23/domestic-abuse-survivors-free-from-entrepreneur-startups.

Sorensen, Susan B., and Rebecca A. Schut. "Nonfatal Gun Use in Intimate Partner Violence: A Systematic Review of the Literature." *Trauma, Violence, and Abuse*, 2016, 1–12.

Sottile, Leah. "Abuser and Survivor, Face to Face." *The Atlantic*, October 5, 2015. https://theatlantic.com/health/archive/2015/10/domestic-violence-restorative-justice/408820/.

Sparks, Anne. "Feminists Negotiate the Executive Branch: The Policing of Male Violence." In *Feminists Negotiate the State: The Politics of Domestic Violence.* Edited by Cynthia R. Daniels. Lanham: University Press of America, 1997.

SpearIt. "Gender Violence in Prison and Hyper-Masculinities in the 'Hood: Cycles of Destructive Masculinity." *Washington University Journal of Law and Policy* 37, no. 13 (2011): 89–147.

Sterbenz, Christina. "Why Norway's Prison System Is So Successful." *Business Insider*, December 11, 2014. www.businessinsider.com/why-norways-prison-system-is-so-successful-2014-12.

Stover, Carla Smith. "Fathers for Change: A New Approach to Working with Fathers Who Perpetrate Intimate Partner Violence." *Journal of the American Academy of Psychiatry and Law* 41, no. 1 (2013).

Strang, Heather, Lawrence W. Sherman, Evan Mayo-Wilson, Daniel Woods, and Barak Ariel. *Restorative Justice Conferencing (RJC) Using Face-to-Face Meetings of Offenders and Victims: Effects on Offender Recidivism and Victim Satisfaction: A Systematic Review.* Oslo: The Campbell Collaboration, 2013.

Strang, Heather, and Lawrence W. Sherman. "Repairing the Harm: Victims and Restorative Justice." *Utah Law Review* 2003, no. 15 (2003): 15–42.

Stubbs, Julie. "Domestic Violence and Women's Safety: Feminist Challenges to Restorative Justice." In *Restorative Justice and Family Violence*. Edited by Heather Strang and John Braithwaite. Cambridge: Cambridge University Press, 2002.

Stubbs, Julie. "Gendered Violence and Restorative Justice." in *A Restorative Approach to Family Violence: Changing Tack*. Edited by Anne Hayden, Loraine Gelsthorpe, Venezia Kingi, and Allison Morris. Surrey: Ashgate Press, 2014.

Taft, Angela J., Rhonda Small, Kelsey L. Hegarty, Lyndsey F. Watson, Lisa Gold, and Judith A. Lumley. "Mothers' AdvocateS In the Community (MOSAIC)—Non-professional Mentor Support to Reduce Intimate Partner Violence and Depression in Mothers: A Cluster Randomized Trial in Primary Care." *BMC Public Health* 11, no. 178 (2011). https://bmcpublichealth.biomedcentral.com/track/pdf/10.1186/1471-2458-11-178.

Taft, Casey T., Alexandra Macdonald, Suzannah K. Creech, Candice M. Monson, and Christopher M. Murphy. "A Randomized Controlled Clinical Trial of the Strength at Home Men's Program for Partner Violence in Military Veterans." *Journal of Clinical Psychiatry* 77, no. 9 (2016): 1168–75.

Thiara, Ravi K., and Jane Ellis. "Concluding Remarks." In *Preventing Violence against Women and Girls: Educational Work with Children and Young People*. Edited by Jane Ellis and Ravi K. Thiara. Bristol: Policy Press, 2014.

Thompson, Martie P., and J.B. Kingree. "The Roles of Victim and Perpetrator Alcohol Use in Intimate Partner Violence Outcomes." *Journal of Interpersonal Violence* 21, no. 2 (2006): 163–77.

Tolman, Richard M., and Daniel Rosen. "Domestic Violence in the Lives of Women Receiving Welfare: Mental Health, Substance Dependence, and Economic Well-Being." *Violence against Women* 7, no. 2 (2001): 141–58.

Tolman, Richard M., Tova Walsh, and Jeffrey Edleson, "Engaging Men in Violence Prevention." In *Sourcebook on Violence against Women*. 3rd ed. Edited by Claire M. Renzetti, Jeffrey L. Edleson, and Raquel Kennedy Bergen. Thousand Oaks, CA: Sage Publications, 2017.

Tolman, Richard M., and Hui-Chen Wang. "Domestic Violence and Women's Employment: Fixed Effects Models of Three Waves of Women's Employment

Study Data." *American Journal of Community Psychology* 36, no. 1–2 (2005): 147–58.

"Transformative Justice: A Liberatory Approach to Child Sexual Abuse and Other Forms of Intimate and Community Violence." *Generation Five,* 2007. www.generationfive.org/wp-content/uploads/2013/07/G5_Toward_Transformative_Justice-Document.pdf

True, Jacqui. *The Political Economy of Violence against Women.* New York: Oxford University Press, 2012.

Ulloa, Jazmine. "What Is a 'Violent Crime'? For California's New Parole Law, the Definition Is Murky—and It Matters." *Los Angeles Times,* January 27, 2017. www.latimes.com/politics/la-pol-sac-proposition-57-violent-crime-list-20170127-story.html.

United Nations General Assembly. *In-Depth Study on All Forms of Violence against Women: Report of the Secretary-General* A/61/122. New York: United Nations, 2006. https://documents-dds-ny.un.org/doc/UNDOC/GEN/N06/419/74/PDF/N0641974.pdf?OpenElement.

University of Miami Human Rights Clinic, Columbia Law School Human Rights Institute, and ACLU Women's Rights Project. *Domestic Violence and Sexual Assault in the United States: A Human Rights Based Approach and Practice Guide,* 2014. http://law.columbia.edu/sites/default/files/microsites/human-rights-institute/files/dv_sa_hr_guide_reduce.pdf.

Usdin, S., E. Scheepers, Susan Goldstein, Garth Japhet. "Achieving Social Change on Gender-Based Violence: A Report on the Impact Evaluation of Soul City's Fourth Series." *Social Science and Medicine* 61, no. 11 (2005): 2434–45.

Veslasquez Rodriguez v. Honduras (Inter-American Court of Human Rights 1988).

Verbitsky-Savitz, Natalya, Margaret B. Hargreaves, Samantha Penoyer, Norberto Morales, Brandon Coffee-Borden, and Emilyn Whitesell. *Preventing and Mitigating the Effects of ACEs by Building Community Capacity and Resilience: APPI Cross-Site Evaluation Findings.* Washington, D.C.: Mathematica Policy Research, 2016.

Vigdor, Elizabeth Richardson, and James A. Mercy. "Do Laws Restricting Access to Firearms by Domestic Violence Offenders Prevent Intimate Partner Homicide?" *Evaluation Review* 30, no. 3 (2006): 313–46.

Vittes, Katherine A., Daniel W. Webster, Shannon Frattaroli, Barbara E. Claire, and Garen J. Wintemute. "Removing Guns from Batterers: Findings from a Pilot Study of Domestic Violence Restraining Order Recipients in California." *Violence against Women* 19, no. 5 (2013): 602–16.

Webster, Daniel W., Shannon Frattaroli, Jon S.Vernick, Chris O'Sullivan, Janice Roehl, and Jacquelyn C. Campbell. "Women with Protective Orders Report Failure to Remove Firearms from Their Abusive Partners: Results from an Exploratory Study." *Journal of Women's Health* 19, no. 1 (2010): 93–98.

Weissman, Deborah M. "Countering Neoliberalism and Aligning Solidarities: Rethinking Domestic Violence Advocacy." *Southwestern Law Review* 45, no. 4 (2016): 915–65.

Weissman, Deborah M. "Law, Social Movements, and the Political Economy of Domestic Violence." *Duke Journal of Gender Law and Policy* 20, no. 2 (2013): 221–54.

Weissman, Deborah M. "The Personal Is Political—And Economic: Rethinking Domestic Violence." *Brigham Young University Law Review* 2007, no. 2 (2007): 387–450.

Whitaker, Daniel J., Christopher M. Murphy, Christopher I. Eckhardt, Amanda E. Hodges, and Melissa Cowart. "Effectiveness of Primary Prevention Efforts for Intimate Partner Violence." *Partner Abuse* 4, no. 2 (2013): 175–95.

Whitfield, Charles L., Robert Anda, Shanta R. Dube, and Vincent J. Felitti. "Violent Childhood Experiences and the Risk of Intimate Partner Violence in Adults." *Journal of Interpersonal Violence* 18, no. 2 (2003): 166–85.

Wilkinson, Richard, and Michael Marmot. *Social Determinants of Health: The Solid Facts*. Copenhagen: World Health Organization Europe, 2003. www.euro.who.int/__data/assets/pdf_file/0005/98438/e81384.pdf.

Wintemute, Garen J., Shannon Frattaroli, Barbara E. Claire, Katherine A. Vittes, and Daniel W. Webster. "Identifying Armed Respondents to Domestic Violence Restraining Orders and Recovering Their Firearms: Process Evaluation of an Initiative in California." *American Journal of Public Health* 104, no. 2 (2014): 113–18.

Wolfe, David A., Claire Crooks, Peter Jaffe, Debbie Chiodo, Ray Hughes, Wendy Ellis, Larry Stitt, and Allan Donner. "A School-Based Program to Prevent Adolescent Dating Violence: A Cluster Randomized Trial." *Archives of Pediatrics and Adolescent Medicine* 163, no. 8 (2009): 692–99.

Wolfe, David A., Christine Wekerle, Katreena Scott, Anna-Lee Straatman, Carolyn Grasley, Deborah Reitzel-Jaffe. "Dating Violence Prevention with At-Risk Youth: A Controlled Outcome Evaluation." *Journal of Consulting and Clinical Psychology* 71, no. 2 (2003): 279–91.

World Health Organization/London School of Hygiene and Tropical Medicine. *Preventing Intimate Partner and Sexual Violence against Women: Taking Action and Generating Evidence.* Geneva: World Health Organization, 2010.

Wright, Emily L. and Michael L. Benson. "Clarifying the Effects of Neighborhood Context on Violence 'Behind Closed Doors.'" *Justice Quarterly* 28, no. 5 (2011): 775–98.

Wright, Emily L., and Michael L. Benson. "Immigration and Intimate Partner Violence: Exploring the Immigrant Paradox." *Social Problems* 57, no. 3 (2010): 480–503.

Yllö, Kersti. "Through a Feminist Lens: Gender Diversity, and Violence: Extending the Feminist Framework." In *Current Controversies on Family Violence.* Edited by Donileen R. Loseke, Richard J. Gelles, and Mary M. Cavanaugh. Thousand Oaks, CA: Sage Publications, 2005.

Yoder, Steven. "Getting beyond Prison: A Vermont Case Study." *The American Prospect,* May 4, 2016. www.prospect.org/article/getting-beyond-prison-vermont-case-study.

Yoshihama, Mieko, Aparna Ramakrishnan, Amy C. Hammock, and Mahmooda Khaliq. "Intimate Partner Violence Prevention Program in an Asian Immigrant Community: Integrating Theories, Data, and Community." *Violence against Women* 18, no. 7 (2012): 763–83.

Zeoli, April, Rebecca Malinski, and Brandon Turchan. "Risks and Targeted Interventions: Firearms in Intimate Partner Violence." *Epidemiology Review* 38, no. 1 (2016): 125–39.

Zolotor, Adam A., and Desmond K. Runyan. "Social Capital, Family Violence, and Neglect." *Pediatrics* 117, no. 6 (2006): 1124–31.

Index

Made in the USA
Middletown, DE
09 August 2021